Contemporary Arab-American Literature

Contemporary Arab-American Literature

Transnational Reconfigurations
of Citizenship and Belonging

CAROL FADDA-CONREY

New York University Press
NEW YORK AND LONDON

NEW YORK UNIVERSITY PRESS
New York and London
www.nyupress.org

© 2014 by New York University
All rights reserved

LIBRARY OF CONGRESS CATALOGING-IN-PUBLICATION DATA

Fadda-Conrey, Carol.
 Contemporary Arab-American literature : transnational reconfigurations of citizenship and belonging / Carol Fadda-Conrey.
  pages cm
 Includes bibliographical references and index.
 ISBN 978-1-4798-2692-6 (hardback)
 ISBN 978-1-4798-0431-3 (pb)
  1. American literature—Arab American authors—History and criticism. 2. Identity (Psychology) in literature. 3. Alienation (Social psychology) in literature. 4. Homeland in literature. 5. Arab Americans in literature. 6. Arabs in literature. 7. Arab countries—In literature. I. Title.
 PS153.A73F34 2014
 810.9'8927—dc23
                                              2013049739

References to Internet websites (URLs) were accurate at the time of writing. Neither the author nor New York University Press is responsible for URLs that may have expired or changed since the manuscript was prepared.

New York University Press books are printed on acid-free paper, and their binding materials are chosen for strength and durability. We strive to use environmentally responsible suppliers and materials to the greatest extent possible in publishing our books.

Manufactured in the United States of America
10 9 8 7 6 5 4 3 2 1

Also available as an ebook

A book in the American Literatures Initiative (ALI), a collaborative publishing project of NYU Press, Fordham University Press, Rutgers University Press, Temple University Press, and the University of Virginia Press. The Initiative is supported by The Andrew W. Mellon Foundation. For more information, please visit www.americanliteratures.org.

Contents

	Acknowledgments	vii
	Introduction: Transnational Arab-American Belonging	1
1	Reimagining the Ancestral Arab Homeland	28
2	To the Arab Homeland and Back: Narratives of Returns and Rearrivals	65
3	Translocal Connections between the US and the Arab World	105
4	Representing Arabs and Muslims in the US after 9/11: Gender, Religion, and Citizenship	139
	Conclusion: Transnational Solidarity and the Arab Uprisings	177
	Notes	189
	Works Cited	217
	Index	237
	About the Author	244

Acknowledgments

This book has traveled with me from one home to another, crisscrossing back and forth between Beirut, Indiana, Philadelphia, and Syracuse. I have been extremely fortunate to have the support of many people in these different places, without whom this project would not have been possible. I am grateful for the thoughtfulness and generosity of Aparajita Sagar, who first guided me through this project when it was still at the dissertation stage, and for the input and feedback of John Duvall, Shaun Hughes, and Nancy Peterson at Purdue University. Special thanks go to Siobhan Somerville, who was instrumental in helping me survive my first year of graduate school and who encouraged me to write about Arab-American literature.

Several colleagues and friends offered advice and feedback on various drafts of the book, enriching and focusing my arguments every step of the way. For that I thank Keith Feldman, Amy Kallander, Nouri Gana, Lisa Suhair Majaj, Susan Muaddi Darraj, Jesse Nissim, Dana Olwan, Therí Pickens, Steven Salaita, and the English Department Faculty Writing Group at Syracuse University, including Manan Desai, Susan Edmunds, Mike Goode, Roger Hallas, Chris Hanson, Kevin Morrison, Patricia Roylance, and Stephanie Shirilan. Any errors in the book, however, are completely my own. I would like to thank Crystal Bartolovich, Steven Cohan, Mike Goode, Roger Hallas, Claudia Klaver, Scott Lyons, and Erin Mackie for their professional advice and guidance. Scholars and artists in the Arab and Arab-American community provided me with a much-needed sense of connection that prevented me from writing in isolation, and for that I am especially grateful to Rabab Abdulhadi, Maysa Abu Youssef Hayward, Layla Al Maleh, Deborah Al-Najjar, Evelyn Alsultany, Amal Amireh, Zeina Azzam, Carol Bardenstein, Lana Barkawi, Leila Ben-Nasr, Yussef El Guindi, Sirène Harb, Waïl Hassan, Syrine Hout, Pauline Homsi Vinson, Amira Jarmakani, Randa Jarrar, Mohja Kahf, Randa Kayyali, Jamil Khoury, Khaled Mattawa, Phil Metres, Susan Muaddi Darraj, Nadine Naber, Hedy Sabbagh Habra, Steven Salaita, Laila Shereen Sakr, the late Michael Suleiman, and Ahimsa Timoteo Bodhrán. A big thank-you goes to Lisa Suhair Majaj, whose kindness and thoughtfulness pulled me through some difficult moments. I am much indebted to her pioneering scholarship on Arab-American literature. I would also like to acknowledge the generous spirit of the late Evelyn Shakir, whose encouragement and groundbreaking work I am deeply grateful for.

The time provided by a Future of Minority Studies Fellowship in spring 2011 was crucial, allowing me to think and to focus on my writing. I am deeply grateful for the mentorship of Chandra Talpade Mohanty and Silvio Torres-Saillant during and well beyond the fellowship period. Silvio's questions helped me think deeper about minority labels and racialized positionings, and Chandra's support helped me build crucial solidarity ties with other feminist and minority scholars within as well as outside the Syracuse University community. A National Endowment for the Humanities Summer Stipend in 2010 allowed me to make progress on chapter 3, and the feedback I received on various sections of the book that I presented at the Radius of Arab American Writers' conferences, as well as the Modern Language Association and Middle East Studies Association conferences, were immensely helpful. I am also grateful to the two anonymous reviewers whose feedback and suggestions helped me produce a stronger book. Jesse Nissim's discerning eye, editing skills, and unfailing encouragement helped me make it through the final stage of the book revisions. Many thanks go to Ruma Sinha and Sarah Barkin for their work on copyedits and the index, respectively, and to the other students in my graduate seminars who helped me think through many of the ideas in this book. Much gratitude and thanks go to Eric Zinner at New York University Press for believing in the manuscript and to Ciara McLaughlin and Alicia Nadkarni for their diligence in seeing the project through till the end.

The time I spent researching and writing this book would have been much less bright and enjoyable were it not for the support and companionship of friends and family members. For warmly opening their homes to me and my family, and welcoming us into new communities, I thank Jenny Spinner and Peter McGahey, Violette Farha Humsi and Amal Humsi, Farha Ternikar and Travis Vande Berg, Mike Goode and Jolynn Parker, and Amy Kallander. Their friendship has been crucial in helping my family and me restart our lives in new places. For always having her door and ear open to both good and bad news, for her art days, and for her intellectual rigor and sense of wonder and fun, I thank Susan Edmunds, who read and commented on every chapter of the book. The late nights spent on campus writing would have been intolerable were it not for the presence and friendship of Stephanie Shirilan. I owe much to her and Ryan Howlett, as well as Katie Beckstrand, Amber Lough, and Jim Lough, for granting me precious periods of uninterrupted work while they entertained my kids. Much thanks and gratitude go to Lisa Bunghalia, Jesse Nissim, Dana Olwan, and Gretchen Purser, whose food and laughter enabled me to see the light at the end of the tunnel as I finalized this project. Dana Olwan's fierce sisterhood and sharp intellect kept me grounded, reminding me that we make our own families as much as we inherit them. Warm thanks and appreciation go to Farha Ternikar, who always made sure that I left the work behind every once in a while to have some fun and relax. I am also grateful for old friends who continue to anchor me in the present while sharing a lot of the past. Tamara Sawaya, Mona Rouayheb, Danielle Khouri, Zeina Misk, I am so thankful for growing up with you physically, emotionally, and intellectually. Tamara, your deep regard for the meaningful shaped my views in formative ways.

My parents and sister were the first to believe in and support this journey. For showing me the beauty of books and reading early on, and for teaching me the importance of humor, I thank my sister, Nada Fadda, whose love and support are a huge part of my accomplishments. The unconditional love of my parents, Wadad (Odette) Wehbe Fadda and Nahi Fadda, is a constant source of encouragement. Their hard work during long years of war and uncertainty taught me the value of perseverance and integrity. Much appreciation goes to my in-laws, Phyllis Conrey and Jim Conrey, as well as to my extended family in Lebanon and in the US, whose support and love are always present with me despite geographical distances.

The love and selflessness of my partner, Sean Conrey, are reflected in every part of this book. Whether through reading various drafts, shouldering parental duties, or journeying back and forth between the US and Lebanon, Sean enabled me to inhabit this book in multiple ways, sharing the beauty and agony of living in two worlds at once. My daughters, Mira and Emily, brightened up every step of writing this book. Their patience and enthusiasm are constant reminders of the delight and wonder brought about by the discovery of words and ideas. May they always face these journeys of discovery and continuity with their usual exuberance and excitement. This book is for them.

Sections of chapters 1 and 3 are revised versions of previously published essays:

"Weaving Poetic Autobiographies: Individual and Communal Identities in the Poetry of Mohja Kahf and Suheir Hammad." *Arab Women's Lives Retold: Exploring Identity Through Writing*. Ed. Nawar Al-Hassan Golley. Syracuse: Syracuse UP, 2007. 155–76.

"Arab-American Literature in the Ethnic Borderland: Cultural Intersections in Diana Abu-Jaber's *Crescent*." *Arab American Literature*. Spec. issue of *MELUS* 31.4 (2006): 187–205.

"The New Transnational Immigrant and the Search for Home in Rabih Alameddine's *I, the Divine: A Novel in First Chapters*." Ed. Layla Al Maleh. *Arab Voices in Diaspora: Critical Perspectives on Anglophone Arab Literature*. Amsterdam: Rodopi, 2009. 163–85.

A section of chapter 4 was previously published as "Arab American Citizenship in Crisis: Destabilizing Representations of Arabs and Muslims in the US after 9/11." Spec. issue of *Modern Fiction Studies* 57. 3 (2011): 532–55. Reprinted with permission.

My sincere thanks go to Khaled Mattawa for allowing me to reprint his poem "Now That We Have Tasted Hope" in the book's conclusion, and to Wafaa Bilal, Annemarie Jacir, Emily Jacir, and Jamil Khoury and Malik Gillani from Silk Road Rising for allowing me to include images from their work in this book.

Contemporary Arab-American Literature

Introduction: Transnational Arab-American Belonging

The past two and a half decades have witnessed an exciting flourishing of Arab-American literature, as made evident by the rapid increase in the number of literary texts published in an array of genres, including fiction, poetry, nonfiction, and drama. With roots in an early-twentieth-century Arab-American literary tradition spearheaded by the Al-Rabita al-Qalamiyya, or the Pen League,[1] contemporary Arab-American literature is currently at an important juncture in its development as a field. More courses are being taught on Arab-American literature and culture across the US, more critical texts are focusing on Arab-American studies, and more Arab-American writers are being published by mainstream presses to national and international acclaim. Yet this increased interest in the current production and circulation of Arab-American literary texts is ironically paralleled by a prevalent and tenacious bias against Arabs and Muslims, one that often erroneously portrays their long presence in the US not only as a recent phenomenon but as a dangerous and unwelcome one to boot.

Such bias against Arabs and Muslims has a long history and has been particularly visible and blatant in US public, political, and legal venues since the turn of the twenty-first century. What with the events of September 11, 2001, and the ensuing US-led wars in Afghanistan and Iraq, as well as the interminable War on Terror, Arab-Americans[2] have found themselves relegated to an increasingly precarious position within the US nation-state. Such precariousness firmly brands Arab-Americans as the racial, religious, political, and national Other of a hegemonic US national identity that has increasingly become more uniform and insular in nature. Of course, Arab-Americans have occupied these precarious positionalities well before 2001, starting with Arab immigration to the US in the nineteenth century and intensifying in the second part of the twentieth century onward. For one, the integration of European colonialist and Orientalist paradigms into the US's neoimperialist agenda beginning around the mid-twentieth century has had major repercussions on Arabs within the Arab world as well as in the diaspora. In this period, the direct and indirect role of the US in major Middle Eastern crises and ensuing wars and conflicts has had particular impact on immigration patterns, pushing millions of Arabs and Muslims into various conditions of displacement, exile, and dispossession. These crises include the establishment of the state of Israel in 1948, the Arab-Israeli wars of 1967 and 1973, the 1970s Arab oil embargo, the Lebanese civil war from 1975 to 1990 and its aftermath, the 1982 Israeli invasion of Lebanon, the First Gulf War in the early 1990s, as well as the invasions of Afghanistan and Iraq in 2001 and 2003, respectively.

The changing geopolitical landscapes resulting from such crises have given rise to negative conceptualizations of Arab-Americans in the US, ones that are deeply entrenched in the binary logics of Orientalist discourse.[3] In this way, derogatory and essentialist stereotypes about Arabs and Muslims, replete with lascivious Arab sheikhs, villains, harem girls, and belly dancers, become the shared vocabulary used to reify the vast differences between a "civilized" US culture on the one hand and a "barbaric" and backward Arab and Muslim landscape on the other hand.[4] Such Orientalist discourse has taken on an additional policing role after 9/11, portraying Arabs and Muslims as perpetual aliens, volatile extremists, and potential or actual terrorists (in the case of men) or oppressed, silenced, and disenfranchised subjects (in the case of women).[5] These labeling acts are not always overtly or directly stated, however. For even seemingly benevolent attempts to depict Arabs and Muslims in a positive light, such as the ones prevalent in various US media outlets and political arenas, ultimately end up affirming their perceived national and religious Otherness.[6]

Arab-American writers and critics (as well as activists, artists, and cultural workers) have been responding in their work to these rigid and limited readings of Arab and Muslim bodies in the US. In doing so, they articulate a rising need among Arab-Americans for a transformative project of communal and individual self-representation, one that captures the complexity and heterogeneity of their communities. Such efforts, however, have hardly forced Arab-American literary output to conform to a didactic and proclamatory platform. Instead, they render it a valuable creative space for delineating shared and individual concerns regarding Arab-Americans' myriad positions and outlooks in the US, their connections to original Arab homelands, and their negotiation of the complexities of citizenship and belonging in the US.[7]

To exemplify these complex and heterogeneous forms of self-representation, I focus in my analysis on literary and occasionally visual texts dating from the 1990s onward that contest blanket and erroneous representations of Arab-Americans. At the same time, these texts endorse, develop, and portray antiassimilationist and transnational modes of Arab-American belonging that ultimately transform dominant and exclusionary US understandings of national membership and citizenship. Throughout the book, I argue that the discursive negotiation of transnational connections to Arab homelands from a variegated and multilayered US perspective has an integral role in creating a space for reformulating hegemonic and unilocal understandings of US citizenship and belonging. In other words, the ways in which original Arab homelands, and their concomitant cultural and political byproducts, are imagined, replicated, portrayed, and lived by multiple generations of Arab-Americans in these texts invite new engagements with US citizenship and belonging that are repositioned outside the frameworks of Orientalism and neoimperialism. By problematizing the binary constructs (such as "us versus them" and "over there versus over here") that inform much of current Orientalist and neoimperial US understandings of national, political, and religious identities, the literary and visual texts analyzed here contest and reimagine the exclusionary and isolationist elements informing dominant enactments of US citizenship and belonging.

More than revising the binary constructs defining US relations with the Arab world, the transnational articulations examined in this book challenge those same constructs as they are applied to the racialized bodies of Arab-Americans within the US landscape. Through Arab-American writers' and artists' strategic reconfigurations of the binary logics inherent in such constructs, Arab-Americans' connections to the Arab world cease to be the ostracizing factor that prohibit them from asserting US belonging. Instead, these transnational connections to original Arab homelands become the main discursive vehicle for defying exclusionary and uniform types of US citizenship. In this way, the figure of the Arab-American body, as it draws on the memories and realities of an Arab homeland from within the US space, posits itself as a US entity to be contended with, despite all hegemonic efforts to define it outside the purview of US citizenship, or as the "enemy-alien" within.[8] Hence, Arab-Americans like the ones portrayed in these texts, by asserting themselves within a US framework while maintaining transnational connections to their Arab homelands, overturn the exclusionary belongings dictated by the US nation-state, thus transforming its strict delimitations of citizenship in the process.

My use of the term *citizenship* draws on its legal as well as its cultural dimensions.[9] Legal citizenship primarily involves the construction of the citizen-subject through the acquisition of legal and civic rights as well as the performance of civic duties and obligations. Cultural citizenship goes beyond legal structures to evoke a type of citizenship that is shaped by connections to and participation in the US social and cultural landscapes. Although the definitions of cultural citizenship offered by Aihwa Ong and Renato Rosaldo somewhat differ one from the other, their definitions of this term are helpful, particularly in their conceptualization of this type of citizenship in the contexts of Asian and Latino immigration, respectively. For Ong, on the one hand, cultural citizenship is often an oppressive state-controlled tool that mandates the inclusion and exclusion of minority groups within the nation-state. Ong states that "cultural citizenship is a dual process of self-making and being-made within webs of power linked to the nation-state and civil society" ("Cultural Citizenship as Subject Making" 738). Rosaldo, on the other hand, defines cultural citizenship as the process by which minority groups such as Latinos negotiate a place for themselves within the dominant cultural sphere, thus laying claim to this sphere despite their difference from it (37).

Building on these theorizations of cultural citizenship, I argue that in the Arab-American context, there is often very little room for negotiating cultural citizenship outside the discourse and practice of inclusion and assimilation, primarily by virtue of Arab-Americans' religious and political affiliations.[10] In fact, for Arab-Americans, both legal and cultural forms of citizenship have been repeatedly denied or questioned since the arrival of the first wave of immigrants from the Arab world in the nineteenth century,[11] a point that I develop in more detail in the following section. The passing of the 1965 Immigration and Nationality Act eased Arab immigrants' entry into the US and in turn bettered their chances of becoming US citizens. Their US cultural citizenship has nevertheless been steadily undermined or even completely negated in the decades from the late 1960s to the present, a period marked by the US's increasing involvement in Middle Eastern affairs. In the years after 9/11 especially, such negations have reached a crescendo, informing the implementation of state and federal laws that have systematically stripped Arab-Americans (as well as Muslim-Americans and other racialized minorities) of their citizen rights, if not their legal citizenship altogether.[12] Moreover, Arab-Americans' cultural citizenship has been severely and consistently undermined due to a widespread perception that they lack true and single allegiance to the US by virtue of their religion, heritage, politics, or transnational perspective, all of which brand Arab-Americans as "forever foreign" in the dominant US imaginary (Shohat, "Gendered Cartographies of Knowledge" 6).

In asserting anti-imperialist and anti-Orientalist forms of US citizenship through transnational articulations of belonging, the texts analyzed throughout this book challenge the idea that assimilating into dominant cultural frameworks in the US is a necessary and adequate goal for Arab-Americans. The critical analyses I present here call attention to an Arab-American literary and cultural discourse that addresses and moves Arab-American communal responses beyond the often limiting strategies that focus wholly on rejecting or refuting the discriminatory labels and harmful stereotypes informing anti-Arab racism and Islamophobia in the US. Such communal responses include attempts to rectify derogatory portrayals of Arabs by exclusively expounding on seemingly apolitical or unthreatening Arab traditions and values such as food, folklore, music, or hospitality. Instead of pursuing an apologetic or defensive track, I argue for the need to forge new critical US citizenships that break through the insularity of dominant US perspectives by privileging the transnational outlook at the heart of Arab-American identities and cultures. Such an outlook tackles the Orientalist and neoimperialist views informing dominant US opinions about Arabs in general by directly handling difficult but necessary discussions of race, religion, nationality, politics, and gender, while simultaneously connecting them to Arab-Americans' transnational negotiations of their place in the US. In other words, Arab-American writers, by focusing in their work on complex and transnational engagements with the self-same constructs that Otherize them in the eyes of a US public, revise hegemonic and binary configurations of racial, ethnic, religious, national, political, and gendered identities. In doing so, they challenge and push against the limits of purportedly inclusive structures of US citizenship and belonging as conceived of and imagined by neoliberal US multiculturalism.

My analysis of discursive reconfigurations of Arab-American identities in this book deploys a theoretical framework developed at the intersections of Middle East studies, US ethnic studies, transnational studies, and diaspora studies. Rather than treating each of these nodes separately, I stress the importance of drawing on the intersections and differences between and among them. In doing so, I show how Arab-American literary and cultural production, with all its variety and complexity, formulates a distinct transnational discourse in its output and focus that defies a facile categorization of Arab-American literary and cultural studies according to traditional US ethnic or diasporic models. Even while drawing on the ethnic and diasporic makeup of Arab-American communities, the transnational discourse that I outline here troubles the specific and often rigid affiliations embedded in ethnic and diasporic labels, with all the structures of belonging and unbelonging they uphold. The ethnic label on the one hand, as applied to minority US communities, has specific historical and political significance that connects these communities to the struggles for representation and civil rights in the US starting in the 1960s (Anthias 558). The diasporic label on the other hand primarily places immigrant or displaced groups and their progeny outside the bounds of an original homeland, which can be defined in national, religious, or even sexual terms (Tölölyan, "Rethinking *Diaspora(s)*" 16; Patton and Sánchez-Eppler). Both the *ethnic* and *diasporic* labels underscore positions of empowerment and disempowerment as they are enacted within the bounds of specific nation-states. The transnational framework calls for a transgression or a traversal of physical as well as imaginative boundaries of such nation-states.[13] I place Arab-American literary and cultural texts within such a transformative framework to examine the ways in which these texts create a discourse of citizenship and belonging that positions Arab-American identities beyond traditional ethnic and diasporic labels.

I am aware that the dividing line between the diasporic and the ethnic is not always obvious or stable, and some scholars consider the diasporic to be a subset of the ethnic, wherein, as Khachig Tölölyan reminds us, "all diasporics are ethnics, but all ethnics are not diasporic" ("Contemporary Discourse" 652).[14] In a similar vein, I would add that even though most transnationals in the Arab-American context are diasporics, diasporics vary in their development of transnational connections to an original homeland. Moreover, diasporics are always defined by their lack of or provisional access to an original homeland, while transnationals embody a simultaneous physical or metaphorical placement in dual or even multiple locations that cut across national boundaries. Transnational enactments among Arab-Americans are far from being uniform or consistent, however. They include physical mobility but also extend to imaginative attachments, all promulgated by the fast development of tools of communication such as the Internet and satellite TV. These transnational enactments vary depending on the conditions that enable or prohibit Arab-Americans' access to ancestral Arab homelands, whether by virtue of geopolitical conditions, generational divides, economic means, or the pressures of US assimilation and integration. It is with these understandings in mind that I argue for the development of a complex transnational discourse like the one I delineate in the literary texts discussed here, a discourse that overturns fixed and conventional adherences to diasporic and ethnic labels. By underscoring larger structures of belonging, citizenship, and national membership that exceed and thus transform the limits of the nation-state, such transnational discourse challenges the stigmatizing racialization of ethnic and diasporic communities within the US. At the same time, it places racial, ethnic, gendered, religious, and sexual identities outside the rigid constructs of traditional or normative cultural and national frameworks.

In this way, the transnational, in all its discursive and physical permutations, becomes a key concept for negotiating a type of Arab-American citizenship and belonging that defies the separation of the "over there" from "over here." By suggesting that the texts I analyze in this book help us rethink the bounds and borders of US citizenship and belonging, I do not intend to privilege the centrality of a US national identity. Instead, I show through my analysis how the types of transnational Arab-American identities offered in these texts underscore the limits of the national rubric defining US citizenship and belonging as it is currently practiced and imagined. Although in the past couple of decades US national literature and culture has experienced a transnational turn, such expansions need to be contextualized and studied alongside an equally expanding US political and military hegemony that undercuts facile claims of diverse and inclusive US landscapes. For this reason, Arab-American cultural production becomes a key site for exploring the effects of such a transnational turn given the positioning of Arab-Americans at the interstices of aggressive military hegemony in the Arab world and a purportedly diverse and multicultural society within the US. The transnational enactments of US citizenship and belonging that these texts portray, then, become the basis for a broader analysis of the kinds of knowledge that mainstream US citizens could embody regarding US military and imperial ambitions in the Arab world. This knowledge would then necessarily inform more critical and transformative responses to US foreign policies and would lead to more in-depth, anti-imperialist, and anti-Orientalist understandings of Arab identities as lived in both the US and the Arab world.

To this end, I prioritize the transnational in framing Arab-American literary studies, especially because it highlights in crucial ways the influences and factors shaping Arab-American identities that lie beyond the US nation-state. It would nevertheless be counterproductive and even possibly dangerous to forgo the ethnic and diasporic structures altogether, particularly due to the potential for inter- and intraethnic alliances, as well as cross-diasporic solidarities, that these structures entail. For it is within these promises of solidarities and connections that US minority identities can avoid the pitfalls of turning into self-referential enclaves and niches that are often the byproducts of ethnic and/or diasporic constructs. Such interethnic and cross-diasporic solidarities facilitate various forms and articulations of solidarity among US racial and ethnic minorities, given their common experience of struggle against marginalization and discrimination, as well as their continuous negotiation of issues related to identity politics, in-betweenness, multiple home fronts, and uneasy belongings.

While identifying Arab-Americans as people of color within the US, this book is not meant to explore the interethnic and cross-racial connections that tie Arab-Americans to the histories and realities of other US ethnicities and races, including Latino/as, African-Americans, Native Americans, and Asian-Americans. Instead, my aim here is to highlight the ways in which Arab-Americans' transnational connections to Arab homelands, as expressed through cultural venues, produce anti-imperialist and antihegemonic modalities of Arab-American citizenship and belonging that pave the way for more solid connections among various communities of color. At the same time, these modalities gesture toward reconfigurations of broader understandings of a US political and national membership as they are enacted and imagined by a dominant white, Christian majority. The main factors determining such reconfigurations lie mainly in geopolitical and historical events shaping relations between the US and the Arab world from around the mid-twentieth century onward. That is, the US military operations and foreign policies in the Arab world play a direct role in molding a strong transnational consciousness among Arab-Americans.[15] As I show in my discussion throughout the book, it is these military operations and foreign policies, as well as their construction of Arabs and Muslims as Other, that primarily position Arab-Americans at the forefront of radical transnational reimaginings of the US nation-state and concomitant reconceptualizations of dominant citizenship and belonging.

The transnational consciousness permeating contemporary Arab-American experiences, however, is neither a new phenomenon nor one exclusively defining the more recent waves of immigrants from the Arab world. For as Sarah Gualtieri points out in her historical study of early Arab immigrants, transnational connections between Arab homelands and the diaspora are very much in evidence during the first period of Arab immigration, from the nineteenth century up till the 1920s. Such transnational connections were shaped by "the ways in which [early] emigrants constructed an imaginary bridge [as well as a physical route] between Syria and Amrika, between the place they had left and the place where they had arrived, between the person they had been and the person they had become" (*Between Arab and White* 19).[16] Even though current articulations of transnational Arab-American perspectives are rooted in these earlier iterations, they are nevertheless distinct in the way they are more directly focused on Arab-American enactments of citizenship and belonging within the US rather than in original Arab homelands. Such enactments are far from being fixed or stable. Instead, as will become evident throughout my analysis in the following chapters, they are constantly being negotiated and renegotiated in relation to the double or multiple national affiliations that shape Arab-American identities.[17]

Privileging a transnational approach to the study of Arab-American literature, however, is not without its own limitations and shortcomings. The performance of transnational identities, for one, operates within its own structures of inclusion and exclusion, given that access to voluntary travel or physical mobility is not readily available to everyone and is contingent on socioeconomic status, as well as political and national backgrounds.[18] Moreover, alongside the prevalence of transnational studies and its focus on the global flow of capital, commodities, bodies, and ideas, the realities of the nation-state and its policing and control of its ideological and physical borders are increasingly stringent and inescapable.[19] My use of the transnational framework in this book acknowledges such limitations and seeks to highlight how they are confronted and addressed in Arab-American articulations of a transnational consciousness. This consciousness is formed through imaginative connections to both the US and the Arab homeland as well as to the spaces of physical travel and mobility between them. I am primarily invested in analyzing, through the selection of literary texts included in this book, the ways in which Arab-Americans live in, negotiate, and subsequently change the landscapes of US citizenship and belonging by superimposing the reimagined Arab terrain onto these landscapes. This simultaneity of visions and belongings, rather than perpetuating the ideological or cultural split between the two terrains, brings them into direct conversation in ways that reconfigure strict definitions of homes, homelands, and national belonging.[20]

In conjunction with the study of Arab-American representations of race, religion, class, diaspora, ethnicity, and citizenship within a transnational framework, I also incorporate a focus on feminist and gender issues as depicted and discussed in the texts I analyze in this book. In doing so, I engage in a larger anti-imperialist approach that challenges the neoliberalist tendency to separate the analysis of Arab-American women from that of Arab-American men. Dominant understandings in the US are governed by a so-called cultural knowledge that considers Muslim, Arab, and Arab-American women to be oppressed and powerless, and Muslim, Arab, and Arab-American men to be agents of oppression and terror. Such simplistic, binary formulations in fact hinge on equal misrepresentations of both genders (while obscuring transgendered and transsexual as well as other nonnormative Muslim, Arab, and Arab-American identities). In my revisions of such hegemonic constructions of gender through close readings of the selected literary and visual texts, I stress how Arab-American writers and artists interweave a focus on gender with issues of race, religion, class, nationality, and political histories to create complex and antiessentialist transnational frameworks of knowledge about Arab-American subjectivities.[21]

This project is firmly positioned within the important nexus of the political, racial, religious, gendered, and literary histories shaping Arab America as discussed by other scholars in the field whose work I draw on and converse with throughout the book.[22] Like these scholars, I have had to confront the problems involved in using general terms, categories, and groupings in reference to Arab-Americans that often gloss over the cultural, religious, and geopolitical specificities of the vast region these terms are meant to represent. For example, like others, I am cognizant of the shortcomings of the term *Arab* as I use it throughout the book, especially as it risks erasing non-Arab ethnic identities and other minority groups in the region, as well as the connections that exist among Arabs and non-Arabs from the larger Middle East region and Central Asia, such as Iran, Turkey, and Afghanistan.[23] I find the term *Arab-American*, despite its shortcomings, to be useful insofar as it denotes a minority collective whose members are connected not only through a shared cultural and linguistic Arab heritage but more importantly through a common investment in shaping and performing a revisionary form of US citizenship that alters the simplistic binary constructs inherent in dominant understandings of the US nation-state. Moreover, I choose to use the umbrella term *Arab-American* while every so often specifying the national affiliations of the various writers and characters discussed here (such as Palestinian-American, Lebanese-American, etc.). Doing so strategically overturns the negative and even racist usages of the term *Arab*, confirming the connections among Arabs within the US as well as their transnational attachments to Arab homelands. As Joe Kadi (formerly Joanna but now self-identifying as Joe) states in the introduction to the anthology *Food for Our Grandmothers*, using the term *Arab-American* "allows us to reclaim the word Arab, to force people to hear and say a word that has become synonymous with 'crazy Muslim terrorists.' It affirms our identity and links us to our brothers and sisters in Arab countries" (xviii). Of course, both terms (*Arab* and *American*) are reductive and conceal the complexity of identities, subjectivities, histories, and politics they entail. The sense of doubleness or splitting of self captured by the *Arab-American* label adequately denotes an inherent tension between these two terms. This tension, however, is not based on some epistemic or originary difference between the two entities but is largely based on history and politics, including colonial histories and neoimperial US ambitions.

I end this section with a note on my use of the terms *Arab* and *Muslim*. While these terms are often erroneously used in the US as synonyms, it is important to emphasize the distinctions between these two identifications. Given my focus in this book on developing an Arab-American critical discourse on the role of Arab homelands in formulating antiassimilative types of US citizenship and belonging, an assertion of the distinctions between the terms *Arab* and *Muslim* becomes central. To this end, I indicate in the following section the variety of religions and nationalities in the Arab world, a move that clarifies my usage of the term *Arab-American* as an umbrella term that incorporates a multiplicity of religious identities, including Muslim ones. Doing so also foregrounds and challenges the dominant US discourse that draws on a long history of US Orientalism, xenophobia, and religious hegemony to frame Arab- and Muslim-Americans as a homogeneous group whose presence in the US remains a precarious and threatening one despite a long and rich history of transnational movement between the Arab world and the US.

Historical and Geographical Backgrounds of Arab-Americans

Arabs and Arab-Americans can trace their national origins to the twenty-two countries of the Arab League states, which are linked through shared cultural and linguistic outlooks.[24] As mentioned earlier, the term *Arab* can be problematically simplistic since member states of the Arab League span vast regions in North Africa and the Middle East, embodying huge variances not only in geographical settings but also in matters of faith, cultural traditions, and even spoken dialects, despite the fact that they all derive from a common classical Arabic linguistic tradition.[25] Moreover, a multiplicity of religious identifications abounds in these member states, incorporating Muslims (Shiites, Sunnis, and minority sects such as Alawites and Zaidis), Christians (Catholics, Greek Orthodox, Protestants, and regional sects such as Copts, Chaldeans, and Maronites), as well as Druze, Jews, and Sufis, among others.[26] The number of Arab-Americans currently living in the US is estimated to have reached around 3.6 million.[27] A large part of this population hails from the Levant area, which encompasses Lebanon, Syria, Jordan, and Palestine.

Arab immigration to the US is characteristically divided into roughly three phases: the first one extends from the 1880s to 1925, the year the Immigration Quota Act was passed, which limited the number of immigrants to the US on the basis of their nationality. The second wave of immigration started with the end of World War II in 1945 and lasted till 1967, a year marked by the Six-Day War between Israel and several Arab countries.[28] The last phase, facilitated by the passing of the 1965 Immigration and Nationality Act, extends from the late 1960s into the current period.[29] The first wave of Arab immigrants, numbering around one hundred thousand by 1914 (Naff, *Becoming American* 2), consisted mostly of Christians from the provinces of Syria, Mount Lebanon, and Palestine, which were ruled by the Ottoman Empire up until 1917.[30] These early immigrants, although initially classified as Syrians or even Turks,[31] were difficult to place within the US racial and national structures of the time, especially since they claimed regional, and more specifically sectarian and familial, identities rather than national ones (Gualtieri, *Between Arab and White* 7; W. Hassan, *Immigrant Narratives* 15; Naber, *Arab America* 19; Majaj, "Arab-Americans and the Meanings of Race" 321).[32] Even though they maintained their cultural and social traditions within their immigrant homes, they sought to assimilate themselves and their children into the US racial structures of the period, with all their dictums of inclusion and exclusion, by lobbying for white status (Naber, "Arab-American In/visibility" 2; Saliba, "Resisting Invisibility" 311).[33] The second and third waves of Arab immigrants, however, although still upholding the official white classification label, proved to be less amenable to assimilation and were largely viewed as nonwhite by the US mainstream. They are largely composed of Muslims who maintain strong Arab national affiliations (Saliba, "Resisting Invisibility" 311–12), despite the fact that these affiliations, accompanied by their Muslim identities, were and continue to be regarded as antithetical to the dominant and favored Christian and European-based identities of the US nation.[34] The rising Arab nationalisms of the 1950s and 1960s, as well as the increasing imperial ambitions of the US in the Arab world during the second half of the twentieth century onward, galvanized stronger transnational political attachments to the Arab world among Arab-American communities across the US.[35] As a result, new trans-Arab solidarities were formed (both within the US and between the US-based Arab diaspora and the Arab world) that were driven by particular political and Arab nationalist concerns while still being firmly grounded in the US geopolitical terrain.

These trans-Arab solidarities, coming into full fruition in the wake of the 1967 war and in the midst of the civil rights movement and the racial, ethnic, and social justice campaigns sweeping across the US in the late 1960s and early 1970s, led to the formation of key Arab-American organizations. Such formations included the Association of Arab American University Graduates (AAUG) in 1967 and the National Association for Arab Americans (NAAA) in 1972, followed by the establishment of the American-Arab Anti-Discrimination Committee (ADC) in 1980 and the Arab American Institute in 1985.[36] All these groups, espousing various organizational methods and approaches, have individually pursued the larger goals of procuring the equal and just treatment of Arab-Americans in the US as well as a greater Arab-American involvement in US foreign policies affecting the Arab world.[37]

This transnational focus lies at the heart of the radicalization of Arab-Americans' civic, cultural, and most importantly political awareness from the mid-twentieth century onward. It helps add a strong, albeit still underrepresented, Arab focus to the range of civil rights issues and transnational struggles defining this period, a focus that highlights Arab-Americans' own positions within the US legal, civil, and social structures. These positions have fluctuated over the years, marked by shifts in the US government's policies on domestic and foreign affairs, as well as the US public's prejudice against Arabs and Muslims, which has accelerated over the past few decades (Y. Haddad, *Not Quite American?* 2). The role that such policies and prejudices have played in the curtailment of Arab-American civil and legal rights dates back to the 1970s and 1980s, made evident by Operation Boulder in 1972, Operation Abscam in 1978, and the case of the LA 8 in 1987 (Naber, "Introduction: Arab Americans and U.S. Racial Formations" 34–36), all of which involved the institutionalized harassment and unconstitutional targeting of Arabs in the US. Such discriminatory treatments were accompanied by the FBI's development of intelligence files on Arab American activists, the surveillance of Palestinian student organizations, and the targeting of ADC offices and the murder of its West Coast regional director, Alex Odeh, in 1986. The 1990s were also marked by the increased subjection of Arab-Americans to racial profiling and to the use of secret evidence against them. With the events of 9/11, these practices have taken on full-blown and normalized proportions. They have been further entrenched with the implementation of new policies such as the PATRIOT Act and John Ashcroft's special registration program, as well as the exponential increase in the number of hate crimes against Arabs, Muslims, and Sikhs in the US (Zogby, "Arab Americans and Law Enforcement").[38]

One important structural framework that captures the difficulties and struggles that have historically defined Arab-American belonging draws heavily on evolving understandings of race, racial formations, and the racialization of minorities in the US. Ever since the first wave of Arab immigration to the US in the nineteenth century, this group's racial identity has been mired in contradictory and changing labels. With the group's official categorization shifting between various identifications such as Turkish, Syrian, and Asiatic in the early years of immigration, its racial status wavered as naturalization laws drew and redrew citizenship rights during the first half of the twentieth century on the basis of changing definitions of whiteness. For instance, in 1910, immigrants from Ottoman-ruled areas, typically referred to as Syrians or Turks, were categorized as Asiatic, rendering them ineligible for US citizenship according to the period's restrictive naturalization laws (Majaj, "Arab-Americans and the Meanings of Race" 321).[39]

Such ambiguous and shifting labels were emphasized in a series of court cases typically referred to as the prerequisite cases, in which individual Arab immigrants had to petition for white classification if they wanted to attain US citizenship. Skin color and religious affiliation were two major factors on which court decisions were based in the cases of George Najour in 1909, Faras Shahid in 1913, George Dow in 1914,

Ahmed Hassan in 1942, and Mohamed Mohriez in 1944.[40] These individual cases necessarily affected the racial classification of the larger ethnic group to which the appealing immigrant belonged, with the result being that Arab immigrants applying for US citizenship, and by extension Arabs in general, "were declared white in 1909 and 1910, non-white in 1913 and 1914, white in 1915, non-white in 1942, and white in 1944" (Majaj, "Arab-Americans and the Meanings of Race" 321, 333n. 6).[41]

Even with the US Census Bureau's consistent adoption of the white label in its official racial classification of Arab-Americans since the 1940s, the Arab-American community still faces a quandary in relation to such a classification.[42] One of the most immediate concerns about such a categorization is that, with the US Census solidly situating Arab-Americans within the white category, this group has no legal position among the spectrum of minority cultures that would enable it to demand minoritarian rights and to articulate its communal concerns about racial and ethnic discrimination. Moreover, the irony of such a white classification is augmented by a dominant US belief permeating much of the nation's collective consciousness that Arab- and Muslim-Americans (as well as Arabs and Muslims in general) are racially different and threatening, a belief that has been expounded on and concretized with every political crisis since the mid-twentieth century. These ambiguous and contradictory racial labels affixed to Arab America drive public figures such as Helen Hatab Samhan, executive director of the Arab American Institute Foundation, to state that the current federal inclusion of Arab-Americans from the Middle East and North Africa within the "white 'majority' context" does not resolve confusions regarding their racial status ("Not Quite White" 219). In fact, such a categorization aggravates these confusions. In order to partly address such ambiguities, the Census Bureau in 1980 initiated a question on ancestry that respondents across the various racial categories can use for the purpose of ethnic self-identification.[43] Even though this ancestry question found its way once again into the 1990 and 2000 census forms, it was omitted from the 2010 forms despite the fact that various ethnic organizations were lobbying for its inclusion.

The instability and ambiguity of Arab-American racial classification has historically generated a variety of responses from within Arab-American communities, with these responses revolving around two opposing political demands. The first demand veers toward complete Arab-American integration into the US mainstream and the continuance of the white classification, while the second seeks the right for Arab-Americans to be granted minority status and to self-identify as "people of color" (Gualtieri, "Becoming 'White'" 52; Majaj, "Arab-American Ethnicity" 322). During the 1990s, a consensus could not be reached among Arab-Americans calling for a specific Arab or Middle Eastern designation under the white racial category. One faction called for the recognition of a Middle Eastern category that would include Iranians and Turks (proposed by the Arab American Institute [AAI]), while another lobbied for an "Arab-American classification" (upheld by the American-Arab Anti-Discrimination Committee [ADC]) (Saliba, "Resisting Invisibility" 309).[44] Presently, such positions are changing to reflect an increasing shift away from the Arab label on the part of the ADC as well as the AAI. Both organizations have been working together to support the adoption of a Middle Eastern / North African (MENA) label as its own category or as a subsection of the white category.[45] To date, a clear decision is still not available on this issue. Such a shift away from the Arab label reflects Arab-Americans' reaction to the increased racialization and demonization of Arab identities, especially in the overbearing post-9/11 atmosphere of surveillance and racial profiling.

Whatever the results of such demands prove to be, the unstable identity of Arab-Americans burdens this group with an ambiguous state of "honorary whiteness," allowing members of this group a tentative and provisional entry into American white society, only to find that status "readily stripped away at moments of crisis" (Majaj, "Arab-American Ethnicity" 321).[46] This type of "honorary whiteness" serves to isolate Arab-Americans from the white category (since they are never actually included in discussions of racial whiteness) and from a racial minority status, situating them in an unstable racial space within the US. Moreover, the stigmatizing racialization of Arab- and Muslim-American bodies by the US mainstream accentuates the ambiguity of Arab-American belonging in the US.[47] Whether imposed on Arab-American bodies through specific hegemonic readings of their religious dress or other religious observances, their political views, their accents, or their skin color, such stigmatizing racializations are instrumental in affirming the foreignness or Otherness of these bodies in the US.[48]

Not all Arab-Americans identify as people of color or adopt a critical approach toward US foreign policies in the Middle East and toward the domestic policies governing the treatment of Arabs and Muslims in the US. In lieu of demanding their civil rights and liberties, many Arab-Americans have opted to remain silent and acquiescent to secure safety for themselves and for their families. Nevertheless, it has become evident in the past couple of decades that the racialization of Arab-Americans and the discriminatory treatment they receive in the US due to their allegedly suspect and foreign character have given rise to a certain cohesiveness or unity of vision shared by many Arab-Americans. This unity often supersedes, but at the same time remains very much cognizant of, the heterogeneity of Arab individuals' ancestral national and religious identities. In other words, the vast differences and fraught histories defining relations among the various countries of the Arab world, even while being replicated and recalled in the US diaspora, do not produce the same rigid boundaries among the different Arab-American identities as they do in the Arab world. In this way, the flexibility characterizing the boundaries between Arab identities in the US enables Arab-Americans to develop and maintain revisionary forms of pan-Arab identifications, ones that, as history has shown, have often been difficult to maintain within the geographical bounds of the Arab world itself.

The Development of an Arab-American Literary Tradition

The fast-growing list of contemporary Arab-American literary texts has its roots in the works of early-twentieth-century Arab-American writers such as Gibran Kahlil Gibran (1883–1931) and Ameen Rihani (1876–1940). Recognized as the founders of Arab-American literature, Gibran and Rihani are hailed as groundbreaking writers in the Arab world and its diaspora. Gibran's numerous publications include the much-touted collection *The Prophet* (1923), written in English and translated into more than fifty languages, and Rihani's multigenre literary output including *The Book of Khalid* (1911), also written in English and usually referred to as the first Arab-American novel.[49] These early writers, known as the *mahjar* (immigrant) writers who traveled from the Arab world to the US and eventually resettled in their original homelands, wrote in both English and Arabic. In 1920, they established in New York what came to be known as Al-Rabita al-Qalamiyya, or the Pen League, consisting of Syrian and Lebanese writers such as Gibran, Rihani, Mikhael Naimy (1889–1988), and Elia Abu Madi (1890–1957). Though based in the US, members of this group were instrumental in transforming modern Arabic literature in important ways, including their introduction of blank verse into Arabic poetry (Shakir, "Arab-American Literature" 3; W. Hassan, *Immigrant Narratives* 59). They maintained a solid transnational outlook in their physical and intellectual negotiations of Arab and American identities.[50]

Critic and translator Salma Khadra Jayyusi sees "a very clear discontinuity" between the mahjar writers and contemporary Arab-American writers (qtd. in Majaj, "Of Stories and Storytellers" 27), especially given that the main contributions of the early mahjar writers were to the enrichment and flourishing of Arabic literature. Rather than a complete break, I see a shift between the transnational perspectives of the earlier group of mahjar writers and contemporary Arab-American authors and artists. While both groups of writers enact transnational belonging, current literary works mark a move away from the mahjar writers' overall tendency to perceive the Arab homeland as the first and final home front for their expatriate identities. Members of the Pen League, despite their investment in fomenting dialogue between the Arab world and the US, ultimately retained a solid grounding in the Arab world (mostly Lebanon), to which many of the group's members retired after their US sojourns. Moreover, most of their work did not directly reference their immigrant lives in the US (W. Hassan, *Immigrant Narratives* 59). Conversely, contemporary Arab-American writers engage first and foremost with the US landscape as a permanent rather than as a provisional home. Their transnational perspective, even though also informed by their strong connections to an Arab homeland, nevertheless claims the US terrain as a permanent home for Arab immigrants and their descendants, with this claim aimed at altering fixed and exclusionary landscapes of US citizenship and belonging. Instead of framing their work primarily in terms of its contributions to an ongoing tradition of Arabic literature, the literary output of contemporary Arab-American writers needs to be read *as* American literature, with a recognition of its formative role in shaping alternative and antihegemonic types of US cultural production.

By 1940, with the passing away of some of the Pen League's members and the return of others to the Arab world, the League had dissolved. The period extending from the 1940s up until the late 1980s / early 1990s is a transitional one in Arab-American literature. Characterized by different phases, this transitional phase starts with the second wave of immigration and stretches into the third wave. Very few texts were published between the 1940s and 1960s, with the handful of available texts reflecting the desire to assimilate that was prevalent among immigrants and their children during the first two waves of Arab-American immigration. This assimilative bent is evident in autobiographies such as Salom Rizk's *Syrian Yankee* (1943), Vance Bourjaily's *Confessions of a Spent Youth* (1960), and William Blatty's *Which Way to Mecca, Jack?* (1960) and even encompasses earlier autobiographies such as Abraham

Mitrie Rihbany's *A Far Journey* (1914).[51] Works such as these, particularly those by Bourjaily and Rizk, while enjoying a great deal of success at the time of their publication, reflect their writers' shared disconnection from their Arab heritage, which they approached with a mixed sense of shame and nostalgia (Majaj, "Of Stories and Storytellers" 27; Shakir, "Arab-American Literature" 7). This sense of shame paradoxically turns into an exoticizing admiration of the "old country" and its traditions upon the protagonists' respective visits to Lebanon (an admiration that nevertheless, in Blatty's case, verges on the farcical).

Between the late 1960s and the 1980s, the paradox of shame and nostalgia pervading these early autobiographies slowly gave way among Arab-American authors to a growing sense of pride in their Arab heritage and ethnicity, marking the second phase of this transitional period. This sense of pride is exemplified in the works of writers such as Samuel Hazo, D. H. Melhem, Eugene Paul Nassar, Jack Marshall, and Joseph Awad. As writers initially "independent of ethnic categorization who later donned the cloak of the Arab-American identity," they became "direct links between Arab American writing and the American literary canon" (Abinader, "Children of Al-Mahjar").[52] These writers' important and formative investigations of a US-based identity that is shaped by an Arab background significantly helped set the stage for a full-blown flourishing of Arab-American literature in the 1990s onward.

It is with the emergence of literary works in this period by Arab-American writers who were either born or who came of age in the 1950s and 1960s onward (a time of increased US intervention in the Arab world) that we can see a clear and consistent development of a transnational critical perspective in Arab-American literary production. This perspective acknowledges the shame and nostalgia inherent in being *bint/ibn Arab* (daughter/son of Arabs) but nevertheless succeeds in transcending such limited and limiting conceptualizations of identity and heritage to map out new pathways for Arab-American articulations of US belonging and citizenship. In addition to maintaining a critique of US foreign policies in Arab countries and the war traumas they incur, these works celebrate inherited Arab cultures but at the same time acknowledge their dark underbelly, which might include patriarchal norms, political divisions, and religious restrictions.

Arab-American writers starting to write and publish in the 1990s (and in the late 1980s) onward differ from their literary predecessors in notable ways, particularly in the kinds of subject matter they take up in their writings. For one, their works for the most part reflect on experiences of displacement, exile, and dispossession caused by the political shifts and military conflicts across the Arab world from the mid-twentieth to the early twenty-first century.[53] These experiences largely depart from the circumstances instigating earlier Arab immigration, such as poverty, the determination to escape conscription into the Ottoman army, or a thirst for adventure and fortune.[54] Whether incorporating a thematic focus on the memory and ongoing experience of the Palestinian Nakba,[55] the Lebanese civil war, or the shifting geopolitical terrains in Egypt, Syria, Kuwait, or Iraq, Arab-American literary texts published from the 1990s onward vividly capture the circumstances of war and dispossession that have driven millions of Arabs to leave their homes. Such representations, and the political implications they hold, become key factors in shaping the connective and transnational attachments to an Arab homeland.

Whether experienced firsthand by Arab immigrants of the third wave or handed down to the US-born generations by immigrants arriving during the earlier waves of Arab immigration, these transnational attachments become integral for developing heterogeneous enactments of Arab-American identities, as featured in the texts discussed throughout this book. These attachments in turn instigate a deeply interrogative rather than an assimilative approach to US identity, largely devoid of nostalgia and sentimentalism. Even if there remains some lingering nostalgia toward the Arab homeland in these contemporary literary texts, it nevertheless differs from the kind prevalent in earlier texts such as those by Bourjaily and Blatty. What distinguishes this version of nostalgia from its earlier counterpart is that in contemporary Arab-American literature, nostalgic remembrances of an original Arab homeland are often undercut by a stark political knowledge of neoimperialist and settler-colonialist agendas and the ensuing traumas of war and dispossession they incur. As I show throughout my analysis of the various literary texts in this book, such knowledge could either be experienced firsthand and brought into the US space by recent Arab immigrants themselves or inherited and replicated by their children.

The 1990s are a significant decade in the flourishing of the current and latest phase of Arab-American literature for several reasons. As I mentioned earlier, many Arab-American writers who either came of age or were born in the fraught political climate defining the Arab world and the US in the 1950s and 1960s started writing, publishing, and sharing their work during the 1990s. Writers who had started publishing prior to the 1990s but whose work gained more recognition during this period and since include poet Naomi Shihab Nye (*Words under the Words* [1995] and *Red Suitcase* [1994]),[56] as well as Lawrence Joseph (*Before Our Eyes* [1993]).[57] The number of first books published by Arab-American writers during this period is notable, with these groundbreaking texts including Joseph Geha's *Through and Through: Toledo Stories* (1990), Elmaz Abinader's memoir *Children of the Roojme: A Family's Journey from Lebanon* (1991), Diana Abu-Jaber's first novel *Arabian Jazz* (1993), Suheir Hammad's first book of poetry *Born Palestinian, Born Black*, and Rabih Alameddine's first novel *Koolaids: The Art of War* (1998).[58]

This surge in literature built on important historical as well as sociological and ethnographic studies on Arab-American immigrant communities that had been published during the 1980s. Some of these notable studies include Sameer Y. Abraham and Nabeel Abraham's edited collection *Arabs in the New World: Studies on Arab-American Communities* (1983), Alixa Naff's *Becoming American: The Early Arab Immigrant Experience* (1985), and Gregory Orfalea's *Before the Flames: A Quest for the History of Arab Americans* (1988). A new wave of historical and sociological studies were published during the 1990s, the most prominent of which is Michael Suleiman's edited collection *Arabs in America: Building a New Future* (1999). These works paved the way for the full-fledged development of the literary sphere in the 1990s onward, driven by the interest in recognizing and locating the Arab-American presence in the US.

The emergence of Arab-American writers' creative work during the 1990s coincided with another high point in the US's direct political and military involvement in the Arab world. Such involvement included the First Gulf War and the US-led invasion of Kuwait in 1991, as well as the US-brokered peace negotiations between Palestinians and Israelis, which culminated in the signing of the Oslo Accords in 1993. These kinds of US interventions in the Arab world were of course preceded in the 1980s by the US role in the Lebanese civil war and the Israeli invasion of Lebanon in 1982.[59] The emergence of a growing Arab-American literary repertoire was timely, albeit ironic, given the increased demonization of Arabs and Muslims in the US during this period, especially with the 1993 bombing of the US World Trade Center and the domestic backlash against Arabs after the First Gulf War. These ongoing national and international crises and military conflicts render Arab-Americans all the more vulnerable to prejudice and anti-Arab racism. In the context of such vulnerabilities, and in the absence of established political leadership among Arab-Americans, literary production becomes an important vehicle to counter the limited venues in which Arab-Americans could enact diverse and antihegemonic forms of transnational US belonging and citizenship.

The importance of such venues is also informed by their power to establish intellectual and creative connections among Arab-American writers, thinkers, and cultural workers scattered across the US. These kinds of connections were instigated, for one, by collaborative publications such as *Grape Leaves: A Century of Arab American Poetry*, a groundbreaking anthology published in 1988 and featuring the poetry of Gibran Kahlil Gibran, Ameen Rihani, Elia Abu Madi, Etel Adnan, D. H. Melhem, Naomi Shihab Nye, Elmaz Abinader, and Sam Hamod, among others.[60] Edited by Gregory Orfalea and Sharif Elmusa, *Grape Leaves* not only exposed a US public to an emergent minority US literature but also spread an empowering awareness among many Arab-American writers of a larger collective with which they could engage to break away from the isolation and invisibility defining their individual struggles. This connection to a larger collective and the increasing visibility of Arab-American literary and cultural production were further solidified by another pioneering anthology published in 1994, titled *Food for Our Grandmothers: Writings by Arab-American and Arab-Canadian Feminists*. Edited by Joe Kadi, this feminist anthology features more than forty contributors of Arab and Middle Eastern backgrounds. It asserted the growing cultural productivity of members of these minority communities in the US, which Kadi refers to in the introduction as "the most Invisible of the Invisibles" ("Introduction" xix). *Food for Our Grandmothers* also cemented the need to acknowledge the heterogeneity of these communities, as well as the need to map their histories and concerns onto the US terrain rather than treat them as perpetual foreigners by virtue of their connections to the Middle East in general or to the Arab world specifically. It is within the coupled contexts of political and historical urgency on the one hand and an increased rate at which Arab-American literary and cultural work was being published on the other hand that the literary organization Radius of Arab American Writers Inc. (RAWI) was mobilized by Barbara Nimri Aziz in 1992. Coined by Mohja Kahf to signify the Arabic word for "storyteller," the name for RAWI was officially adopted in 1994. Initially featuring a handful of Arab-American writers, scholars, and artists, RAWI's membership has grown exponentially over the years and is currently in the hundreds.

Moreover, the ushering in of a new phase of Arab-American writing with a sizable and expanding literary repertoire was confirmed in 1999 with the publication of *Post-Gibran: Anthology of New Arab American*

Writing, edited by Khaled Mattawa and Munir Akash. Including a collection of mostly new voices and a range of previously unpublished work, this anthology sought to assert a marked departure in turn-of-the-twentieth-century Arab-American literary texts from their earlier counterparts, especially in issues pertaining to "cross-genre" and literary experimentation (Mattawa and Akash, "Introduction: Post-Gibran" xiii). In fact, in the case of all three Arab-American anthologies published during the 1990s, the editors' selections reflect the different and often contradictory approaches undertaken to define and delineate Arab-American literature during this formative decade. For while *Grape Leaves* features a selection of the most notable Arab-American poetry from the twentieth century, *Food for Our Grandmothers* focuses on the writings of feminists working in various venues and in different genres, and *Post-Gibran* incorporates a range of new and experimental pieces. All three anthologies, however, engage the question of how to capture and define an evolving Arab-American identity through the lens of literary and cultural production. As Michelle Hartman notes in her insightful analysis of the anthologies' introductions, the importance of these works also lies in the strategic positioning of Arab-American identities in each anthology along specific US racial lines. Such positionings differ from one anthology to another, thus reflecting the shifting and multiple enactments of racial identities among Arab-Americans, as well as the evolving depictions of cross-ethnic and cross-racial struggles between Arab-Americans and other minorities in the US (Hartman 177–201).

Since the 1990s, there has been a burgeoning of the Arab-American literary and cultural scene, made evident by the publication of more anthologies, novels, poetry collections, nonfiction, and critical texts, as well as new and emergent genres such as spoken-word poetry, drama, stand-up comedy, film, and graphic narratives, to name a few. The appearance of separate anthologies on Arab-American fiction and poetry attest to the prolific contributions of writers in both genres, even though poetry has been, and still remains, the dominant genre in Arab-American literature. Edited by Pauline Kaldas and Khaled Mattawa, *Dinarzad's Children: An Anthology of Contemporary Arab American Fiction*, first published in 2004, was revised and reissued in 2009, while *Inclined to Speak: An Anthology of Contemporary Arab American Poetry*, edited by Hayan Charara, appeared in 2008.[61]

The events of 9/11, while exacerbating the demonization and racialization of Arabs and Muslims in the US, have also ironically rendered more available the space for voicing the Arab-American perspective, whether in the form of literary or scholarly publications, conferences, university programs, or artistic shows and forums.[62] Such spaces have become more prevalent especially in light of a national realization, which increased with the wars in Afghanistan and Iraq, that mainstream America is for the most part ignorant about the Arab world and about Muslim cultures. Occupying these scholarly and creative spaces without a self-reflexive understanding of the structures and powers controlling and shaping minority representation, however, can be dangerous and limiting. In moments of national crisis, certain Arab-Americans and Muslim-Americans, by choice or not, have often acted as singular representatives of what is in fact a wide variety of backgrounds and opinions defining the Arab and Muslim communities in the US. In such tense and volatile contexts, mobilizing the discursive spaces of literary production becomes important for enacting multiple and complex forms of Arab-American self-representation and also for creating artistic and cultural spaces that reimagine hegemonic forms of US citizenship and belonging.

These discursive spaces nevertheless become a point of contention within Arab-American literary and artistic communities when it comes to determining what constitutes Arab and Arab-American identities and whether or not certain criteria should be set for determining what makes a certain text or a writer "Arab-American." One question that arises from such discussions is "Does anything written by an Arab-American qualify *per se*, or is 'Arab-American writing' restricted to Arab-American themes?" (Majaj, "Of Stories and Storytellers" 30; see also Salaita, *Arab American Literary Fictions, Cultures, and Politics* 25). My approach in this book maintains as a basic premise the idea that writers should at least have an Arab background or heritage to qualify as Arab-American. However, rather than setting up strict parameters for Arab-American writing, I believe the criteria for determining whether texts can be considered Arab-American should remain as flexible as possible to avoid replicating the exclusionary methods that have and continue to relegate minority voices to the peripheries of US literatures and cultures. Moreover, instead of repeatedly returning to questions geared toward determining what is or is not eligible for inclusion in the Arab-American literary category, I believe that a constant assessment of the nature, makeup, and changing genre boundaries of this field should instead be part of an ongoing discussion within the community, with a clear emphasis on maintaining its rich and heterogeneous literary makeup.

A wide array of themes and representations is present in contemporary Arab-American literature, including Arab-American engagements with issues of cultural and transnational in-betweenness, collective and individual marginalization, US assimilation, food and cultural memory, language, gender, heritage, and religious identity, to name a few. Thematic engagements also handle the racialization of Arab-Americans in the US, as well as a concern about military and political conflicts in Arab homelands, with all the negative consequences on Arab-American communities that these conflicts instigate. Throughout the book, my argument highlights the role of these Arab homelands in shaping complex, transnational, and antihegemonic forms of US citizenship and belonging for Arab-Americans. To this end, I have selected texts that portray direct or indirect engagements with Arab homelands (whether experienced firsthand or through the memories of a parent or grandparent). More specifically, I argue that these texts, rather than employing the memory and knowledge of original homelands to privilege a permanent return to the Arab world, in fact challenge understandings of *US* belonging and citizenship by discursively reconfiguring racial, religious, political, and gendered US landscapes. In doing so, I emphasize for the most part texts depicting connections to specific Arab homelands, particularly the geopolitical terrains of Lebanon, Palestine, Jordan, Syria, and Egypt. Most of the writers whose works I discuss hail from these countries. I also emphasize texts that convey military conflicts in the Arab world, the most prominent of which are the Palestinian Nakba and the Lebanese civil war, given their prevalence in Arab-American literature and their effects on Arab-Americans' transnational experiences. Beyond these frameworks of specific geopolitical terrains and military conflicts, however, the transnational outlooks as well as individual and communal traits featured in these selected texts are widely varied. For while some Arab-Americans have never been to the Arab homeland (and thus rely for their knowledge of it on their elders' memories) or cannot return to these homelands due to the conditions of war and occupation, other Arab-Americans either grew up in these homelands and then immigrated to the US or return to them for short-term visits. Moreover, connections to Arab cultures and traditions are highly varied among the Arab-Americans featured in these texts, with some, for example, being able to speak and read Arabic and others not. Some grew up in households where both parents were Arab, while others come from mixed marriages, self-identifying as "half and half."[63]

This selection of texts is meant to be neither exhaustive nor absolute in its representation of the field. It is geared toward emphasizing the diversity of Arab-American literature despite the fact that the book's thematic approach necessitates a more focused consideration of those texts that most exemplify discursive formations of transnational Arab-American citizenship and belonging. To show the diversity of genres in Arab-American literary production, I include analyses of poetry, fiction, nonfiction, and drama, occasionally branching out into discussions of Arab-American visual works to discuss how Arab-American artists undertake similar themes and concerns in various cultural venues.[64]

In tracing the various discursive iterations of transnational Arab-American citizenship and belonging in contemporary Arab-American literature, I focus on texts primarily published from the 1990s onward. A few texts published in the late 1980s are nevertheless included due to their formative contribution to the field, such as Lawrence Joseph's poem "Sand Nigger," for instance. Throughout the book, I outline four major thematic approaches to the study of the transnational in Arab-American literary and cultural production, with these approaches forming the framework of my analysis as well as the book's chapter divisions. The first theme, discussed in chapter 1, revolves around representations of Arab homelands as embodied and performed by immigrant parents or grandparents, with these memories subsequently internalized but also revised by second- and third-generation Arab-Americans (who came of age or were born in the second half of the twentieth century).[65] Revisions of the first generation's[66] fragmented memories of original Arab homelands are addressed in this first chapter through the works of Lawrence Joseph, Therese Saliba, Suheir Hammad, Naomi Shihab Nye, Joe Kadi, David Williams, D. H. Melhem, Diana Abu-Jaber, Joseph Geha, Elmaz Abinader, Mohja Kahf, Elmaz Abinader, and Susan Muaddi Darraj. The second thematic focus, developed in chapter 2, portrays second- and third-generation Arab-Americans undertaking temporary return journeys to ancestral homelands. The revisionary perspectives resulting from such journeys, a concept I refer to as *rearrivals*, are exemplified in the works of writers such as Kahf, Samia Serageldin, Pauline Kaldas, and Muaddi Darraj. This chapter also features some nonliterary pieces that focus on the significance of return journeys in the Palestinian context, such as Annemarie Jacir's film *Salt of this Sea* (2008) and Emily Jacir's visual art. Chapter 3 delves deeper into the thematic diversity of transnational articulations to investigate how Arab-American rootedness in and production of transnational identities produce specific translocal spaces that alter our understanding of US national, diasporic, and ethnic belonging. In doing so, I analyze novels, essays, memoirs, and poetry by Patricia Sarrafian Ward, Haas Mroue, Rabih Alameddine, Etel Adnan,

Edward Said, Laila Halaby, and Randa Jarrar. These writers' antinostalgic stances and critical perspectives, mostly but not solely reflecting a contemporary immigrant perspective, produce complicated constructs of homes and homelands that incorporate the stark effects of lingering war traumas and political tensions on current Arab-American identity formations. Chapter 4 focuses on literary texts that develop articulations of transnational Arab-American citizenship and belonging that are directly related to the events of 9/11. These texts encompass an array of poems, essays, short stories, novels, and plays by Geha, Kahf, Halaby, Hammad, Dima Hilal, Rabab Abdulhadi, and Yussef El Guindi. I include in the last part of this chapter a discussion of artist Wafaa Bilal's installation work in order to acquaint readers with other artistic venues in which similar questions and concerns about Arab-American citizenship and belonging are being raised. In the conclusion, I outline some exciting new directions in the field and briefly discuss the impact of the Arab uprisings on Arab America.

Rather than simply compartmentalizing Arab-American writers and their texts into the divisions just outlined, however, I preserve the complexity of these thematic strains by showing, across the scope of the book, how various literary engagements with Arab homelands can coexist and intersect within the same Arab-American text or within the range of a writer's literary repertoire. In treating Arab-American literary and visual texts as important discursive sites in which such confrontations and negotiations become manifest, I am particularly invested in studying how cultural production ultimately gives shape to transnational and transcultural Arab-American epistemologies, ones that stress antiessentialist reformulations of Arab-American identities as well as antihegemonic types of citizenship and belonging in the US. This book enables, then, through literary and cultural analysis, the delineation and development of a transnational language of Arab-American belonging that is revisionary and radical in nature. This revised language of citizenship and belonging as performed by contemporary Arab-American writers, artists, and cultural critics simultaneously reshapes the US landscape as a whole, ultimately offering new vistas for reimagining and reenacting US identities and the power structures they entail.

1 / Reimagining the Ancestral Arab Homeland

Palestinian-American writer and literary critic Lisa Suhair Majaj claims her belonging and attachment to the city of Jerusalem, which she repeatedly visited as a child and as an adult, and describes this city in her essay "Journeys to Jerusalem" as living deep inside her "like the stone of a fruit" (101).[1] Such a weighty and incipient core (which can extend beyond Jerusalem to stand for various Arab locations) holds what Majaj calls the "traces [that] register at the deepest layers of consciousness" (88). Assorted renditions of such a visceral representation of an original Arab homeland, in slightly varied guises, accents, and flavors, lie at the core of contemporary Arab-American literature, in which the theme of inherited memories of ancestral homelands is prominent. Tracing such representations in several contemporary Arab-American literary texts, I highlight in this chapter the ways in which second- and third-generation Arab-American identities are shaped by specific articulations of transnational belongings that complicate the link between, in poet Lawrence Joseph's words, "what is furthest from us / and what deepest in us" ("Inclined to Speak" 164, lines 22–23).[2]

Focusing on literary representations of second- and third-generation Arab-Americans who were born or raised in the US from the mid-twentieth century onward,[3] this chapter shows how these generations, most of whom have never been to the Arab world, revise inherited understandings of and connections to that "furthest" and "deepest" point of origin, or the "old country." Instead of replicating the older immigrant generations' nostalgic memories of Arab homelands, however, these younger generations of Arab-Americans destabilize such nostalgia by moving depictions of original homelands beyond a celebratory focus on ethnic and cultural traditions to incorporate accounts of the harsh realities of war, dispossession, gender politics, and exile.[4] Through such portrayals, Arab-American writers whose work is featured in this chapter (as well as other writers throughout the book) carry out the important task of "de-mythologizing the homeland" (Shakir, "Imaginary Homelands" 23).[5] This generational shift in perspective becomes noticeable in the works of writers who either were born or came of age in the 1950s and 1960s onward, a watershed period for the development of a critical and interrogative outlook among Arab-Americans generally, primarily due to major political and military upheavals as well as social change occurring in the US and in the Arab world.[6]

In producing antinostalgic literary mappings of original homelands, these writers draw on transnational frameworks of knowledge production to imagine, exemplify, and enact in their work a revisionary approach to Arab-American citizenship and belonging. This approach ultimately alters dominant understandings of US national membership by inserting the complex political, religious, and national landscapes of Arab homelands into discursive constructions of US space. Such insertions challenge binary constructions of national belonging, which pit the US against the Arab world and posit any simultaneous claim to both locales as a contradiction in terms. Instead of espousing a "split vision," or a sense of having to constantly oscillate between two (or more) cultures, Arab and American, which are often regarded as being at odds with each other (Majaj, "New Directions" 123; Salaita, "Split Vision"),[7] many of the texts explored in this chapter express a critical transnational vision that is simultaneously linked to, and informed by, the inescapable pull of an Arab homeland *as well as* a US locale. It is this particular vision that distinguishes the majority of immigrants' children coming of age during the second half of the twentieth century onward from their older counterparts.[8]

The transnational vision that I trace in this chapter lays claim to the spatial, material, and temporal positionalities of Arab-American identities within the US as mediated by an older immigrant generation. In this way, the US becomes the central locus from which the Arab homeland is explored, identified with, and reimagined, but not forgotten. But instead of it becoming an ostracizing factor in constructions of Arab-American belonging in the US, it is asserted and reconceived as an elemental part of transnational formulations of Arab-American identities that challenge the binaries of exclusion and inclusion inherent in dominant understandings of US citizenship and belonging. It is exactly this type of transnational vision that enables Arab-American writers to challenge any docile and unquestioning forms of ethnic identity (despite lingering assimilative tendencies within Arab-American communities that might indicate otherwise). This type of revisionary perspective, however, even though it ultimately destabilizes a secure and unchanging notion of home and homeland, does not necessarily lead to an inevitable sense of homelessness.[9] Instead, it opens up new vistas of belonging in the US, which create new understandings and maps of home by simultaneously laying claim to and transforming both the Arab and the American sides of Arab-American identities.

Rather than pursue a chronological analysis of literary narratives shaping and giving voice to the ongoing development of Arab-American transnational belonging, and in order to delineate the continuance of certain concerns and the revision of others, this chapter and the book as a whole trace specific thematic threads that place side by side texts by an older generation of writers (who came of age in the 1960s and 1970s) alongside others by a younger generation (who came of age in the 1980s and 1990s). This approach shows that the revision of nostalgic representations of original homelands in Arab-American literary texts published from around the 1990s onward has been highly diverse, representing a whole range of national, religious, political, and regional, as well as generational, concerns. Irrespective of such diversity, however, these texts share a clear investment in retaining the Arab homeland as a central trope in the production of revised forms of spatial, material, and temporal Arab-American positionalities.

To analyze such discursive revisions and the new mappings of home they create, I start by tracing second- and third-generational representations of immigrant memories as manifested within the confines of domestic Arab-American spaces. In the absence of the US-born-and-raised generation's direct experience of an Arab homeland, the immigrant parents' and grandparents' reproduction of it from memory within the space of the immigrant home becomes the primary site through which this generation first comes in contact with it.[10] The reproduction of this Arab homeland occurs primarily through material fragments, including food, Arabic text, photos, music, plants, and religious icons and scripture. The persistence of such fragments is exemplified in the first section of this chapter through poetry and nonfiction by Lawrence Joseph, Therese Saliba, Suheir Hammad, and Naomi Shihab Nye. An analysis of these writers' revised engagements with the domestic fragments embodying immigrant memories leads to an exploration in the second section of this chapter of the gendered aspects of these memories and the role that parents/grandparents play in perpetuating patriarchal mores in the diaspora. Drawing on texts by Joe Kadi, David Williams, D. H. Melhem, and Diana Abu-Jaber, I focus specifically on the grandmother and father figures to analyze the ways in which their cultural knowledge is received and renegotiated by their children and grandchildren. After exploring some of the ways in which these writers strategically delineate and question nostalgic and gendered memories within the insular confines of the Arab-American immigrant household, I turn in the third and final section of the chapter to analyze how they depict the movement of the second and third generations from the insular immigrant mold into a more public US domain. Such movement is analyzed in the context of works by Lawrence Joseph, Hayan Charara, Elmaz Abinader, Mohja Kahf, and Susan Muaddi Darraj. The transformative aspects embedded in such reconfigurations of homes and homelands are essential for the placement of transnational Arab-American belonging in the US outside neo-Orientalist and imperialist frameworks.

The Presence of Absence:[11] Fragments of Arab Homes Re-membered

The revision of nostalgic and fragmented deployments of an absent Arab homeland within the present of a domestic immigrant space is captured most effectively in Lawrence Joseph's poem "Sand Nigger" (1988).[12] Considered to be a landmark piece in Arab-American literature, this poem delineates the ways in which the physical artifacts of an Arab homeland, in this case Lebanon, within the confines of the narrator's "house in Detroit" inform his developing consciousness as a young child as well as his negotiations of Arab-American heritage and identity as an adult. Within the space of his childhood home, the narrator recollects fragments of food, language, history, and religion that embody the inherited memory of a Lebanon left behind but not forgotten:

> Lebanon is everywhere
> in the house: in the kitchen
> of steaming pots, leg of lamb
> in the oven, plates of kousa,
> hushwee rolled in cabbage,

> dishes of olives, tomatoes, onions,
> roasted chicken, and sweets;
> . . . .
> Lebanon of mountains and sea,
> of pine and almond trees,
> of cedars in the service
> of Solomon, Lebanon
> of Babylonians, Phoenicians, Arabs, Turks
> and Byzantines, of the one-eyed
> monk, Saint Maron,
> in whose rite I am baptized. (lines 15–21, 26–33)

Despite the poem's piecing together of such culinary, historical, and religious fragments that capture nostalgic, if not mythical, remembrances of Lebanon, its larger depiction of an original homeland falls far from being elegiac or ideal. The nostalgic remembrances of the narrator's grandparents (whose presence in the narrator's childhood home informs the wistful tone captured in the lines just quoted) exist in harsh juxtaposition with another fragmented version of Lebanon permeating the poem, one that is neither palatable nor sumptuous. This darker version, which the speaker's parents try to suppress, is dominated by war, conflict, and death and stands in stark contrast to the nostalgic backdrop of his grandparents' lyrical representation of "Lebanon of mountains and sea":

> Lebanon of my mother
> warning my father not to let
> the children hear,
> of my brother who hears
> and from whose silence
> I know there is something
> I will never know. (lines 34–40)

This concealed knowledge of a war-torn Lebanon is followed by a cousin's graphic description over dinner of his "niece's head / severed with bullets, in Beirut, / in civil war" (lines 56–58). In emphasizing the multiple Lebanons that exist within this childhood home (ranging from the ideal to the horrific), Joseph evokes a complexity of Arab history and Arab-American heritage that flies in the face of nostalgic essentialism, pointing to the generational shifts in perspective vis-à-vis the homeland within the same household. This perspective is inevitably shaped and revised by evolving events in the Arab world, specifically here the Lebanese war (1975–90). In this way, despite the predominance of an idyllic "Lebanon of mountains and sea" in the speaker's household, other contradictory versions of this homeland emerge to contest such idyllic representations and to underscore that nostalgic immigrant remembrances of original homelands often omit or conceal harsh realities that extend to violence and death.[13]

Notwithstanding these fragments' power to evoke a sense of an original homeland, albeit one pieced together from contradictory versions, Lebanon remains not only inaccessible but for the most part incomprehensible to the speaker. For the legacy of the Lebanon(s) to which he is exposed within the domestic space holds disorienting elements, including a language (Arabic) that he finds hard to read "word by word from right to left" (line 5), a political history that he is not privy to, as well as a budding doubt toward an inherited religion, leading him to question his grandmother's belief "that if I pray / to the holy card of Our Lady Of Lebanon / I will share the miracle" (lines 12–14). In this way, the various fragments of Lebanon evoked in this home do not create a link to an original homeland but instead highlight the speaker's disconnection and alienation from it. Such disconnections and gaps, however, become the key factors instigating the children and grandchildren of immigrants to develop alternate, demythologized, and individualized forms of attachment to Arab homelands that extend beyond the nostalgic and the celebratory.[14] In doing so, they mobilize new critical understandings of these ancestral homelands that in turn enable them to engage more directly and critically with the larger social and racial US structures, as I discuss in this chapter's second section. In other words, the impossibility of connecting to mythological immigrant renditions of an Arab homeland that we see in Joseph's poem gives rise to a multilayered understanding that transcends singular constructions of home, with all the exclusionary and conditional forms of belonging such constructions entail.[15] In "Sand Nigger," the speaker's awareness of the multiple narratives within his home about Lebanon is the first step toward reenvisioning his national belongings and allegiances, thus producing more informed and critical versions in the process. This awareness accompanies him in his efforts to self-identify along the black/white racial binaries outside the confines of the domestic space, a self-identification that I discuss in more detail in the thematic context of this chapter's second section.

Therese Saliba's nonfictional essay "Sittee (or Phantom Appearances of a Lebanese Grandmother)" (1994), published in Joe Kadi's anthology

Food for Our Grandmothers, similarly depicts the development of a critical and multilayered vision from the perspective of a child also reacting to her grandmother's nostalgic remembrances of a lost Arab homeland.[16] In this piece, Saliba pays homage to her deceased grandmother Victoria, who immigrated to the US at the age of twenty-four never to return permanently to her native Lebanon. In an evocative statement, Saliba acknowledges her grandmother's embodiment of a homeland, stating, "If a woman could be a land, then Sittee ["grandmother" in Arabic] was Lebanon to me" (10). Yet for the young Saliba, this Lebanon remains relegated to her grandmother's domestic realm: "On weekdays I lived in an American world. But on weekends, I lived in a world of foreign foods, strange language, incense, ritual, bazaar, and bizarre" (9). Together, the heady intermingling of "lemon jasmine . . . from Lebanon and Jean Nate from France . . . with the steam from the chicken boiling on the stove" in her grandmother's kitchen (11), as well as the grandmother's love of the French language and her inability to talk about her beloved Lebanon except in Arabic, reproduce for the young Saliba the "fragmented history of Victoria's homeland" (9). Unlike in Joseph's poem, however, where a complex, intergenerational layering of memory exists within the domestic space, Saliba's piece emphasizes the centrality of Victoria's nostalgic reminiscences of home, which "her memory had fixed in a pastoral painting" (14).

It is only as an adult that Saliba can start reconceptualizing the fragments of her grandmother's memory, replacing nostalgia with an acknowledgment of the harsh realities and histories that were glossed over and elided in Victoria's selective narrative of home. It is through such reconceptualizations that Saliba recognizes and incorporates "the scars of French colonization," the imprint of civil war, and the transformative effects of US naturalization on her grandmother's uprooted female body (10).[17] Such recognitions, like those in Joseph's poem, stress the gaps rather than the links between immigrant memory and the actual Arab homeland, which remains beyond reach for Saliba. Like the speaker in "Sand Nigger," the adult Saliba seeks to formulate a more coherent version of Lebanon, one that is not riddled with her grandmother's nostalgic yearning. More than negotiating this version of Lebanon within the US space, Saliba tries to visit Lebanon in her effort to transcend the gaps and fissures propagated by her grandmother's narrative of the Lebanese homeland. However, even after accessing her grandmother's Lebanese passport to circumvent the ban on American travel to Lebanon in the 1980s and 1990s, Saliba is still unable to reach her grandmother's homeland. In the summer of 1991, due to civil unrest and regional tensions, "too many borders seemed closed," writes Saliba. "And though I spent the summer instead in the West Bank, just miles from Lebanon, I couldn't enter Sittee's country because Southern Lebanon was under siege from Israel and the borders were closed" (16).

The fissures and gaps prevalent in an older immigrant generation's fragmented memories of an original Arab homeland are not always typified by the nostalgic and the mythical. As exemplified in "Sand Nigger," the stark realities of war and dispossession seep into domestic reenactments of the homeland, despite the older generation's efforts to suppress them. Moreover, these realities are not always absent from older immigrants' stories about the homelands they left behind. They often permeate the Arab-American home, replacing celebratory visions of these homelands with fragments that more transparently evoke the violence of exile and displacement brought about by particular political and historical conditions. Suheir Hammad's poem "Argela Remembrance" (1996), which references the dispossession of Palestinians after the Nakba in 1948, grounds the autobiography of a Palestinian-American community within a very tactile and tangible narrative of exile as told and retold within the domestic space.[18] This space, in its every aspect, becomes the claustrophobic antithesis of a lost Palestine that permeates the poem but is never explicitly named. The speaker, referred to as "my father," addresses his daughter "suheir," delineating the fragmented contours of exile as lived individually and collectively within the Palestinian-American household:

>   we are a people
>   name our sons after prophets
>   daughters after midwives
>   eat with upturned hands
>   plant plastic potted plants
>   in suffocating apartments
>   tiny brooklyn style
>   in memory of the soil once
>   laid under our nails (lines 21–29)

The overwhelming sadness punctuating this poem's brutal imagery revolves around a gaping spatial and temporal absence that pervades every aspect of Palestinian relocation, specifically here domestic spatiality. But rather than symbolizing a larger whole (the Palestinian homeland) that was left behind, the fragments punctuating the domestic space in this poem evoke the lack and even the artificiality of a continuous, seamless link between the original homeland and the US space of exile. For instead of olive and orange trees (emblems of Palestinian land and identity),[19] the exilic generation is reduced to "plant[ing] plastic potted plants," an act that embodies the truncation and rootlessness of exile and one that encapsulates the artificiality of the speaker's new surroundings.

Plastic potted plants, disheartening replacements of Palestine's olive trees and fruit orchards, and metaphors of displaced Palestinian identity, possess no roots and bear no fruit. They are plastic and sterile, reminders of an alienating location to which the speaker feels no connection and evoking only a memory of the richness of Palestinian "soil once / laid under our nails" (lines 28–29).[20] The use of the past tense in this line conveys the severance of a deep attachment to the physicality of the homeland, a severance that continues to have strong reverberations as it is passed down from one generation to another. The absence and loss of this land is augmented and rendered intolerable when juxtaposed against the "suffocating apartments / tiny brooklyn style" as rooted in the present (lines 26–27). Moreover, this poem's Palestinian-American autobiographical collective, captured by the term "we," is one that registers communal mourning for a lost homeland, a mourning that stresses the need to remember while emphasizing the pain involved in such acts of memory:

> We've become a people of
> living room politics and tobacco
> stained teeth,   painfully
> reminding each other
> reciting quranic verse and
> um kolthom scripture
> of how jasmine can
> fill your head on a clear night and
> mint tea dawned you to morning (lines 35–43)

By reviving the memory of Palestine, such fragmented evocations are in fact mourning the loss of a past homeland and its disconnection from an exilic present. Evocations such as these enact what Roberta Rubenstein calls "the presence of absence," or "an absence that continues to occupy a palpable emotional space" (5). More than merely occupying an emotional space, however, this absence is often replicated in material fragments within the exilic household. The piecing together of these fragments and the revision of any lingering nostalgic elements in them become the main tools through which the second and third generations of Arab-Americans not only can connect with or metaphorically reoccupy the past but can also reevaluate it from the critical yet informed vantage point of a US-based present.

This type of engagement with an Arab past from within the present space of the US disrupts traditional ethnic, immigrant, and diasporic tendencies that keep these two temporal and spatial realms separate. At the same time, dominant US national discourse perpetuates such separations by insisting on uniform and singular affiliations to the nation-state. Disrupting such tendencies produces a transnational vision that insists on drawing on informed, albeit painful, understandings of original homelands to negotiate antihegemonic and antiassimilative forms of US belonging. Various iterations of this vision are evident in the texts discussed in this chapter, serving to portray and revise the nostalgia inherent in an immigrant generation's memories of an original homeland, at the same time mapping out radical and transformative paths for the US present.

Sometimes, the figure of the immigrant him- or herself is the one who adopts such a reevaluative vision. In Naomi Shihab Nye's poem "My Father and the Figtree" (1994), for one, the speaker repeatedly evokes her immigrant father's stories and memories of Palestine, especially his yearning for the taste of fresh figs of his Palestinian childhood that is ingrained in his memory:[21]

> In the evenings he sat by our beds
> weaving folktales like vivid little scarves.
> They always involved a figtree.
> . . . .
> At age six I ate a dried fig and shrugged.
> "That's not what I'm talking about!" he said,
> "I'm talking about a fig straight from the earth—
> Gift of Allah!—on a branch so heavy
> It touches the ground. (lines 4–6, 13–17)

Like "Argela Remembrance," the poem is permeated by a sense of rootlessness evoked by the poignant absence of Palestinian native soil and trees from the US space of exile. The absence of these fig trees becomes the emblem of the father's homesickness and his dislocation from the Palestine of his memories. Yet unlike "Argela Remembrance," in which the mourning of this absence is a lingering and constant presence, there is a shift in the father's perspective and actions at the end of "My Father and the Figtree." This shift replaces mournful absence with the promise of an altered present that, while not exactly replicating the homeland (or its fragments), still offers viable alternatives. After the speaker's father has spent a lifetime in the US yearning for the plump and delicious fresh figs of his homeland, he moves to a new house in Dallas where he finds a fig tree already planted in the yard:

> There, in the middle of Dallas, Texas,
> a tree with the largest, fattest,
> sweetest figs in the world.
> "It's a figtree song!" he said,
> plucking his fruits like ripe tokens,
> emblems, assurance
> of a world that was always his own. (lines 35–41)

The intriguing closing lines of this poem portray a world that embodies the father's yearning for the homeland he left behind when he immigrated to the US. At the same time, a close reading of these lines necessitates the recognition of the fact that this world does not replicate, neither partially nor fully, the Palestinian homeland.[22] The roots of this world lie in new soil, US soil, and its fruit, although ripe and delicious, is not after all the same as Palestinian fruit. The claim to memory and homeland in this poem, however, while mourning the loss of past rootedness, nevertheless ends up charting new configurations of belonging to US soil/land. These configurations are based on a remembered past landscape as lived and experienced in the US present. Configurations such as these produce a simultaneity of temporal and spatial perspectives that draw on both the past and the present—the over there and the over here—in formulations of Arab-American identities within a wider US public space beyond the private and domestic immigrant and ethnic domains.

Before turning to public assertions of identity and the way they are shaped by racial, religious, and political factors, I focus next on the relationship between memory and gender within the immigrant household in works by writers such as Joe Kadi, D. H. Melhem, David Williams, and Diana Abu-Jaber. In doing so, I highlight the revision of gendered and patriarchal roles in transnational reconfigurations of immigrant, ethnic, and diasporic connections between past and present, the Arab world and the US.

Gendering Immigrant Memories:
Of Grandmothers and Fathers

In many literary texts by second- and third-generation Arab-Americans, the memory of the homeland as mediated by the first generation is not only nostalgic but also overwhelmingly gendered. Reassessing the fragmented memories of home entails addressing and revising the patriarchal gender roles that are embedded in Arab immigrant perspectives.[23] As made evident by Joseph's and Saliba's texts discussed earlier, the important link between memory, original homelands, and gender, especially as enacted within the Arab-American domestic sphere, is often embodied by the grandmother figure, whose knowledge often takes on mythical proportions.[24] A first step toward "de-mythologizing the homeland" (Shakir, "Imaginary Homelands" 23), therefore, involves a direct and difficult engagement with the figure of the grandmother and all the cultural and gendered elements she stands for. Her towering presence within the domestic immigrant space in many cases determines which fragments of the Arab homeland get to be reenacted within that space, with the production and consumption of Arabic food taking center stage.

Even as many Arab-American texts seek to move the role of the grandmother beyond the purely celebratory domestic sphere (thus releasing her from such staple roles as "the bearer of culture" or the "static carrier ... of 'tradition'" [Civantos]), they still position her as an authoritative representative of (for the most part) an unattainable ancestral homeland. Whether kneading dough, rolling grape leaves, or preparing homemade remedies, the grandmother becomes a symbol of cultural and domestic practices from which the second and third generations of Arab-Americans are largely disconnected. In *Food for Our Grandmothers*, Kadi describes these kinds of practices as a "body memory" that her grandmother has "inside her," one that Kadi herself is not privy to ("Five Steps" 233).[25]

The acknowledgment of the grandmother as an influential figure and symbol is evident in Kadi's introduction to the anthology.[26] Paying tribute to Arab grandmothers, Kadi asserts the need for "giv[ing] something back to these women" (xx).[27] Instead of limiting these grandmothers to the domestic realm, Kadi, self-identifying as female at the time of writing and publishing the anthology, locates their labor within the larger framework of diasporic cultural production. At the same time, Kadi notes their role as "cultural worker[s]" and her own inheritance of that role, albeit in a "different medium" (represented by her writing and political activism) ("Five Steps" 232). Despite bridging the gap between domestic, intellectual, and activist work, however, Kadi still expresses a deep sense of inadequacy in performing the cultural heritage embodied by her grandmother, even in its broader cultural framework. For unlike her grandmother, whose roots are deeply grounded in an unmistakable Arab cultural and geographical terrain, Kadi feels constantly unhinged and uprooted from both an original homeland and an ethnic or diasporic setting. Kadi writes,

> But there is a big, big difference between my grandmother and I. The knowledge is inside her. . . . She is secure in the knowledge of what to do. I am not. I am foraging for a recipe, a tradition, one that originated in the east and will serve me well in the west. . . . So I am floundering, looking for recipes that will serve us, looking for recipes that let people know the place from which we came and the place where we are now. ("Five Steps" 233)

Such recipes become the key to formulating a type of belonging that is neither alienating nor assimilative but one that is transnational and transformative in nature. As discussed in the preceding section, one type of recipe for enacting critical and antiassimilative forms of Arab-American belonging is to acknowledge painful and traumatizing Arab histories and the memories they generate within the intimate space of the Arab immigrant home. Additional recipes include disrupting patriarchal structures and constricting gender roles within Arab-American ethnic and diasporic spaces as well as within mainstream US landscapes.

Literary renegotiations of cultural knowledge, memory, and home through the body of the grandmother contribute to the figurative release of grandmothers (or for that matter mothers, sisters, or aunts, as well as fathers, brothers, and uncles, etc.) from the tight stranglehold of patriarchal "traditions," whether they be carried over from the Arab homeland or constructed within US social milieux. Some literary texts that interrogate the fixity of such patriarchal and gendered roles within Arab-American immigrant communities include David Williams's poem "My Grandmother and the Dirbakeh" (1993), in which the speaker reevaluates the role of his grandmother within a constricting domestic sphere by imagining her playing the *dirbakeh* (traditional Arab drum), which "by tradition a man played" (line 1).[28] Instead of the grandmother pounding the grain in her pestle, the speaker imagines her pounding on the drum:

> . . . It's her
> touch I want to bring to the drum,
> playing steady past the erratic
> heartbeat that couldn't sustain her
> body . . . (lines 33–37)

By the speaker's bringing to life (even if only in his imagination) his grandmother's unexplored or perhaps unfulfilled talents and desires, he releases the memory of his grandmother from the traditional and strictly delineated gender roles that often dictate the domestic sphere of Arab-American communities. D. H. Melhem echoes such a stance in *Rest in Love* (1975), a book-length elegy to her mother. Melhem records her childhood observations of the painstaking labor being carried out in her grandmother's house, where her "mother [and] grandmother sit at the white enamel kitchen table, kneading dough, shelling peas, measuring pine nuts into the chopped lamb and onions" (17).[29] Rather than being a participant in such labor, however, the young narrator merely "bears witness to [the] daily translation of two women's / lives into pots and pans, the circumscription of kitchen walls" (17). Moving from an observer of such cultural performances to a more active participant, the speaker conjures up another medium of expression (namely writing) for her mother. She imagines rescuing her mother from the tight control of the grandmother, who in the poem stands in for conservative cultural and gendered codes:

> o mother I'll pick you right out of her eyes
> off her skin that is thick with you
> I'll give you a room with a nice view of life
> and a pen and some ink and paper in sheaves (22, lines 15–18)

The revisions that are merely imagined by the speakers in Williams's and Melhem's poems become more concrete when it comes to the second and third generations' enactments of these gender roles. After years of Kadi's rejecting her heritage due to the anti-Arab racism she suffered as a child and the abuse meted out by her father, she describes in her memoir *Thinking Class: Sketches from a Cultural Worker* how she "re-connected with [her] roots" by playing a *dirbakeh* similar to the one her grandmother had carried with her from Lebanon (116). It is only by drawing on such an alternative connective link to her grandmother, one that lies outside traditional gender roles, that Kadi can then affirm a strong, albeit revised, sense of her "racial/cultural heritage" (115).[30] Playing the *dirbakeh* and rediscovering Arab music, then, become for Kadi a means to create new "recipes that let people know the place from which we came and the place where we are now," recipes that lie at the core of the Arab-American second and third generations' transnational and transformative visions (Kadi, "Five Steps" 233). When conceived of in this way, such cultural work releases the second and third generations from restrictive ethnic and diasporic performances of homeland rituals that are dictated by immigrants' nostalgia and by constricting gender roles.

Sometimes it is a male rather than a female figure whose memory connects the second and third generations to an Arab homeland that they do not know firsthand.[31] In the work of writers such as Diana Abu-Jaber and Naomi Shihab Nye,[32] the figure of the uprooted immigrant father is a central one, often portrayed as constantly piecing together symbolic remnants of the homeland (whether represented as food, fig and olive trees, or folkloric stories).[33] In Abu-Jaber's work, specifically her second novel *Crescent* (2003) and her memoir *The Language of Baklava* (2005), the articulation of the fragmented, predominantly male memories of Arab homelands is enacted through the production and consumption of Arabic dishes.[34] Even though in *Crescent* these dishes are prepared by the second-generation Iraqi-American Sirine, their preparation is very much informed by the memory of her father's yearning for his native Iraq (which he had left as a young man seeking better opportunities), as well as by her love for her Iraqi boyfriend, Hanif, and her eagerness to replicate the lost dishes of his childhood.[35] Living with her uncle after her parents (American Red Cross volunteers) had died in Africa when she was a child, Sirine rediscovers and reproduces the foods that her father had cooked for her. She works as a chef in a Middle Eastern café that is strategically located in a part of Los Angeles nicknamed Teherangeles and that is frequented by a gaggle of homesick Arab students from the nearby university.[36]

In preparing lentils fried with rice and onions, roasted lamb, baba ghanouj, rice and pine nuts, fava-bean dip, *laban* sauce, and eggplant, Sirine seeks to (literally) replicate fragments of a homeland that she knows only by way of her father's memory of Iraq (and her memory of him). Lacking a deep connection to a sense of place, even though she has lived in LA all her life, Sirine tells Hanif, "I have this feeling that my real home is somewhere else somehow. . . . Work is home" (118). In this way, preparing the food that helped her father maintain his connections to his lost homeland becomes a way for Sirine to find her home, not back in Iraq but in the US. Piecing together a fragmented memory, however, does not merely involve the replication of an inherited homeland within the diaspora but ultimately leads to its reinvention. For rather than reproducing an "authentic" or unchanging Iraqi (or for that matter a wider, more comprehensive Arabic) cuisine, Sirine in fact produces hybrid culinary fragments that seemingly embody or reproduce an original homeland but are nonetheless rooted in the immediacy of the US cultural landscape. Referring to how "good food" "taste[s] like where it came from, . . . so the best butter tastes a little like pastures and flowers," Sirine states, "things show their origins" (69).

The origins that Sirine mentions here are complex and multiple, mirroring her own transnational and transformative vision that straddles and revises both sides of her hyphenated identity. Such a vision, unlike that of her immigrant father, is neither nostalgic nor assimilative, producing instead a unique concept of home that is entrenched in a US present, while retaining vivid, albeit revised, traces of mediated memories of an Arab past.[37] As the novel's effusive Arab poet tells Sirine, "Cooking and tasting is a metaphor for seeing. Your cooking reveals America to us non-Americans. And vice versa" (197). For Hanif, Sirine embodies what he calls "the place I want to be—. . . the opposite of exile" (140). Such revised belongings are best exemplified in *Crescent* in the description of what Sirine dubs her "Arabic Thanksgiving" (192). This event highlights the hybrid mixture that emanates from the culinary intermingling of "origins." In addition to the "[onions, cinnamon,] rice and pine nuts and ground lamb in the turkey instead of cornbread, and yogurt instead of cranberries" (184), this "Arabic Thanksgiving" is replete with eclectic dishes such as "sauteed greens with bittersweet vinegar, and lentils with tomato, onion, and garlic, . . . maple-glazed sweet potatoes, green bean casserole, . . . pumpkin soufflé" (191), as well as "stuffed squashes and grape leaves, . . . creamed spinach, . . . [and] smoked frekeh" (196), Hanif's favorite Iraqi dish. This improvisatory and transformative relationship to one's Arab origins enlarges understandings of home and the construction of individual and communal subjectivities, emphasizing the transnational aspects at the core of Arab-Americans' negotiations of their lives in the US.[38]

A similar transformative relationship with an Arab origin is also underscored in Abu-Jaber's memoir, *The Language of Baklava*. Starting with Abu-Jaber's childhood, spent between Jordan and Syracuse, New York, and ending with her year of residency in Jordan and her move to Portland, Oregon, *The Language of Baklava* delineates an intriguing journey abundant with the smells, tastes, sights, and spirit of the world in which Abu-Jaber grew up. This world is overwhelmingly colored by her Jordanian immigrant father, Ghassan Saleh Abu-Jaber (better known as Bud), whose gregarious and engaging character, tinged with homesickness and a nagging sense of displacement, dominates the narrative. In fact, his yearning for his homeland and his love of cooking Arabic food suffuses the memoir to such an extent that he becomes the main vehicle through which Abu-Jaber articulates her own second-generation Arab-American story.[39] She writes, "I believe the immigrant's story is compelling to us because it is so consciously undertaken. The immigrant compresses time and space—starting out in one country and then very deliberately starting again, a little later, in another. It's a story of fantasy—to have the chance to re-create yourself. But it's also a nightmare, because so much is lost" (*Language* xi).

The revision of Bud's nostalgic and fragmentary reconstructions of home through food is most effectively undertaken in the memoir by Abu-Jaber's paternal aunt, the formidable Aunt Aya. A delightfully willful and colorful character, she reinstates, while on a visit to Syracuse from Jordan, a young Diana's love for Arabic food. Echoing Sirine's emphasis on the importance of origins in *Crescent*, Aunt Aya announces to her niece,

> People say food is a way to remember the past. Never mind about that. Food is a way to forget. . . . Your father? He's the worst of the worst. He thinks he cooks and eats Arabic food, but these walnuts weren't grown from Jordanian earth and this butter wasn't made from Jordanian lambs. He is eating the shadow of memory. He cooks to remember, but the more he eats, the more he forgets. (189–90)

"Eating the shadow of memory," then, inevitably grounds Bud's production of home within the US landscape, which changes and at the same time is changed by that production. In other words, more than being a venue for Arab-Americans like Bud to replicate a version of Jordan in the US, preparing and eating Arabic dishes alter Arab-Americans' connections to original homelands, despite the immigrant generation's lingering nostalgic reminiscences.[40] Aunt Aya's pronouncements, even though not entirely propagating an agenda of culinary authenticity, stress the importance of acknowledging the origins of cultural fragments, specifically food, when they travel, change, and are adapted into new national and multicultural contexts. Pronouncing that "food is robbery," she draws up for the young Diana a peace plan that hinges on powerful nations such as "America, Israel, [and] England" consuming the food of underrepresented nations as a way to acknowledge rather than appropriate their labors and contributions (189, 190).

Years later, Diana is reminded of her aunt's words when she sees the poster for a Jewish Foods Day event sponsored by the Hillel student organization at her college. Seeing the advertisement for the familiar dishes that, to Diana, are synonymous with her father and her father's Jordan, she wonders, "Does falafel belong to a nation? A culture?" (219). Driven by homesickness, Diana attends the event, only to find "the hummus . . . dull as clay, the baba ghanouj thick and bitter," and "the dried-out falafel . . . cold and overcooked" (220, 221). The answer to Diana's question about the rights of nations and cultures is not directly addressed. However, like the father figure in Nye's poem "My Father and the Figtree," Diana is still able to identify and reclaim the specific Arab traces at the heart of cultural symbols and fragments that have been altered within the US landscape. Biting into the "cold and overcooked" falafel, Diana can "still taste fried chickpeas, the golden, mellow fundament of falafel, and, embedded deeper within, the sun-soaked air of Jordan" (221). This reclamation of the food's Arab origins, however, is not so much an affirmation of her father's nostalgia as it is an assertion of her own Arab identity within a landscape that often omits such a presence from its genealogy and history or that presents it as perpetually foreign. This scene is crucial to Diana's own formation of an Arab-American identity, one that is deeply influenced by her father's worldview but is at the same time informed by her Jordanian aunt's critical and insightful perspective on the production of Arabic food and cultural identity within the US landscape.[41]

What is most relevant about Aunt Aya's perspective is that it provides the young Diana with an alternative lens that diverges from her father's take on the role of food in reproducing an intact sense of Jordan within the US. The most important lesson that Diana learns from her aunt is the limitation of her father's male perspective in transmitting the knowledge of what he sees as true Arab culture. In fact, Aunt Aya starts out her lesson on the origins of food by stating, "Food is not sweetness and families and little flying hearts. . . . Food is aggravation and too much work and hurting your back and trapping the women inside like slaves" (189). Diana's reeducation in the domain of "womanliness" at the hands of Aunt Aya (who had never married) opens up an alternative route to the strict gender rules that she had grown up with. These rules manifest themselves, for instance, in her father's distinction between "Good-Arab-girls" and

"Bad-boy-crazy-American-girls," with the presumption that his daughters naturally belong in the former camp (194). As Diana ruminates on her aunt's advice that she should not have "babies unless it's *absolutely necessary*," it dawns on her that there is more than one way to tackle gender roles within her immigrant father's household: "After years of assuming that the purpose of all this cooking and working . . . was to produce and grow babies, this [Aunt Aya's advice] is the first intimation I have heard of *another way through life*" (186; emphasis mine).

In this way, despite the fact that Diana grew up "with Bud's idea that Jordan" is the family's "truest, essential home," we nevertheless find her, single and childless at the end of the memoir, embracing a more fluid version of an inherited sense of home and belonging, one that retains a looser interpretation of cultural and national rootedness (235). She writes, "Even if I had somehow, down the line, brought myself to have babies and to stay in my hometown in a house with an easy, wide-hipped porch, none of that would have made any difference to the sleepless part of me." Calling herself "a reluctant Bedouin," Diana expands on the term's Arab and more specifically Jordanian context by embracing a larger and more inclusive version of her father's fixed and gendered concept of home. She states in the novel's closing chapter, "I miss and I long for every place, every country, I have ever lived" (327).

The revision of male-centered and selective memories of the homeland is not only found in *The Language of Baklava* but is also evident in Abu-Jaber's first novel, *Arabian Jazz*. Published in 1993, this novel features another displaced Jordanian father, Matussem Ramoud, who is raising his two daughters, Melvina and Jemorah, in upstate New York. Matussem's memories of his homeland, even though not as idealistic or effusive as Bud's, retain strong traces of the male privilege with which he grew up as the only son of Palestinian refugees in Jordan. Matussem "knew, watching and overhearing his sisters at night, that it was a bitter thing to be a woman" (187). Abu-Jaber explains that "it was almost impossible for Matussem to think fondly of his old home [in Jordan] through the smudge of years, the sense of poverty, so many lonely sisters, the social restrictions that kept them home," and "the way his parents had married several of his sisters to men they had never seen before in their lives" (233, 237). Despite all this knowledge, there still exist stark gaps in Matussem's memory that do not enable him to easily transmit the knowledge of this home to his daughters. His sister Fatima, however, who occupies the same diasporic location and who is constantly extolling the virtues of Jordan, harbors a different and secret memory of their original home. At a young age, Fatima took part in the unutterable act of participating in not one but "two, possibly three, . . . furtive burials" of infant sisters while they were still alive (119).

Abu-Jaber, however, does not fall into the easy trap of ascribing Fatima's memory of burying her baby sisters alive to what is often condescendingly defined in the West as an example of Jordan's (or for that matter the Arab world's) repertoire of backward cultural and religious practices. In fact, Fatima's impulse to reveal this act to her nieces toward the end of the novel is brought on by her need to explain the painful history of loss and displacement that her family had to go through as Palestinian refugees in Jordan after the establishment of Israel in 1948. She states, "What of my parents' shame, driven off the good land and sacred home the father's fathers built . . . [w]hen we were homeless and dying without food" (334). Fatima expands on Matussem's memory by underscoring the dismal living conditions brought about by dispossession and exile, which might explain why her anguished parents would carry out the incomprehensible act of burying her infant sisters alive. The patriarchal privilege sheltering her brother from knowing about these acts is nevertheless not lost on Fatima, who emphasizes the gaps in Matussem's memory by relating her own memory of the act. "What of the four starving babies I had to bury still alive," she asks, "so my baby brother can eat, so he can move away and never know about it[?] . . . Born a *man*, not to know the truth" (334). Despite recognizing the limits of patriarchal memory, however, Fatima does not fully succeed in overturning it. We find her at the end of the novel still insisting that her nieces carry out what she deems to be the essential norms of marriage and motherhood.[42]

The recognition that the immigrant generation might in fact be transmitting not only fragmented but also selective gendered versions of Arab homelands leads the second and third generations of Arab-Americans to adopt more critical strategies in negotiating transnational belonging.[43] Such strategies challenge patriarchal constructions of original homelands and at the same time address racialized representations of Arab-Americans as an Othered or foreign presence within the US national sphere.[44] After highlighting the ways in which gender is mobilized in formulations of Arab homelands within the domestic immigrant space, I move on in the following section to focus on the ways in which transnational enactments of Arab-American citizenship and belonging are produced by second- and third-generation Arab-Americans in public US domains. I place special emphasis on the interconnected frameworks of race, religion, and politics as portrayed in the selected texts.[45]

Crossing the Threshold: From Arab to Arab-American

The cultural divide separating the immigrant generation's insular domestic space from the larger US cultural landscape is a poignant source of dilemma for second- and third-generation Arab-Americans. The pervasiveness of a fixed set of traditions and values within the immigrant household, which also extends into a collective Arab enclave, in many cases engenders a sense of shame about being the daughter or son of immigrant parents (*bint/ibn Arab*). This sense of shame is often connected to the cultural practices in which immigrant households and communities partake, extending to the production and consumption of Arabic food, participation in Arab-American social events, and the practice of religious traditions within the confines of the communities' churches or mosques. For many US-born Arab-Americans, all of these practices become ostracizing factors that need to be omitted or concealed from their lives in mainstream America, especially those practices that render them more susceptible than others to the ridicule of their "all-American" white peers. Arab-American writers who came of age before the 1960s equally express this sense of shame, highlighting their strong desire to escape the confines of their parents' households and to integrate themselves into mainstream US culture.[46] The difficulties that Arab-Americans face in their negotiation of the private and the public realms, however, is not a self-imposed one. As Andrew Shryock emphasizes in his piece on familial ties in Arab Detroit, the pervasive shame produced by such disconnection is primarily caused by the US mainstream's denigration of Arab familial traditions and viewpoints, which are often regarded as "intrinsically flawed" ("Family Resemblances" 589). "The Otherness of Arab domestic cultures," writes Shryock, "is shaped by the American mainstream against which new immigrants struggle to define themselves. Immigrants from the Arab world must contend with the abnormalization of things that, in Lebanon, Yemen, or Iraq, seemed perfectly normal" (583).

This agonizing process of separating private from public performances of identity takes on specific political dimensions in the works of contemporary second- and third-generation Arab-American writers. For in addition to the cultural traditions that distinguish them from the US mainstream as well as from other ethnic and racial minorities, the political becomes more and more of a defining factor in Arab-American lives, especially from the 1960s onward. As various countries in the Arab world have been caught in the net of national, regional, and international conflicts, and as US imperial ambitions in the Arab world have grown more evident and powerful in this period, Arab-Americans have become increasingly aware of the negative effects that their attachments to their original homelands continue to have on their presence in the US. Mainstream America sees in these attachments an allegiance to a geographic region that poses a danger or an impediment to US hegemony and is regarded as antithetical to white Christian US values and traditions. But rather than Arab-Americans from the mid-twentieth century onward opting for the assimilative route favored by their predecessors, we see them take more critical, interrogative, and direct measures in incorporating their cultural as well as political identities into the US dominant culture. Notwithstanding the sense of trepidation and insecurity accompanying this kind of revisionary and transnational approach to individual and communal representation, it produces discursive articulations of Arab-American identities that do not necessitate denying, suppressing, or excising Arab self-identifications in public performances of US citizenship and belonging.[47]

The challenges involved in straddling (both mentally and physically) an Arab immigrant space and a public US landscape are often at the basis of the revisionary Arab-American perspective examined in the texts discussed in this section. This simultaneous claim to both spaces challenges the either/or formula of American versus Arab inherent in dominant US discourse. It doing so, such a claim incorporates double and multiple national allegiances and memberships that are based on complex articulations of ethnicity, race, sexuality, gender, and religion. The immigrant space discussed in this section is not restricted to the domestic domain but can extend to the surrounding neighborhood / ethnic enclave in cities with a dense Arab presence, such as Dearborn and Toledo. These enclaves embody (on a larger scale) nostalgic reenactments of the Arab homeland and are often perceived to be its diasporic replications. For instance, in Joseph Geha's seminal collection of short stories, *Through and Through: Toledo Stories* (1990), which is regarded as a benchmark text in contemporary Arab-American fiction, the immigrant setting overshadows the narrative as a whole, becoming the main entity against which some of the characters struggle to reformulate inherited notions of identity and belonging.[48] Even though both of the protagonists in the two stories "Everything, Everything" and "Almost Thirty," for instance, manage to escape the overbearing climate of their immigrant parents' households by choosing to live alone, they are still bound by the larger framework of Toledo's Arab community and its cultural norms.

In "Almost Thirty," Haleem is only able to break from those norms of culture and tradition when he marries what his Aunt Afifie calls a "crazy American" (41). But such acts of defiance are not readily available to some of the other characters in this collection of short stories. In "Everything, Everything," for instance, Barbara Saleeb struggles to escape from her meddling mother, who is constantly urging her to get married. By the end of the story, however, this struggle is left unresolved, with only a hint of a promise that she will become fully independent. Throughout the story collection, Geha shows how, within such tight-knit communities, the Arab-American immigrants' mental disconnect from and suspicions of mainstream America are intense and palpable. The children and grandchildren of these immigrants often replicate such suspicions, turning the US into a foreign country despite their being physically present in it. In another short story from the collection, titled "Holy Toledo," the young protagonist, Nadia, observes the infringement of that alien "America" on her grandmother's East Detroit neighborhood,

> the little Syria centered at Congress Street and Larned. . . . On Saturday mornings Americans came . . . . to shop [for] woven artifacts and brass from the old country . . . [and for] pressed apricots, goat cheese, sesame paste and pine nuts and briny olives. . . . Nadia wished that she were one of them, returning with them into that huge strangeness, America, luring her despite the threat it seemed to hold of loss and vicious homesickness. (87–88)

When Nadia wonders aloud about the whereabouts of her father, who had left her and her brother with her grandmother and gone off without a trace after the death of his wife, her grandmother retorts by "only saying 'America'" (92). This laconic response leaves Nadia trying "to imagine [this] America, how it will be, and what they [she and her brother, Mikhi] should take with them when they go" (99).[49]

Such imaginative acts of crossing the threshold that separates immigrant enclaves from mainstream America take on more literal forms in the works of other contemporary Arab-American writers such as Lawrence Joseph, Elmaz Abinader, Mohja Kahf, and Naomi Shihab Nye. The claims that they assert to a US landscape in their work, claims informed by an Arab cultural and political lens, produce a complex type of transnational citizenship and belonging that flies in the face of the assimilation-versus-ethnic-insularity model. This type of transnational citizenship and belonging privileges complex understandings of history, geography, religion, politics, diaspora, race, and ethnicity as they are shaped by an Arab-American presence within the US as well as across the US and the Arab world. In other words, these texts show how Arab-Americans' presence within the US and their enactment of transnational forms of citizenship and belonging complicate, question, and change the racial, religious, ethnic, historical, diasporic, and political landscapes of mainstream America.

A focus on race is especially pertinent here especially given that Arab-Americans are officially categorized as white according to the US Census Bureau. This categorization is problematic and ironic given that Arabs and Muslims are a racialized Other in the dominant US imaginary. Arab-Americans' white status is also an impediment to forming internal communal cohesion since many Arab-Americans in fact espouse this categorization, leaving those who do not choose to or cannot pass as white (due to identifiable bodily markers) in ostracized and ambiguous positions. My own framing of Arab-Americans as people of color is meant to replace the negative and harmful racialization of these communities with empowering racial self-identifications. Self-identifying as a racial minority points to the ways in which Arab-Americans are well positioned to resist the hegemonic demands and privileges inherent in the white label. These demands often result in the erasure or the mainstreaming of cultural differences, which is particularly dangerous in the case of Arab-Americans given the vast range of their national, religious, and cultural backgrounds. Additionally, identifying as people of color enables Arab-Americans to develop transformative connections and alliances with other US racial minorities.[50]

The importance of race and racial self-identification in discursive articulations of Arab-American identities in US public spaces is vividly evoked in the second half of Joseph's poem "Sand Nigger." After exploring the multiple and fragmented memories about Lebanon pervading his "house in Detroit" in the first section of the poem (as discussed at the beginning of this chapter), the speaker in "Sand Nigger" crosses the threshold of the domestic immigrant domain to directly engage with a more public enactment and reception of his racialized identity within Detroit's 1960s terrain. This terrain is characterized by increasing racial tensions and widespread riots:

Outside the house my practice
Is not to respond to remarks
about my nose or the color of my skin.
"Sand nigger," I'm called,
and the name fits: I am
the light-skinned nigger
with black eyes and the look
difficult to figure—a look
of indifference, a look to kill—
a Levantine nigger
in the city on the strait
between the great lakes Erie and St. Clair
which has a reputation
for violence (lines 72–85)

The loaded and problematic term "Levantine nigger," despite its derogatory and racist connotations, becomes the entryway for navigating a complex form of Arab-American racial self-identification. The speaker, by defining himself as a racial Other, refutes the bleaching effects of assimilation as carried out by a large part of an older generation of Arab immigrants and their children, including his parents and grandparents.[51] At the same time, defining himself as a "Levantine nigger" acknowledges the effects of raced readings of his body, as embodied in remarks about his nose or the color of his skin. By calling himself a "Levantine nigger," then, the speaker challenges the equally harmful effects of assimilation on the one hand and stigmatizing racialization on the other hand, the two primary options available to most Arab-Americans in public enactments of their individual and communal identities.

Even while self-identifying as a racial minority, however, the speaker challenges the black/white racial binary that dominates the US mainstream's performance and understandings of race. In other words, even though the speaker's nonwhite self-identification squarely positions him alongside an African-American minority in Detroit,[52] it nevertheless stresses the Levantine, specifically Lebanese, aspects that give his racial identity a national and geographic specificity. This specificity alters dominant historical delineations of race in the US and their placement along a white/black racial binary. Rewriting dominant racial discourse in this way is crucial for asserting and carrying out the transformative vision at the heart of transnational Arab-American belonging. That is, the emphasis placed in a poem such as Joseph's on the intersection of transnational and cross-racial identifications formulates distinct articulations of US citizenship and belonging that transcend simplistic classifications of minority identities in the US, specifically here as they pertain to race.

Signaling the continuance of such racial struggle among the younger generation of Arab-American writers, Hayan Charara,[53] another Detroit-born poet, pays tribute to Joseph in an autobiographical piece titled "Becoming the Center of Mystery." In it, he describes himself as "a slightly lighter-skinned nigger from the city on the strait" (404), thus directly referencing the self-definition of the speaker in "Sand Nigger" as "the light-skinned nigger / with black eyes and the look / difficult to figure." Charara further echoes Joseph's poetic construction of Arab identity by writing, "I am dark-skinned and have a look to kill—I am an Arab and from Detroit. I am ill-tempered and sorrowful, gentle and filled with life, stubborn but eager to listen, patient yet always in a hurry—I am an Arab and from Detroit" (412). Instead of Joseph's term "Levantine nigger," however, Charara refers to himself as an Arab. Rather than distancing him from a racial minority, Charara's use of the Arab label asserts the place and prominence of Arab identities in Detroit's and, by extension, the US's racial landscapes. The litany of seemingly contradictory attributes through which Charara describes himself affirms the complexity of this writer's outlook. The repetition of, and emphasis on, being "an Arab *and* from Detroit" (emphasis mine) points to the need to acknowledge the simultaneity as well as multiplicity of national, racial, religious, and ethnic affiliations in the US, by which to be *both* Arab and from Detroit, Arab *and* American, is not a contradiction in terms. Furthermore, what these affiliations assert is that one *can* be grounded in a US space without having to give up emotional and material allegiances to another homeland, specifically an Arab one. This assertion comes at a historical and political moment overwhelmingly permeated by a continued insistence on the part of the US mainstream to constantly present and imagine Arab and US spheres, and by extension the religious, cultural, and political identities they encompass, as two separate and diametrically opposed entities.

Insisting on multiple and complex attachments to place and identity within a US public space, however, necessitates the development of a complex political and racial consciousness that is not always easy to come by for Arab-Americans, let alone a wider US public. In many contemporary second- and third-generation Arab-American writers' ruminations on their childhood years, in light of the split between the insular (domestic space / communal enclave) and the wider US landscape that characterizes their parents' and grandparents' immigrant lives, they express deep anxieties about their insular lives coming in contact with broader forms of public US life. In other words, the solid separation of worlds with which many of them grew up does not lead to a smooth and unproblematic induction of these immigrants' children into the public sphere. As several of these writers make evident, racialized readings of the Arab-American body are the most immediate and effective approach to marginalizing and alienating Arab-Americans from a US mainstream.

In an autobiographical piece titled "Just Off Main Street," poet, activist, memoirist, and playwright Elmaz Abinader asserts the formative effect of the physical and mental threshold separating the private world of her Arab household from the public realm of her school and neighborhood.[54] Pointing to what she calls "the magic door" separating her life inside the home from her life at school, Abinader emphasizes how the racial markers on her body become an indication, if not an extension, of the perceived foreignness of her life behind that door:

> Despite sharing the same school uniform, being in the Brownies, singing soprano in the choir, and being a good speller, my life and theirs [her schoolmates] were separated by the magic door. And although my classmates didn't know what was behind that portal, they circled me in the playground and shouted "darkie" at my braids trying to explode into a kinky mop, or "ape" at my arms bearing mahogany hair against my olive pale skin.

Inherited physical markers, then, encapsulated here in unruly black hair (in contrast to her girlfriends' blond braids) as well as darker skin color are telltale indicators not only of racial but also of cultural differences. These markers become signifiers of Abinader's other life behind the door (one that is directly linked to a foreign locale), characterized by extensive family gatherings, an abundance of Lebanese food, and *debke* dancing. What these physical markers indicate, then, is that the Arab-American body becomes the site on which separations between inside and outside, private and public, and by extension here and there are inscribed and read. Unlike earlier Arab-American generations, Abinader does not succumb to such stigmatizing racialization and does not try to erase or disguise her racial and ethnic identities. Instead, she lays out an alternative route for enacting and articulating Arab-American belonging within a wider US and Arab landscape, one that does not hinge on replicating either the insularity or the assimilative tendencies typical of immigrant communities. Such a form of belonging is constructed through literary and artistic expression, which eventually enables her to transcend and in turn to transform the metaphorical threshold of her childhood house by giving voice to the inherited stories of her family.[55] These discursive articulations reshape singular and stigmatizing representations of individual and communal Arab-American identities, placing them within multiple and complex transnational frameworks of belonging.

Abinader's work not only broadens dominant conceptualizations of race and national belonging by imbuing them with antiessentialized articulations of Arab-American lives. She alters rigid landscapes of belonging by imagining and enacting strong connections between Arab-American and other writers of color in the US. These alliances further disrupt the constructed boundaries that dictate the production of knowledge about US racial and ethnic minorities. She ends her essay "Just Off Main Street" by alerting us to the various routes of belonging that diverge from the constraints of the US mainstream:

> I have a new small town. It's not anywhere in particular, or maybe it's everywhere. In this village, people live with their doors open, moving back and forth over the threshold of what has been exclusive to what will some day be inclusive. As a writer, I make my life known and woven into the fabric of literature. As an activist, I look toward other young writers of color and let them know, they might have to lean with their shoulder, put their whole body into it, but if they push on that door it will eventually open.

Envisioning multilayered and public forms of Arab-American identities that integrate complex understandings of Arab landscapes into imaginative and actual enactments of US citizenship and belonging extends to the realms of religion and politics. These realms are of extreme importance since they are the primary sites through which, whether directly or indirectly, dominant US discourse formulates and brands Arab identities as a foreign presence in the US. Mohja Kahf is one writer whose work draws on such stigmatizing formulations to constantly push against exclusionary conceptualizations of US citizenship and belonging. Born in Damascus, Syria, and having immigrated to the US with her parents at the age of four, Kahf is a self-proclaimed feminist Muslim whose poems and prose reconfigure dominant religious and political terrains in the US.[56] Such reconfigurations incorporate complex and multiple types of Muslim-American identities that defy the rampant and indelible stereotypes prevalent in the US of oppressed

Muslim women and terrorist Muslim men. The socioreligious space created in Kahf's poetry collection *E-mails from Scheherazad* (2003) extends beyond the confines of the home/mosque/neighborhood. This space is drawn by Kahf with a complexity that teases out the nuanced ethnic, cultural, and religious distinctions among Muslim-Americans on the one hand and between Muslims and other US minority groups on the other hand.[57] The poem "Lateefa," for one, offers the perspective of a second-generation Arab-American narrator who is torn between the allegiance that she was taught to uphold toward an ancestral Palestine and the connectedness that she feels toward the US, more specifically toward New Jersey, the city she was born and raised in:

> I was born here—BORN!
> INNA YOU-ESS-AY—oh Bruce,
> oh Connie, I
> got nowhere to go back to
> > (*Daddy, you can talk to me*
> > *all you want about Palestine*
> > *and I'll be faithful to the end*
> > *but I don't know it, never*
> > *smelled its rainwet streets, don't know*
> > *its stoops and backyards and chicken coops*
> . . . .
> I know New Jersey. I've run
> my fingers up and down its spine,
> scaled the vertebrae of official buildings
> on Broad Street, in Newark,
> taken Uncle Ali to Immigration. (lines 36–45, 52–56)

Despite the speaker's fierce dedication to her father's Palestine, which nevertheless remains shadowy and unreal, she is committed to her roots in the US, and specifically in New Jersey, where she was "BORN." By evoking Bruce Springsteen's song "Born in the USA,"[58] the narrator draws on a broader and more popular understanding of New Jersey, evidenced in Springsteen's own acclaimed attachment to the city, which in turn claims him as its own.[59] By using anthropomorphic imagery to describe her connection to the city, such as running her "fingers up and down its spine, / scal[ing] the vertebrae of official buildings," the speaker asserts an intimate and sensual relationship with her surroundings. This landscape, however, is far from being the homogeneous and one-dimensional US space that the Arab immigrants in Geha's short stories, for instance, imagine "Americans" to live in. Instead, it is teeming with a complex racial, religious, and national mix of Arab-, non-Arab-, and Muslim-American identities that irrevocably changes the makeup of the US terrain.

The speaker's ruminations, delivered against the backdrop of the interracial Muslim wedding of Pakistani-American Constance Mustafa and West Indian Muhammad Smith in New Jersey's Bayonne Park, evoke an intimate but complex knowledge of New Jersey's Muslim communities:

> I know where the Sister Clara Muhammad Schools,
> white *kufis* and black *khimars* bobbing, hold their fairs
> . . . .
> I know like uncles the bearded immigrant shaikhs,
> Cringed as they've stammered into microphones,
> . . . .
> I've visited the gated suburban developments where
> Upwardly mobile Egyptian teenagers lose their *shib-shibs*,
> heard Qawwali music spiral up condominium stairwells
> and twirl over the heads of the great-great-great-grandchildren
> of Leif Eriksson and Akbar and Zobaidah and Son-Jara
> as they play and slide together and tumble into each other
>   (lines 57–58, 63–64, 68–73)

In this way, national and religious heritage intermingle, with the predominantly African-American Islam of the Sister Clara Muhammad Schools[60] existing alongside immigrant sheikhs' freshly relocated Islam and rubbing against the more assimilated, well-to-do Islam of a younger group of Egyptians. Kahf points out, however, that the racial and economic factors that might distinguish one Muslim-American community from another often give way to the stronger hold of a shared history and a common religious culture. For it is this enlarged and flexible sense of religious and cultural expression, exemplified by Kahf's reference to Qawwali music (a form of devotional Sufi music characterized by its inclusive features) that unites not only the descendants of the Mughal ruler Akbar (who reigned between 1556 and 1605), Zobaidah (wife of Abbasid caliph Harun al-Rashid, who ruled from 786 to 809), and Son-Jara (founder of the Mali Empire in the eleventh century) but also the Caucasian descendants of Leif Eriksson (believed to be the first European to land in North America). At the end of the poem, despite the uninformed perspective of the policeman who threatens to give everyone parking tickets, proclaiming that there was no evidence of a wedding because he "don't see no priest" (102), Kahf remains optimistic. The last lines, stating, "if we love what we are we can make it / survive here / . . . / there's room here for all of us" (lines 86–87, 94), gesture toward the possibility of achieving inclusive belongings that would alter the predominant tendency to define the US religious landscape in primarily Judeo-Christian terms.

A similar "we" appears in "Move Over," another poem in Kahf's *E-mails from Scheherazad*. This poem takes a more direct and unequivocal stance against simplistic and binary forms of US belonging that leave no room for transnational or transcultural identities, let alone any complex racial or religious identity formations. Similar to Charara's statement cited earlier that he is "Arab and from Detroit," Kahf, by pointing to the seemingly discordant aspects of Muslim identities in US public space, succeeds in overturning the bias informing such binary formulations. She writes,

> We are the spreaders of prayer rugs
> in highway gas stations at dawn
> We are the fasters at company banquets
> before sunset in Ramadan
> We wear veils and denim,
> prayer caps and Cubs caps
> . . . .
> We will intermarry and commingle
> and multiply, oh, how we'll multiply
> Muhammad-lovers in the motley
> miscellany of the land. (lines 1–6, 16–19)

The type of hybridity portrayed in the intermingling of "veils and denim" and "prayer caps and Cubs caps," rather than pointing to a jarring juxtaposition of disparate religious and cultural markers, opens up a space where the constructed notion of a "pure," essential, and hence exclusionary US identity can be questioned and subsequently altered. The intermingling of Muslim and mainstream white cultures then revises dominant understandings of US identity to make way for complex formulations of transnational citizenship and belonging. Such revisionary formulations supersede the politically vacuous agendas of liberal multiculturalism by offering critical and radical approaches to articulating US identities outside the frameworks of assimilation or political correctness. These approaches are informed by cultural and religious connections that exceed the physical and ideological boundaries of the US nation-state.

Moreover, as in "Lateefa" and despite the repetition of a seemingly united "we" at the beginning of the poem, Kahf's articulation of multiple Muslim voices in "Move Over" also leads to the rejection of fixed and unchanging Muslim-American identities. As we see at the end of the poem, the demand for a much-needed shift in cultural, racial, and religious mappings in "the motley miscellany of the [US] land" is also brought about by the "intermarry[ing] and commingl[ing] and multiply[ing]" of "Muhammad-lovers," thus denoting a racial, national, and ethnic hybridization of Muslim identities in the US. The title, "Move Over," which might initially be taken to mean a Muslim-American's call to "take over" a center dominated by white Christian Americans, lends itself to a more intricate reading that not only facilitates a recognized public place for a Muslim minority but complicates simplistic and singular spatial understandings of race, religion, ethnicity, and national identities in the US as a whole.[61]

In many ways, the suspicion faced by Muslims and Arabs is rooted in forms of intolerance and bigotry that are deeply entrenched in and informed by (whether implicitly or explicitly) US foreign policies in the Middle East. Although other US racial and ethnic minorities have been and continue to be discriminated against due to US relations with their countries of origin, Arab-Americans occupy a distinct position both nationally, in histories of racial and ethnic struggles within the US, and transnationally, in ongoing neocolonial and imperialist US expansion in the Middle East. Such positionalities are noteworthy and distinct given their relatively long historical trajectory, starting with the budding imperial powers of the US at around the middle of the twentieth century. They also stand unique in their lingering and lasting demonization of Arab-Americans, renewed and redeployed with every new US venture and adventure in the Middle East.

Even though deliberations about Arab-American belongings in the US can be traced to the beginning of the twentieth century with attempts to racially categorize newly arrived Arabs (referred to as Syrians or Turks), second- and third-generation Arab-Americans from the mid-twentieth century onward face much more intense forms of racialization and discrimination that are directly linked to US foreign policies in the Middle East over the past several decades.[62] In this way, crossing the threshold of the domestic space (which, as we saw earlier, holds many immigrants' fragmented, nostalgic, and mythical memories of the original homeland) into a more public articulation of Arab-American identity involves directly confronting the political factors that continue to shape Arab-Americans' transnational connections to Arab homelands. Speaking of the poets included in *Inclined to Speak: An Anthology of Contemporary Arab American Poetry*, editor Hayan Charara points out the extent to which "the link to the Middle East, via U.S. foreign policy, is almost always present" in their work, although this link in no way determines the content of all Arab-American writing or oeuvres (xxiv). In mapping out revised connections to inherited Arab homelands and in formulating new, more critically informed trajectories of US citizenship and belonging, we find that many second- and third-generation Arab-American writers place the wars and conflicts plaguing the Arab world and the role of the US in them at the center of their revisionary transnational vision. Chapter 2 focuses on how political and military conflicts in the Arab world inform Arab-American writers' representation of the transnational movement of Arab bodies between the US and the Arab world. Therefore, I end this chapter by discussing a few texts that exemplify how some second- and third-generation writers process such painful and violent realities within the context of a completely oblivious and uncaring US social landscape.

One such writer is Naomi Shihab Nye, whose poem "My Father and the Figtree" was discussed earlier in the chapter. In "Blood," another poem from Nye's collection *19 Varieties of Gazelle*, the speaker juxtaposes her father's humorous proclamations about the exceptional capacities of a "true Arab" (which include catching a fly in one hand and knowing the healing powers of watermelon) against the helplessness of this Arab in the face of a disheartening war and the killing of innocent civilians:

> Today the headlines clot in my blood.
> A Palestinian boy dangles a toy truck
> on the front page.
> Homeless fig, this tragedy with a terrible root
> is too big for us. What flag can we wave?
> . . . .
> I call my father, we talk around the news.
> It is too much for him,
> Neither of his two languages can reach it.
> I drive into the country to find sheep, cows,
> to plead with the air:
> Who calls anyone *civilized*?
> Where can the crying heart graze?
> What does a true Arab do now? (lines 18–22, 25–32)

The effusive fragments of the father's supposedly innate knowledge of "true Arab" identity are overshadowed and even rendered ineffective by the painful circumstances of death and violence that continue to haunt the immigrants' present, with the poem specifically referencing the killing of thousands of Palestinian refugees during the Sabra and Shatila massacre in Lebanon in 1982. The reminder here is that the figurative as well as literal rerooting of the emblematic fig tree in US soil (as enacted by the father figure in "My Father and the Figtree") does not automatically ensure facile rerootings of Arab identity in US soil. For this identity is easily engulfed by that ever-present "tragedy with a terrible root"—specifically here Palestinian dispossession—and is critiqued and cross-examined with every massacre and house demolition in Palestine or other parts of the Arab world. In other words, rather than normalizing or even privileging Arab-Americans' pursuit of a secure type of citizenship and belonging in the US, what these texts assert is that such security remains impossible and even undesirable as long as Arab homelands are embroiled in wars, conflict, and military occupation. It then becomes elemental to consciously bring these tense geopolitical histories into the realm of everyday US lives in order to emphasize their relevance and impact not only within the framework of the Arab world but within the US as well, especially since the US is often directly involved in the perpetuation of violence and political instability in many Arab countries. Such recognitions of violence and conflict consequently shape Arab-Americans' engagement with their US surroundings in ways that produce radical and challenging forms of public engagement. These new forms of citizenship do not hinge on the separation of geographical spheres into "here and there" or the subsequent division of national identities into "us and them."

Driving "into the country . . . / to plead with the air," the speaker in Nye's poem "Blood" faces a US landscape that remains uninformed, unresponsive, and disconnected from the anguish of the Palestinian plight. Interestingly enough, with the father's helpless inability to articulate his dismay about the news, it becomes the second generation's responsibility (as well as that of subsequent generations) to utter and render the challenging experience of negotiating such seemingly disparate locations and identities. These negotiations, though they are eventually translated into more publicly defined Arab-American identities, originate and remain entrenched in the fragmented, selective memories of an original homeland that the younger generations have witnessed their parents/grandparents enact within the insular space of the immigrant home or ethnic enclave.

As discussed earlier in the chapter, the immigrant parents'/grandparents' traumatic memories of the homeland are not readily or easily processed by the younger generations, a fact that adds to their disconnection from an Arab homeland. Susan Muaddi Darraj's collection of short stories, *The Inheritance of Exile* (2007), written from the perspective of four Arab-American women and their mothers, exemplifies such disconnection, especially in the figure of Hanan, who decides at an early age that "she was not an Arab": "Her father was an American, born to Arab parents, but her mother, . . . [who had] grown up in the hilly town of Ramallah, had fled a series of wars, had left behind camps strewn with shrapnel, legless corpses, wailing women, and eyes too weary to weep. But Hanan had been born right here, in Philadelphia, in St. Agnes Hospital on Broad Street" (81).[63] Just like the speaker in Kahf's poem "Lateefa," Hanan claims her American roots first and foremost. However, also like Kahf's speaker, she eventually realizes that the binary option of choosing either an Arab or an American identity is not a feasible one, leading to constricting and limited understandings of US identities.

After Hanan's marriage to and divorce from John, whose parents "hailed originally from . . . the entrenched Irish community" in northeast Philly (125), she supports herself and her baby by selling the gift baskets that she learned to make from her mother, who herself learned how to make them through a Palestinian refugee camp's UNRWA program in order to earn some money (118).[64] The act of preserving the legacy of skills and memories, themselves inherited from the experience of war and dispossession, is taken a step further by Reema, another character in the book, who becomes the "collector of stories," taking on the task of recording her mother's memories of immigrating with her family to the US after being driven out of their home in Haifa and living in a Palestinian refugee camp. The collection of stories actually ends with the oral testimony of Reema's mother, who, addressing her daughter, states in closing, "Just shape the words I said the way you want—fix them and make them sound good" (196). Such a poignant statement strongly acknowledges the effective role that the second generation has in maintaining their parents' memories/legacies in the diaspora. Reema, however, rather than "fixing" her mother's language as she is instructed to do and rendering it more amenable to a US audience, leaves it as it is. In doing so, Reema, and in turn Muaddi Darraj, challenges the dominant standards that regulate immigrant stories, and by extension immigrants themselves, by preserving the accented (and hence nonassimilative) aspect of these articulations.

Despite the outspokenness of many Arab-Americans (writers and nonwriters alike) about the conflicts in the Middle East, there often remains a lingering sense of guilt triggered by an Arab-American allegiance to a US that is regarded as a source of war and suffering in the Arab world. Gregory Orfalea writes in his poem "The Bomb That Fell on Abdu's Farm,"[65]

> Next door, in my great-uncle's newly-
> Irrigated fields, a bomb fell.
> The mud smothered it. The mud
> talked to it. The mud wrapped
> its death like a mother. And
> the bomb with American lettering
> did not go off. (lines 18–24)

Dropped on a village outside Damascus, this American-made bomb starkly positions the US as a major player in many of the Arab world's conflicts in its role as manufacturer, seller, and user of deadly weapons and bombs. One can even argue that the poem might be implicitly asserting the complicity of an American public, whether it be of Arab descent or not, by virtue of its taxpayers' money or political leanings.

The need to record immigrant, ethnic, and diasporic testimonials and to incorporate them into the larger mosaic of US histories is threatened by the fact that many Arab-Americans, well before 9/11, have found themselves perceived as "members of a demonized community" (Mattawa and Akash, "Introduction" xii), leading many Arab-Americans to favor assimilation over discrimination. When it comes to the interconnected histories of the US and the Arab world, the silence ensuing from such assimilative tendencies is a dangerous one. Instead of an either/or vision, what such transnational and transgenerational links to the Arab world make evident is a transformative vision that incorporates the "over there" into the "over here," the past into the present, in ways that inevitably alter the shape of US citizenship and belonging to underscore its exclusionary constructs and its emphasis and privileging of assimilation as well as uniform patriotic allegiance. In other words, by asserting that "we are the stories we tell about ourselves; our words map the spaces of home" (Majaj, "Beyond Silence" 46), Arab-American writers delineate paths for renegotiating fixed and unchanging constructions of belonging, selfhood, and citizenship in the US. Such renegotiations are not enacted at the expense of a connection to the ancestral homeland, which is kept alive in the antinostalgic memory of the various generations of Arab-Americans.

One way to keep this memory alive is through writing and the endurance of artistic creation. In the poem "Fifty Years On / Stones in an Unfinished Wall," Majaj affirms the need to keep the memory of dispossession alive by recapturing and reinstating the names of Palestinian villages that were lost and razed after 1948, as well as the individual stories about the horrific experiences of Palestinian refugees:

> *all that remains*
>   *a scattering of stones and rubble*
>   *across a forgotten landscape*
>
> fifty years on
> the words push through
>
>   a splintered song
>   forced out one note
>   at a time
> . . . .
> we pick our way amid shards
> heir to a generation
>   that broke their teeth on the bread of exile
>   that cracked their hearts on the stone of exile
>   necks bent beneath iron keys to absent doors (lines 69–76, 186–90)

It is through these songs, then, no matter how splintered or broken they may seem, that US-born and US-raised Arab-Americans can maintain a connection to a lost ancestral homeland, asserting what Lawrence Joseph defines in his poem "Inclined to Speak" as "A sort of relationship / [that] is established between our attention / to what is furthest from us / and what deepest in us" (lines 20–23).

2 / To the Arab Homeland and Back: Narratives of Returns and Rearrivals

In 1960, Lebanese-American writer William Blatty published his autobiography, *Which Way to Mecca, Jack?*, a humorous account of being raised in New York City by an immigrant single mother. It also recounts his visit as an adult to his mother's native Lebanon, where he worked for the United States Information Agency for two years. Blatty's narrative, verging on the absurd or even the "burlesque" (Shakir, "Arab Mothers" 6), touches on the important trope of Arab homecomings as carried out and depicted by generations of Arab-Americans whose experience of an original homeland is primarily shaped by their parents' and grandparents' nostalgic memories of it. Published in the same year as Blatty's *Which Way to Mecca, Jack?*, Vance Bourjaily's autobiographical *Confessions of a Spent Youth* also features a second-generation Arab-American returning to his ancestral Arab homeland. In the chapter titled "A Fractional Man," Bourjaily travels in the Middle East as a bus driver for the British army, and his itinerary includes a formative stop in his father's ancestral Lebanese village of Kabb Elias. During his stay there, he reconnects with his heritage and starts feeling less of a "fractional man, ... uselessly complicated and discontent" (272).[1]

Despite being portrayed as the writers' attempt to reconcile with their heritage, Blatty's and Bourjaily's respective return to their ancestral homeland does not leave either of them with a renewed self-awareness that revises the essentialist and nostalgic versions of Arab identities with which they had grown up in the US. For many second-generation Arab-Americans like Blatty and Bourjaily (who grew up before the mid-twentieth century), "to speak of Arabs," even after visiting Lebanon, is to confirm rather than challenge dominant representations of Arabs in the US (Shakir, "Arab Mothers" 10). Such representations portray Arabs as a peculiar, exotic, and for the most part undesirable Other.

Blatty's and Bourjaily's portrayals of a return to an ancestral Arab homeland constitute an earlier version of the return theme prevalent in late-twentieth-/early-twenty-first-century Arab-American literature. Like these earlier counterparts, most contemporary literary portrayals of such returns also depict second- or third-generation Arab-Americans who were born and came of age in the second part of the twentieth century onward embarking on temporary visits to an original homeland. Unlike those in the earlier texts, however, the Arab-Americans depicted in literary narratives published since the 1990s are invested in achieving a complex and multilayered understanding of an Arab homeland. This type of understanding leads them to develop revised engagements with both the Arab and the US locales, a process that reconfigures the models of assimilation and exoticization preferred by earlier US-born and US-raised Arab-Americans. Primarily carried out by immigrants' children or grandchildren, these contemporary narratives of return can also feature immigrants themselves who had originally left their homelands willingly or unwillingly, either due to war, dispossession, and exile or in search of a better economic future.

The journeys to an Arab homeland featured in many of the texts discussed in this chapter are often instigated by a desire to return to the geographical and national roots of diasporic Arab identities, or to what is simply defined as the familiar (even if this familiarity is an inherited construct, as shown in chapter 1). Such desires are informed by the urge to gain a deeper self-knowledge and some reprieve from the ambiguities of belonging that plague Arab-Americans in the diaspora. However, most of these narratives raise challenging questions about the complexities of physical returns to Arab homelands, such as, Who is eligible for such returns? Are such returns in and of themselves exclusionary in nature? If so, whom do they exclude? How do these journeys differ depending on the gender and nationality of the traveler? With the constant political shifts and conflicts in the Arab world, are permanent resettlements in Arab homelands feasible or even desirable for Arab-American returnees?

In pursuing such questions in this chapter, I analyze how the narrative trope of return journeys in contemporary Arab-American literature produces a transnational discursive paradigm that contends with assimilationist, nostalgic, and essentialist articulations of Arab-American belongings in the US. At the basis of this transnational paradigm is what I refer to as the concept of *rearrival*, by which short-term returns to original Arab homelands ultimately lead to the reassessment and reclaiming of the *US* terrain.[2] In other words, the paths of return to an Arab country undertaken by the protagonists in these texts ultimately lead them back to the US, where they rearrive with new self-understandings of their Arab identity. These self-understandings enable them to ultimately rethink the ways in which they interact with, belong to, and claim the US as a permanent home. It is the self-reflection gained during their time in the Arab homeland that enables many of these characters to reassess the version of Arab identity they grew up with or developed in the US. At the same time, this self-reflection enables them to formulate alternate routes to US belonging that replace the pressures of assimilation and ostracization. That is, instead of being depoliticized and nostalgic (especially as propagated by an older generation of Arab immigrants) or demonized and Othered by virtue of their religious and cultural ties to the Arab world, Arab-Americans use the awareness and knowledge they gain on their return visits to the Arab homeland to develop a type of vision that transcends monolithic and mononational modes of belonging in the US. Such a vision enlarges the political, religious, and cultural knowledge available to Arab-Americans *as well as* to a wider US public. It is through such discursive interventions, then, that Arab-Americans develop a language of transnational belonging and citizenship that holds specific yet complex understandings of Arab-American identities at its center, extending to issues related to politics, religion, class, and gender.

By using the insights gained from a return to an Arab homeland to foment new conceptualizations of diasporic and ethnic Arab-American identities in the US, texts such as the ones discussed in this chapter destabilize neatly spatialized understandings of homes, homelands, and host lands, showing how these concepts are forever shifting and evolving. My readings of such destabilizations focus on the gendered geopolitical dimensions of transnational movement that determine, facilitate, or even deter returns and rearrivals.[3] My focus on the ways in which the Arab-American body travels to, experiences, and reconnects with the Arab homeland, as well as the ways in which it travels back to the US, is determined by particular gendered enactments of this body. To elucidate this point, I focus on literary texts featuring female protagonists and their revisionary negotiation of Arab-American identities through their return journeys to an Arab ancestral homeland. This emphasis on female travelers helps us consider the ways in which the notion of home itself (and by extension the homeland) is heavily loaded with gendered implications, by which creating a home, or homemaking, is perceived as the domestic female role par excellence.[4] Reformulating homemaking in these texts develops versions of homes and homelands outside patriarchal and conventional social and cultural structures, which in turn produces transformative mappings of transnational Arab-American citizenship and belonging.

In investigating gendered patterns of returns and rearrivals as they emerge in contemporary Arab-American texts, my analysis in the first part of the chapter incorporates a discussion of Mohja Kahf's novel *The Girl in the Tangerine Scarf* (which features a return to a Syrian ancestral homeland), as well as Samia Serageldin's novel *The Cairo House* and Pauline Kaldas's memoir *Letters from Cairo* (both of which focus on Egyptian homecomings). All three texts capture the intense and intimate physicality of original homelands and the sensory details evoked through the lens of return journeys, with various emphases placed on compelling intersections of gender, religion, race, class, and politics. In my analysis of each text, I pinpoint specific aspects of such intersections, with my discussion of *The Girl in the Tangerine Scarf* yielding a closer focus on gender and religion, and my discussion of *The Cairo House* and *Letters from Cairo* emphasizing the interconnections among gender, class, and race. These intersecting factors nevertheless remain rooted in the fraught political histories defining the relations between the US and the Arab world. Renegotiating the place of the Arab-American body, specifically the female body, in light of such political relations inscribes transformative understandings of the Arab homeland onto the US terrain. For instead of the homeland being regarded as the root cause of Arab-Americans' foreignness in the US, a more complex, transnational, and less binary-based knowledge of this homeland becomes an important conduit for reimagining the place occupied by the Arab-American subject within the US. This type of transnational knowledge also reconfigures broader conceptualizations of US belonging by challenging a mainstream's simplistic approaches to issues of patriotism, US foreign policy, and US involvement in Middle Eastern conflicts.

The Israeli-Palestinian conflict and the unwavering US support of the state of Israel is central to transnational formations of Arab-American identities, specifically in relation to the most contentious and heretofore unresolved question of the Palestinian right of return (as articulated in the UN General Assembly's much-disputed Resolution 194). To elucidate this point, I discuss in the latter part of the chapter the limitations and impossibilities of Palestinian returns to historical Palestine as featured in a selection of Palestinian-American texts. The Palestinian right of return, then, forms a crucial component of my conceptualization of Arab-American returns and rearrivals. It renders visible and immediate the material, historical, and political conditions that make a return to an original homeland impossible or unfeasible for many Arab-Americans.[5] After discussing a section of Susan Muaddi Darraj's short story collection *The Inheritance of Exile*, I supplement my focus on literature with a look at other contemporary representations of Palestinian returns and rearrivals, looking at Annemarie Jacir's film *Salt of This Sea* and Emily Jacir's visual art. A focus on these visual renditions of return journeys and rearrivals introduces a broader framework for analyzing the articulation of transnational Arab-American citizenship and belonging, thus gesturing to the prevalence of this thematic concern in a variety of creative Arab-American outlets. Such articulations are crucial in positing a solid narrative stance against the US as a controlling and imperialist power in the Arab world. In doing so, they participate in the reappraisal of the US nation-state as an uncomplicated home for Arab-Americans by exposing and challenging its policies in the Arab world. Even though the literary and visual texts discussed in this chapter do not all delve in full detail into the lives of the featured Arab-American women once they are back in the US, the awareness that these female protagonists develop in the Arab homeland is strongly indicative of their transformative enactments of transnational citizenship and belonging upon their return to the US.

"Reimagining the Umma":[6] Intersections of Religion and Nationality in Mohja Kahf's *The Girl in the Tangerine Scarf*

Mohja Kahf's first novel, *The Girl in the Tangerine Scarf* (2006), is a coming-of-age story of Khadra Shamy, who immigrates from Syria to the US with her family as a young girl and grows up in a tight-knit Muslim community in Indiana during the 1970s.[7] With the novel's time frame stretching into Khadra's adult life (including her experience of college, marriage, and divorce), the narrative opens with a description of the protagonist's return visit to central Indiana after a seven-year absence in Philadelphia, where she works as a photographer for the magazine *Alternative Americas*. In fact, Khadra is sent to the Midwest on assignment by the magazine to do a feature on Indianapolis's Muslims. Crossing Indiana's state line, Khadra is filled with dread, which trumps any sense of anticipatory homecoming. The "unbearable flatness of Indiana" not only triggers in her "the feeling that the world's been left behind her somewhere" but embodies for Khadra the forbidding isolation and discrimination that she and her Muslim community endured at the hands of white supremacists in Indiana, whose bigotry is very much reminiscent of the Ku Klux Klan's (1). Despite the fact that she spent her formative years in Indiana, Khadra's sense of home is not tied to this midwestern state as much as it stems from a small community of Muslims (constituted of a mix of African-Americans, South Asians, Africans, Arabs, and Caucasian converts) that ran the Islamic Dawah Center, which her father helped establish.

The novel's time frame traverses between a present describing Khadra's temporary return to her Muslim community in Indianapolis and a past featuring insightful snapshots of her formative experiences in Indiana as well as in Mecca, Damascus, and Philadelphia. In doing so, the narrative includes representations of multiple and varied return journeys or homecomings, incorporating the physical as well as the spiritual. The immediate sense of trepidation that overcomes the adult Khadra when she crosses into the state of Indiana in the novel's opening pages is a testament to the deep scars she maintains from the bigotry directed at her Muslim community while growing up in that state. Rather than being a homecoming, then, Khadra's return to Indiana as an adult becomes an entryway into reassessing the trajectories of belonging to the places and homes to which she has been imaginatively and physically connected throughout her life. In this way, Khadra's return "to this ground that didn't love her" (i.e., midwestern ground) gives way to accounts of other journeys of return and rearrival, starting in the first part of the novel with Khadra traveling with her family to the bosom of Muslim belonging, namely Mecca (17).

Embarking on hajj halfway through the novel, the teenage Khadra looks out the plane window and proclaims that she would not care if she never set eyes on Indiana again. This part of the narrative is indicative of the conflicted and complex factors informing Khadra's Arab-American, specifically midwestern, Muslim identity. Such complexity is evident in Khadra's disconnection from Indiana despite the fact that it is the main site of her childhood and adolescence. It also shows through in her efforts to define herself primarily in relation to Mecca, a place to which she feels a deep sense of belonging despite the fact that she has never visited it. Her vehement disavowal of Indiana as a home place rings hollow, for despite the phrase running through her head that "a true Muslim feels at home wherever the call to prayer is sung," Khadra still gets a "lump in her throat" as the plane rises away from Indianapolis (157). However, all thoughts of the Midwest (and the US as a whole for that matter) are dispelled once the family lands in Saudi Arabia, where Khadra feels that they are finally "*someplace where [they] really belong*. It's the land of the Prophet. The land of all Muslims" (159). Arriving at the Sanctuary in Mecca, and elated by the sight of the Kaaba, Khadra is overcome with emotion, repeating again and again the *talbiya* (prayer): "*Here I am, O my Lord, here I am*" (162). Ironically, Khadra's prayer gets muddled in her head with the lyrics of a Phil Collins song: "*I've been waiting for this moment for all my life, oh Lo-ord*" (162), an important, albeit tongue-in-cheek, reference to the ironies, contradictions, and confluences of multiple and overlapping religious and cultural attachments.

Despite Khadra's expectations of this moment, her spiritual homecoming brings her face-to-face with some of the ways in which the practice of Islam differs from one culture to another. The mores governing women's practice of Islam in Saudi Arabia come in direct contrast with Khadra's own experience of living out her faith as a woman in the multinational, multiracial sphere of her parents' Dawah Center in Indiana. During the Shamys' visit to Mecca, they are invited to stay with a Syrian friend of Khadra's mother who had married a Saudi. Entranced by the "real adhan," or the call to prayer, of "the kind that rang out over the rooftops," which she had never experienced before in the US, Khadra slips out at dawn for *fajr* prayer at the nearby mosque (166). What Khadra does not know is that in Saudi Arabia, women not only are forbidden to pray in mosques but are not allowed to leave the house if not properly dressed according to the kingdom's modesty norms. A bewildered Khadra is led back to the Saudi house complex, to her hosts' and her father's horror, by a couple of *mattawa* policemen whose primary responsibility is to monitor religious and ethical behavior and to maintain strict modesty regulations in the kingdom.[8] Upon Khadra's insistence that "women have always gone to the mosque. It's part of Islam," she is stunned by her father's response. "You're used to America, binti," he tells her. "In most of the Muslim world, it hasn't been the custom for hundreds of years" (168). Thus, Khadra's American practice of Islam directly contradicts its enactment in the birthplace of the Prophet Muhammad, a place that Khadra, alongside millions of Muslims around the world, considers to be at the heart of Islam. The novel, however, is quick to show that it is not the much-touted American freedom per se that allows Khadra to emulate the religious practices of the first Muslim women, including the Prophet's wife, Aisha. As Khadra realizes later on in the novel during her visit to Syria, she is in fact enabled to do so through her parents' insistence on forging a relatively nonpatriarchal, nonhierarchical approach to the practice of Islam in Indiana.

Khadra's journey to Mecca presents her with another perspective on her Arab-American identity. Even though, throughout her childhood and adolescence in the US, she repeatedly distances herself from what she thinks of as a white mainstream's American identity, while in Saudi, she is primarily regarded as an American. Going out with her hosts' daughter Afaaf on what she initially believes to be a friendly visit to an aunt's house, Khadra finds herself in the middle of the desert with a gaggle of partying Saudi teenagers. Khadra is introduced by Afaaf to the mixed-gender group as "my American cousin," despite her insistence that she is Arab and not American. She scrambles to defend herself from the heavy-handed advances of Ghazi, one of the young Saudi men with whom she is left alone in the limousine, aside from an unresponsive driver (174). This experience creates a fissure in the untenable wall that Khadra has constructed (with the help of her protective parents and a general midwestern intolerance) between the supposedly separate categories of Arab and American. Rather than the Arab, and more specifically Muslim, wholesomeness that she had consistently set up against the backdrop of American depravity, she discovers, in no holier place than Mecca to boot, that strict adherence to blanket labels such as American and Arab or Muslim and non-Muslim can become a limiting and limited form of self-identification. Khadra flirts with the possibility of forging an alternative, antihomogeneous type of mixed American identity by acknowledging on the plane back to the US that a place like Indianapolis could be called "Home" (179). In this way, the journey to what Khadra perceives to be her unquestionable place of religious belonging, namely Mecca, opens up for her a heretofore unexplored path to some initial reformulations of the US, specifically Indiana, as a possible home front. This type of acknowledgment, however, and the weighty role that return journeys to ancestral and spiritual homelands play in reassessing the rigidity of the landscapes of belonging in the US, remains elusive and underdeveloped in the mind of the young Khadra. It does not reach its full potential until she decides, as an adult, to embark on another journey of discovery, this time to her native Syria.

Because Khadra arrived in the US at a young age, her memories of Syria are reduced to a handful of images, tastes, and smells. These memories, however, despite coming to her in intermittent "flashes," still ground her in a tangible Arab place, one that irrevocably counteracts the foreignness of exile. Describing Khadra and her brother's developing perception of their family's surroundings in the US, Kahf writes, "Here in 'Mreeka [America], no one looked like them and they looked like no one," as opposed to a Syria filled with "people whose faces bore . . . [their] parents' features" and "who spoke Arabic in the same rhythms" (16). Such lingering connections to Syria continue to shape Khadra's adult perception of the US. They take on a formative role when Khadra, emotionally raw from the rigors of an abortion and a failed marriage, decides to take a regenerative trip back home. Questioning the cultural and religious tenets she was raised on in the overlapping spheres of Arab and Muslim diasporas, and feeling completely unhinged, she grasps for a base, a point of origin that will anchor her: "It was time for a retreat. She would betake herself unto an eastern place. Back where she came from: Syria" (266).

And with that, Khadra embarks on a journey east, which culminates in her arriving unannounced at her Téta's (Arabic for "grandmother") doorstep in Damascus.[9] The words Téta welcomes Khadra with, "I have been waiting for you" (269), emphasize the way in which the absence of immigrants, exiles, and diasporics from their home countries creates a physical and metaphorical space that can develop into a form of cultural haunting, especially for those who stay behind.[10] In other words, just as exiles/immigrants are haunted in the diaspora by the specter of a country left behind, their absence, represented generally as *al-ghurba*, pervades the homeland's collective consciousness. The term *al-ghurba* refers to "the absence from the homeland; separation from one's native country, banishment, exile; life, or place, away from home" (Wehr 783). Furthermore, a closer look at the term and its linguistic roots links it to its opposite meaning, *al-sharaqa*, with *al-sharq* denoting the East, or the direction from which the sun rises. Juliane Hammer points out these linguistic nuances to underscore their significance in Islamic philosophy, in which the sun, and thereby the East, becomes a "symbol for God, who is the One from whom all light originates. . . . Thus, the term *ghurba* means religiously and philosophically barred from the light" (60).

Within the context of the novel, this notion of *al-ghurba* plays a major role in Khadra's dual sense of spiritual and cultural exile (from a Muslim as well as from an Arab origin). I would moreover argue that the juxtaposition of *al-ghurba* with the Syrian homeland carries deep and significant gendered implications. For shortly after referencing Téta's statement "I have been waiting for you" (269), Khadra informs us that "Syria was Téta" (270). Such a proclamation posits Khadra's return to Syria as a gendered one through and through, particularly the way her statement (and subsequently her return to Syria) equates the ancestral/maternal figure of the grandmother with a feminine homeland (or motherland) that is awaiting its exiled and estranged daughters. This feminization of the homeland has of course been historically problematic especially in colonial and postcolonial contexts, particularly given the ways in which the trope of the helpless female (and by extension the feminized land) is used to enact expansionist and imperialist agendas. However, in the case of Kahf's novel, the gendered representation of the Syrian homeland as a female entity is linked in crucial ways to the recuperation of lost, hidden, or buried stories about the most important female figures in Khadra's life, namely her mother and her Téta.

For it is in the female-dominated setting of the kitchen of Khadra's Aunt Razanne, between one batch of fried eggplant and another, that Khadra finds out that her teenage mother was raped by her Syrian teacher while on a school trip to France. The telling of these secrets is carried over into the intimate space of her Téta's bathroom. While scrubbing her Téta's back, "in the warmth and the vapor" of her grandmother's ritualistic bath, Khadra listens for the first time to the older woman reminisce on how she eloped with a Circassian from Palestine and lived in Haifa till 1948, when he was shot and killed by "one of the Zionist militias" (274). This gendered knowledge about her mother's and grandmother's past enables Khadra to recuperate a more complex sense of self in light of her female ancestry. Moreover, the fact that such weighty secrets are imparted within the intimacy of a domestic space challenges its dominant representation as a source of safety and comfort. Instead, this space becomes an empowering, albeit disturbing, background for the development of Khadra's act of re-vision and rearrival. Equipped with this gendered knowledge, Khadra is better positioned to enact a demythologized version of home not only within the confines of the domestic space but within the larger context of both the Syrian and, subsequently, the US landscapes.

In addition to recuperating these lost gendered histories, Khadra's return to Syria reveals and at the same time revises the mythical nature of home and homeland as they exist in the mind of her immigrant parents. The Syria that Khadra grew up with is relayed mainly through "the inherited lenses of her parents' memory" (268), while the version she encounters firsthand as an adult is a "sweet relief from the myth of Syria that had hung over her life" in the US (278). Although fascinated by the real Syria and the real Damascus to which her return journey takes her, where "the shape of things was different" (267), Khadra quickly realizes that "there were many Damascuses" (292), and not all versions are magical. The political and social anxieties plaguing Syria often overshadow and exceed its magical aura. They can grate on the Arab-American returnee's sensibilities and ultimately render his or her return a temporary one. Khadra realizes that, along with enfolding the delight of "little tea glasses on hammered copper trays . . . [and the novelty of] rooms [that] had doors with keyholes you could see through" (267), Syria also harbors "small-town" and "mediocre minds," rendered even more stultified and cautious by the oppressive ruling regime that instills fear and paranoia in its citizens, including none other than her own uncles and cousins (291). In fact, Khadra's parents had left Syria to escape the Baathist government's crackdown on religious and political dissidents, nevertheless continuing their oppositional stance from the diaspora by publishing tracts against the Syrian regime in Arabic and Islamic journals.[11] Seeing the extent to which her relatives in Syria have been brainwashed by the oppressive logic that the government uses to control its citizens, Khadra is filled with a sense of pride about her parents' decision to leave all they had known behind in Syria so as not to compromise their political and religious beliefs. They "had not twisted their minds to fit into a cramped space. . . . Her parents had flown into new air. Home had been left behind, given up. For the utter unknown. What a bitter and marvelous choice" (282–83). This emphasis on "new air," however, in no way reinforces the much-touted rhetoric of US freedom. For, as mentioned earlier, this new air brings with it its own stultifying conformity in the shape of social and religious norms and anti-Muslim bigotry experienced firsthand by Khadra's immigrant family.

The sketch of a larger and more ominous Syria harbors a smaller, more intimate Syria, one that Khadra experiences in the company of her grandmother and friends. This encounter leads her to a renewed vision that allows her to assess her identity from a different vantage point. Similar to the Mecca trip, Khadra's journey to Syria as a place of origin(s) is crucial for her revised self-understanding. Unlike her experience in Mecca, which in many ways validates her stringent, albeit more racially and ethnically nuanced, religious upbringing, Khadra's trip to Syria ends up having the opposite effect. It shatters the well-defined spiritual and intellectual parameters of the Muslim Arab-American identity that she had fastidiously developed throughout her life in response to US bias. In a scene that echoes the revisionary approach of second- and third-generation Arab-Americans discussed in chapter 1 (nevertheless here enacted within the sphere of the Arab homeland), Khadra undergoes a physical and spiritual breakdown.

Upon visiting the Jobar synagogue and meeting its Damascene rabbi, Khadra is suddenly overwhelmed by what she recognizes as her replication of the "us versus them" rhetoric she grew up with in the US. But instead of the binary of a Christian us and a non-Christian them that informs much of US bias against religious minorities, the dividing line in the Syrian context is between Muslim and non-Muslim, specifically here Jewish minorities. She realizes that the rabbi, "drawling out the last syllable [of every word] . . . like such a Damascene" (306), has as much claim to Damascus as a home as she does, if not more: "Of course, of course; she knew there were Arab Jews. . . . It's just that—all this time, she'd thought of them as *Them*, these people over *There*, not all the same of course, she knew that, but, still not part of *Us*. Never" (305–6). Such cognitive dissonance between what she sees and what she knows (or thinks she knows) makes all the beliefs she had grown up with seem illusory: "This whole other life opened up in her mind. It sent her whirling in mad agony. This incidental skin, this name she wore like a badge . . . what was it again? Had it changed? Who was she?" (306).[12] Such recognition of a "whole other life" that she had previously shunned (consciously or unconsciously) or denied because it differed from her bounded and well-defined beliefs throws Khadra into a deep crisis. Slowly emerging from it, she evokes redemptive quotes from the Quran and the Prophet's Hadith that bring her to a place of spiritual tranquility and help her find peace in prayer again. But her return to prayer leads her to a cognizance and practice of Muslim faith different from the one with which she had initially arrived in Syria. After her breakdown, "Khadra . . . felt as though she were praying . . . for the first time, as if all that long-ago praying, rakat after rakat, had been only the illusion of prayer, and this—what she began to do now—was the real thing. All that had been lost was returning. All that had been disconnected was connected again" (307).

Accompanying Khadra's reassessment of her Arab identity is her act of taking off the hijab, baring herself to the "soul-sickness" that she carried with her from the US.[13] This crucial moment of unveiling occurs when Khadra, on a trip to a cherry orchard with her grandmother and friends, lets the hijab slip off her head. This small act triggers an intense spiritual reaction in Khadra, by which she recognizes that "the sunlight on her head was a gift from God. . . . Veiling and unveiling are part of the same process." Describing this unveiling process, Kahf writes, "She opened her eyes, and she knew deep in the place of *yaqin* [certainty] that this was all right, a blessing on her shoulders.... Here was an exposure, her soul an unmarked sheet shadowing into distinct shapes under the fluids.... Her self, developing" (309). Khadra's encounter with this developing self in the "real" Syria becomes the perfect foil for her revision of the deeply entrenched and clearly demarcated parameters delimiting the identities and labels that she had grown up with in Indiana (Muslim, Syrian, Arab, immigrant, halal, haram, etc.).

In this way, Khadra's discovery of this developing version of herself in Syria is at the basis of her transformative rearrival in what she refers to as "Homeland America" (313). This rearrival marks a further step toward the state of "*yaqin*" she first experiences while in Syria. This redefinition of physical veiling while in her ancestral homeland leads Khadra to reassess her place within the US, which is then transformed in her process of spiritual growth and grounding. On the plane back to the US, Khadra drapes a tangerine scarf loosely over her head as a way to claim "the many signs of the heritage" (313). Such a reclamation of the hijab as an expression of Muslim belief is important for two reasons. First, it enables Khadra to assert her veiling as a personal choice rather than a communal or familial imposition. Second, it flies in the face of dominant US depictions of the hijab as a physical marker of a foreign and un-American religion. Thus, by reclaiming the hijab upon returning to her "Homeland America," Khadra rejects the binary logics of belonging embedded in dominant understandings of US citizenship. Such logics dictate clear and unambiguous national allegiance to a Judeo-Christian US space, an over here, that is distinctly separate from an over there marked by irrefutable Muslim difference. By traveling into the space of the US, Khadra's state of *yaqin* leads her to a broader understanding of her own place as a Muslim Arab-American woman in the US. This understanding shapes what I refer to as Arab-Americans' rearrivals in the US after return journeys to an Arab homeland, rearrivals that lead to revised and transformed conceptualizations of citizenship and belonging.

In this way, the trajectory of Khadra's return journey to Syria leads her straight back to the US, where she further delves into the process of self-discovery and self-awareness. The novel makes it clear that "going overseas was what enabled her [Khadra] to see that she was irrevocably American, in some way she couldn't pin down.... Yet even ... [after returning to the US], she never thinks of herself as American, not really. When she says 'Americans,' 'Americans do this or think that,' she means someone else" (391). But instead of reiterating the Arab-American conundrum of being Arab in the US and American in the

Arab world, what this statement actually makes clear is that both the Arab and the American identities inherent in such labels are changed by virtue of Arab-Americans' transnational acts of mobility, return, and rearrival. Instead of being a space of inevitable assimilation and compulsory Americanization, the US becomes a home for counterhegemonic and antiessentialist identities, particularly here Muslim Arab ones. Even though the construction of a hegemonic and mainstream US identity as being white and Christian is a lingering and entrenched one, what Kahf's novel shows is that such a construction is ultimately an untenable one.

In earlier drafts of the novel, Khadra removes her headscarf once and for all at the end of the narrative. In the final published version, however, she ends up covering her hair on the plane ride back to the US. This act becomes her way of asserting a visible Muslim identity in a country that supposedly cherishes and values plurality and diversity of faiths and backgrounds but in fact falls short of fully realizing such ideals, particularly in relation to Muslim minorities. A *New York Times* article about Kahf's work includes a quote from Kahf justifying her ultimate decision to have Khadra wear the veil, albeit loosely, by the end of the novel. She states, "People would have read it [Kahdra's removal of the veil at the novel's end] as 'We won! She is an escaped Muslim woman!' . . . People think that all Arab women are dying to uncover" (Macfarquhar).[14]

Along with revising dominant US religious and cultural mores, Khadra's US rearrival also signifies a reassessment of the Arab and Muslim tenets she grew up with. It is within the US space, then, that she forges a full reenactment of her Muslim Arab-American identity, one nevertheless initiated by her return to Syria. Back in the US, Khadra, seeking "new air," consciously chooses to disengage herself from her parents' community in Indiana. She moves to Philadelphia, where she has more of an opportunity to develop her revised sense of self. Kahf writes, "Here in Philadelphia, America didn't seem so dead-against what Khadra was. . . . In Philly, it almost feels as if she, Khadra Shamy, she and her kind, are just the latest in a series of Americans, instead of trespassers on the homestead of the real Americans" (391). Philadelphia, with its large African-American Muslim community and its multinational Arab Muslim immigrant population, becomes the prime terrain for Khadra's revision of the form of traditional Islam dominating her childhood. Upon her return visit to Indiana, which is featured at the beginning and at the end of the novel, Khadra seems to have retained a good grasp on a still-developing transnational belonging. Her version neither adheres to the strict bounds of the Muslim identity of her youth nor subscribes to the exoticizing or assimilative tendencies typical of earlier second-generation Arab-Americans such as those featured in Blatty's and Bourjaily's narratives.

Khadra's journeys of return and rearrival ultimately reveal the multitudinous and shifting terrains that Arab-Americans from various generations have to constantly contend with in their antinostalgic, antihegemonic negotiations of dual or even multiple national belongings. In doing so, such journeys constantly question and problematize fixed notions of homes and homelands. The type of longing that drives Arab-American immigrants and their descendants back to their ancestral homelands, then, ultimately reshapes fixed enactments of US citizenship and belonging, rendering them more transnational in nature. In this way, the rearrival of the Arab-American female returnee in the US as evoked in Kahf's novel should not be read as an overt selection of one locale over another as a permanent home place. Instead, it becomes an entryway into complex and multilayered formations of Arab-American subjectivities that draw on and simultaneously inhabit multiple spatial, temporal, and national homes.[15]

Inscriptions and Reinscriptions of Race and Class in *The Cairo House* and *Letters from Cairo*

The intermingling of locations, as well as pasts and presents, and the impossibility of reclaiming unchanged versions of original homelands in the wake of exile and displacement is the central theme of another coming-of-age narrative, Samia Serageldin's novel *The Cairo House* (2000). Both Kahf's and Serageldin's novels capture the stories of two female protagonists, Khadra and Gigi (short for Gihan) and depict their return as adults to ancestral Arab homelands. The bulk of *The Cairo House*, however, more so than *The Girl in the Tangerine Scarf*, is set in the Arab world, specifically in Egypt.[16] Opening with Gigi's arrival at the Cairo airport after a long absence in the US, the narrative immediately meanders back in time to capture Gigi's memories of growing up in Egypt during the Nasserite years and the treatment that her well-known and influential family endured under President Gamal Abdel Nasser's sequestration rules.[17] The novel depicts Gigi's personal struggles with the upper-class Cairene social sphere she was born into, with a focus on her arranged marriage, subsequent estrangement from her husband, and ten-year self-imposed exile, first in France and then in the US. She moves to the US with her second husband, Luc, a French journalist whom she had initially met in Egypt. Though the book's narrative is set primarily in Egypt, it nevertheless includes sections on Gigi's life in London, France, and the US. Its depiction of the protagonist's return as an adult from her US exile to her childhood home offers readers an insightful comparative lens that juxtaposes the two different (albeit interconnected) Cairos that Gigi knows firsthand. One Cairo forms the backdrop to Gigi's past, and another one permeates the novel's present. Both versions take on multiple and layered characteristics.[18]

Even though Gigi's return to Egypt is carried out in the name of rediscovering her own childhood and reconnecting with her son, whom she had to leave in the care of her mother and ex-husband, such a return also takes on the more practical purpose of resolving the fate of her grandparents' house, aptly called the Cairo House. Despite the fact that Gigi had grown up in her parents' Zamalek villa, what primarily shapes the landscape of Gigi's past and present is this sprawling and impressive family estate. It is the house in which her father, Shamel, had grown up and in which her widower uncle, the Pasha, as the eldest brother and the family patriarch, lives and presides over the affairs of the extensive Seif-el-Islam clan. The materiality of Gigi's memories of herself as a child and as a young adult is embodied in the Cairo House, which becomes a symbol of Gigi's personal, familial, and national histories. It becomes clear that the fate of this house will also determine Gigi's future connections to Egypt.

With the change in the family's political, social, and economic standing in the period following the assassination of Anwar Al Sadat in 1981 and with the Pasha's dwindling health, as well as the prevalence of foreign investors in Egypt, the family (including Gigi) must choose between selling the house to the Saudi Prince Bandar or leaving it to fall into disrepair and possible devaluation. At the family meeting held to discuss the sale offer, which most of her cousins and uncles are in favor of, Gigi surprises herself by voicing her unwillingness to forgo what to her is the primary symbol of her heritage, as well as that of her son. Speaking up against rushing into the sale, Gigi thinks to herself, "Because I had been uprooted, I needed to know that the house would be here for me to come home to. Because my past and present were irreconcilable, I needed to be able to touch base, to reconnect to my old self. The house was my link to the past. . . . It was part of Tarek's [her son's] heritage" (222). This statement becomes a clear indication of the extent to which Arab-American return journeys not only entail a spatial return to an ancestral homeland but involve a temporal return to a past as experienced in this homeland.[19]

In this way, the returnee's presence in the Arab homeland signals his or her material grounding in a palimpsest landscape (both on the spatial and temporal levels) that is simultaneously familiar and unfamiliar.

Gigi's assertion in the novel's opening pages, then, of why she has returned to Egypt—to "claim what's mine. . . . To find two children I left behind: . . . one child is my son and the other the girl I once was"—remains incomplete without a material grounding of such a claim (2). More than merely being a symbol of Gigi's past, the Cairo House specifically embodies the class privileges with which she had grown up, so much so that the loss of the house would inevitably signal the loss or at least the denaturalization of that privilege. It is not till the novel's end, however, that Gigi hints at the implications involved in losing the "material debris" of her childhood, or the material embodiment of her childhood years (Boym 258).[20] Surveying the grand hall, "the monstrous crystal chandeliers," and the sweeping "marble staircase" of the Cairo House after paying a visit to her uncle, the Pasha, Gigi acknowledges the end of a significant chapter in her family's, as well as the country's, history (Serageldin, *Cairo House* 171). She states, "It [the Cairo House] was the last private home in this row of houses that had once belonged to friends and relatives and had now been turned into embassies, one after the other. One day soon I would only be able to drive past the Cairo House, and it would be flying a foreign flag" (171). Even though, at the time of Gigi's return visit, her own parents' villa in Zamalek had already been purchased by an American company, which had turned it into offices, the inevitable loss of the Cairo House (despite the Pasha's efforts to reside in it till he dies) signifies what Gigi describes at the end of the novel as the futility of future return journeys to Egypt: "I might go back to Egypt, but I will never go home again" (233).

Such a pronouncement is couched in Gigi's sense of being unable to close the physical and emotional gaps separating her from the present Egypt, specifically from her son Tarek and her cousin Tamer (to whom she had developed a romantic attachment during her sojourn). More than that, however, I would argue that social class plays a pivotal role in determining Gigi's future connections to Egypt as her home in the event that the Cairo House is sold. For in spite of the outsider status that Gigi assumes during her return visit—especially her weariness of the age-old familiarity of social obligations, gossiping relatives, and bustling traffic, as well as the new phenomena of "all-Filipino staff in the midst of the *fellahin*, . . . *Infitah* millionaires and Islamists" (213)—she nevertheless retains from her childhood days the class-based social separations distancing her from the lives of working-class Egyptians. Such a disconnection becomes most obvious during her interaction with the household help during her return visit, especially with the Nubian gatekeeper Ibrahim, whom she regards with a mix of fascination and condescension. In a scene that evokes the hierarchical social relations governing her childhood and adolescence, Gigi asks Ibrahim to place rat poison in the garbage bins to deter foraging animals from breaking the garbage bags open. Initially reading Ibrahim's unresponsiveness as possible insolence, Gigi realizes later on, upon waking up early one day, that rather than foraging animals, it is desolate children (part of the community of *zabaleen*, or garbage collectors) who are in fact strewing the garbage around in search of food for themselves and their farm animals.

Such a reality, to which Gigi had been oblivious throughout her sheltered and privileged upbringing, offers her a glimpse of the teeming layers of everyday Egyptian life that she had never been privy to before. Moreover, listening to the muted conversation of Ibrahim and the other Nubian doorkeepers congregated in front of her parents' old villa, and seeing in their uprooted status within Cairo a reflection of her own alienation from her ancestral home place, Gigi wonders if they too, like her, felt homesick. Gigi's social status, however, renders her sense of alienation in Cairo very different from that of the Nubian doorkeepers, who "migrate north from their far-flung villages in the Nubia and the Sudan, leaving wives and children behind, and take up a monastic life in the basements, stairwells, and garages of villas and buildings all over the city" (214).[21]

In addition to Gigi's limited acknowledgment of the privileges that her social position offers her in Egypt, her perspective is also shaped by racial difference, another important factor of Egyptian identity politics that remains outside the conscious realm of Gigi's critical evaluations of her ancestral homeland. Although Gigi is well aware of her inability to be part of this "formidable basement grapevine [constituted by the coterie of Nubian workers] running through the streets of the capital," her proclamation that they "all seem to be related to one another" underscores her internalization of the racial and class hierarchies within Egyptian society (214).[22] Rosemary Marangoly George's statement that "the basic organizing principle around which the notion of the 'home' is built is a pattern of select inclusions and exclusions" is helpful here (2). In Serageldin's novel, we see this sphere of inclusions and exclusions playing out within the class and racial hierarchy governing Egyptian social life, with the huge gulf of privilege, money, and education separating Gigi's milieu from the life of the average Egyptian.[23] But Gigi, despite her privileged upbringing and her status as a member of the novel's financially challenged upper class, feels upon her return to what is supposedly her inalienable home that she has lost her grasp on the unquestionable sense of belonging with which she had grown up. Looking back at her life in the US, she tries to reinvent her sense of home by seeing in her quiet and predictable New Hampshire lifestyle the kind of belonging she realizes can no longer be easily accessible to her in Egypt. She finds herself yearning for the quiet life she had developed in "the northern town of snow-capped steeples and ice hockey that she has called home for . . . ten years" (139). Suddenly, the object of her homesickness is reversed, so much so that it is New Hampshire that she misses, not so much the physicality of it but rather what it offers in solitude, introspection, and "an uncomplicated existence" (211).

Like Khadra in *The Girl in the Tangerine Scarf*, Gigi's return to an ancestral Arab homeland triggers crucial reconfigurations of homes and belongings, reshaping the protagonist's connections to both her Arab homeland and to the US terrain. Khadra carries out such negotiations by focusing primarily on her religious identity. Even though Gigi's reformulations of home and identity occur at the fault lines of class and race, they still, as in Kahf's novel, convey a specifically gendered narrative of return and rearrival. *The Cairo House* portrays a young Gigi who, forced to choose between being free from her unhappy first marriage and staying close to her son, chooses the former. She finds herself exiled in Paris, with a return to Cairo inevitably resulting in possible state prosecution and inevitable social judgment. For, with her departure, her first husband, Yussef, revokes the divorce ruling that she had obtained with the help of her uncle, which means that "to go back [to Cairo], a runaway wife returned, would be to put herself at Yussef's mercy" (124). Even when her first husband does go through with the divorce, Gigi remains in Paris in order to secure her mother's custody of her son Tarek. In this way, even after Gigi marries her second husband, Luc, and moves to the US, the narrative of her return to Egypt automatically implicates the sexist labels of runaway wife and irresponsible mother, labels that she implicitly has to contend with upon her return visit a decade later.[24]

Moreover, the type of national and familial belonging with which Gigi is faced upon her return to Egypt is a highly patriarchal one. Despite the relative independence that Gigi possesses in Egypt due to her upper-class status, such independence is undercut by the ways in which her female body is read within the larger constructs of Egypt's patriarchal society.

Her quest to recover the girl she once was in Egypt collides with prevalent understandings of the role she is expected to play as an Egyptian woman (albeit one belonging to the influential Seif-el-Islam family), especially were she to decide to stay in Egypt and give up her life in the US. Gigi witnesses such weighty gender expectations as carried out by her cousin Leila, who has to simultaneously negotiate the roles of the gracious and elegant hostess, the accomplished doctor, the devoted wife and mother, the pious Muslim woman, and the indefatigable caregiver to her ailing grandmother. Such demanding gender roles are of course not restricted to Egypt or the Arab world for that matter but are an intrinsic part of patriarchal structures in the West, including the US. Gigi nevertheless sees in her life in New Hampshire a path to escape the constricting gender roles with which she grew up and which she sees being perpetuated by close family members in Egypt.

But the "uncomplicated existence" Gigi yearns for in New Hampshire is not that uncomplicated (211). For even before her return to Egypt, Gigi struggles with the seismic cultural, linguistic, and social shifts posed by her move to the US with her second husband, Luc. With what they both thought was going to be a temporary job assignment for Luc inevitably stretching into ten years, Gigi finds herself adapting "to their new life in an alien world," despite the fact that "they gradually became strangers to each other" (139). Throughout the novel, Gigi often refers to herself as a chameleon, a characteristic that she claims had come in handy for adapting to a new US, specifically New England, environment. She states that "chameleon-like, ... [she] had tried to blur her edges and lose her accent since they had immigrated to this neutral territory, [unlike] Luc, [who] had somehow managed to accentuate his foreignness" (142). But Gigi's insistence on her "chameleon-like" qualities remains unconvincing, even to her. Despite the fact that she "had made friends, ... she felt like one of those 'sleeper' agents that were popular in Cold War fiction.... There was no place in this world of snow-capped steeples and ice hockey for her memories of dust and jasmine" (141). More than cultural alienation, Gigi's life is also governed by a lingering sense of class privilege that she alludes to but never fully acknowledges. The lifestyle she leads in this New Hampshire university town, which retains "a clear distinction ... between town and gown" and where most of her friends and acquaintances are university people, in many ways resonates with the social elitism dictating her Egyptian milieu throughout her childhood and adolescence (141). That is not to say, however, that class is the only factor shaping Gigi's expatriate experience, for as discussed earlier, class is inevitably linked to issues of race and gender.

To a certain extent, Gigi echoes Khadra in her reassessment of her attachment to and conceptualization of an Arab space in *The Girl in the Tangerine Scarf*. But unlike Khadra, who has the support back in the US of an extended Muslim- and Arab-American community in her determined efforts to carve out a permanent home for Arab-American identity in "Homeland America" (313), Gigi remains isolated and unsure in her explorations of transnational US citizenship and belonging. Her future in the US is merely alluded to in the novel, the ending of which stops short of fully delving into it. For this reason, the return journey depicted in *The Cairo House* denotes a revisionary perspective that for the most part remains fixed on reassessing the protagonist's ties to the Arab world more so than to her US space. But it is the changed perception brought about by Gigi's return visit to Egypt that promises a shift in her vision at the end of the novel. Despite the novel's somewhat bleak ending, what remains clear is that Gigi, by way of her return journey to Egypt and her US rearrival, is in no way ready to replace the restrictions she battled against within the Egyptian terrain with similar pressures of assimilation and conformity faced by Arab-American and other immigrant communities in the US.

Despite the disparity between the two US rearrivals depicted in Kahf's and Serageldin's novels, they both affirm that the US terrain could and should be reconfigured as a space for Arab-American transnational belongings. In other words, instead of characterizing a constant state of in-betweenness and yearning, these journeys of return and rearrival revise the US terrain so much so that rather than being a temporary abode—with the return to the true homeland always barring complete US belonging—the US is claimed, and subsequently altered, by the Arab-American presence within it. To be more specific, Arab-American writers' transnational and transcultural investigations of home and homeland, more than just being antinostalgic or antiessentialist, affirm the need for a transformative rootedness in the US, one that is not assimilationist but one that generates a particularly American type of Arabness or, even more so, an Arab type of Americanness.

But carving out such a space is not an easy task. Again, as George reminds us, "Homes are not about inclusions and wide open arms as much as they are about places carved out of closed doors, closed borders and screening apparatuses" (18). As Egyptian-American writer Pauline Kaldas suggests, such screenings are not restricted to the US but are also fully operational within the Arab world as well. In a collection of travel essays, letters, poems, illustrations, and email correspondence titled *Letters from Cairo* (2007), Kaldas chronicles the six months she spent in Egypt in 2002 with her two daughters and husband, who had been offered a Fulbright grant to teach American literature at Cairo University.[25] In fact, this six-month stay does not constitute Kaldas's first return to Egypt, for she had previously returned in 1990 with her husband for a short-term teaching position at the American University of Cairo. Comparing the two trips, Kaldas writes, "My first trip to Egypt as an adult ... allowed me to reclaim a sense of who I was, to own the knowledge of my cultural identity, and to create a unified identity rather than the fragmented one that had been thrust on me by my American experience. The second trip allowed me to release the sense of loss that comes with the immigrant experience" (153). This shift in perspective enacted by repeated returns to original homelands is a valuable one, given the multiplicity of contexts and factors defining the return journeys discussed in this chapter.

Kaldas, who was born in Egypt and immigrated with her parents to the US at the age of eight, presents in *Letters from Cairo* a narrative collage that captures the elusive and transformative effects of her return to her country of birth in 2002. Such a return, underscoring "the sense of loss that comes with the immigrant experience," renders Kaldas hyperconscious of the ways in which she is perceived (or screened) in Egypt. For despite her characteristic Egyptian features, she realizes that her body is read and perceived by Egyptians as "foreign." Detecting a similar reading being applied to the bodies of her parents visiting from the US, she notes, "Immigration changes the body, the way you move, the way you dress, your facial gestures, and the tone of your complexion" (54). Ironically, her husband, T.J., with his "brown skin and African American features," blends effortlessly into the Egyptian racial landscape, to the extent that he is often called on to prove his Americanness, given the prevalent assumption in the Arab world that "all Americans are white and blond" (5, 21).

The framing of the immigrant body within a native-versus-foreign binary is most importantly informed in Kaldas's text by what could be described as deeply ingrained colonialist residues determining gender- and race-informed understandings of natives and Westerners in Egypt. Commenting on the treatment she receives from university staff members during her time teaching in 1990 at the American University in Cairo (itself a Western-based academic institution), Kaldas notes the evident shift in their attitude depending on whether she spoke in Arabic or English:

> If I . . . spoke in English, people were very polite and I could get what I needed, but there was a distance that disturbed me. Their manner of responding to me placed me as a foreigner. If I spoke in Arabic, people were very friendly and I felt included, clearly perceived as one of them. However, I also sensed a diminished respect, perhaps because I did not seem to be sufficiently "westernized," and it was difficult to get whatever I was requesting. (32–33)

Kaldas's narrative troubles such rigid placements of bodies and identities into seemingly clear-cut and transparent categories such as Egyptian and American. Like Khadra and Gigi in the two novels discussed earlier, Kaldas takes up this questioning stance within the space of an original homeland. Instead of perceiving her return to Egypt as an act of personal and cultural recovery, as in the case of Khadra and Gigi, however, Kaldas is well aware, even prior to embarking on her 2002 sojourn, that this return will define her American as much as her Egyptian identity, her future as much as her past. Rather than perpetuating a split between the two aspects of her identity, Kaldas's multiple returns to Egypt act as a springboard for questioning the binary logics separating the two cultures to which she feels an equal and simultaneous connection. As in Kahf's and Serageldin's novels, the image of a plane permeates the text, representing the protagonist's straddling of multiple locations. Kaldas states, "I'm beginning to think I can only belong on a plane between both countries, suspended in flight" (23). This kind of imagery stresses the simultaneity of transnational belonging that sutures the seemingly separate spheres of "over here" and "over there." Such a positioning shifts fixed concepts of national affiliation and connection to reach a complex and multilayered understanding of place and identity, specifically here pertaining to Arab-Americans.

One of the main venues in which Kaldas develops an understanding of such transformative and transnational approaches to identity formation is the classroom setting, where she seeks to alter both her Egyptian and American students' perspectives about the cultures of the US and the Arab world. While teaching at the American University of Cairo (AUC) in the early 1990s, Kaldas finds herself confronted with Egyptian students' sweeping generalizations about the US, based on what they see of it on such popular TV programs as *Dallas* and *Knots Landing*. They are appalled to hear from Kaldas about the social problems that pervade the US, such as homelessness and poverty. One student asks her, "America is so rich.... How could anyone be homeless?" (28). Another student wonders, "But everyone in America, they live like people on *Dallas*, right?" (28).

When in the US classroom, however, Kaldas attempts to render Arab identities more conceivable to the American students taking her Arabic literature class. At one point in the book, Kaldas recalls an incident in which one of her American students, after reading a novel by Palestinian writer Sahar Khalifeh, asks her "why someone . . . [would] become a terrorist." She responds by explaining the complexities of history and human oppression, nevertheless feeling uneasy with her role as a "cultural" and "political translator" (35). She writes, "My answers felt inadequate.... My attempts were as futile as trying to explain U.S. actions to Egyptians. I have been thrust into a role that disturbs me, yet whether in Egypt or in the United States, it seems I must take it on" (37).[26] Embedded in such negotiations is an insistence on recognizing one's own role, and one's own possible culpability, in reaffirming binary conceptualizations of citizenship and belonging that propagate fixed Arab and US national belongings.

An admittance or awareness of how we are all implicated in reproducing, challenging, or reformulating these larger normative and limiting structures is not only central to Kaldas's classroom pedagogy. It also lies at the forefront of her overall portrayal of the ways in which her Arab-American female body moves across transnational space and the complexity of belonging engendered by that movement. Assessing the effects of her physical and metaphorical returns and rearrivals, Kaldas writes, "I existed on both sides of the divide: the colonizer and the colonized. I found myself tumbling and losing my footing. In this case, I learned to embrace my shifting pronouns [we, they, us]; it was the only way to articulate the complexity of my own position" (33). The complexity that Kaldas demands and enacts through her journeys of returns and rearrivals flies in the face of the hegemonic pressures that read the pull of an over there (in this case Egypt) as a deterrence to true belonging over here (the US), or vice versa.

Yet fulfilling the promise of returning to an Arab homeland is not easily accessible to all Arab-Americans. For many, the gates of the Arab homeland remain firmly closed, whether due to financial, political, or religious reasons, with the dream of homecoming perpetually delayed or canceled. In some cases, as in the context of the forbidding realities created by dictatorial Arab regimes,[27] as well as the Israeli occupation, Arab-Americans' dissident politics and opposition to the governments in their Arab homelands render a visit, let alone a permanent return home, an ostensibly dangerous, if not a fatal, venture. In other cases, as best exemplified by the Palestinian diasporic condition, the loss of land through dispossession and exile, especially in its pre-1948 contours, renders any attempt at permanent return an exercise in futility, frustration, and humiliation.[28] For while the land remains in place, any claim to it is perpetually mired in the political complexities of Israel's occupation of Palestinian lands as well as in exclusionary constructions of Israeli citizenship.

Several texts by Palestinian-Americans capture the sense of mental and emotional yearning for a pre-1948 Palestine that many had directly known or had heard about through their parents' or grandparents' exilic memories. While many of these texts do depict return journeys carried out to (re)discover and reclaim a connection to Palestinian land, such returns are for the most part temporary ones due to the geopolitics of Palestinians' right of return, circumventing any permanent rerootings of Arab-American identities in ancestral landscapes. More than merely asserting a reconnection to Palestine, what the texts discussed in the following section underscore is how fragmented, impossible, or partial returns to Palestine bring about particular rearrivals in the US (whether actual or metaphorical). Such rearrivals remap the US space and reconfigure the exclusionary nature of dominant US citizenship and belonging to make it more transnational and malleable. It is exactly through this transnational type of belonging that Arab-Americans as well as a mainstream US public become better equipped to assess and critique the foreign policies governing US relations with the Arab world, policies that are largely determined by US hegemony and US imperial power.

"Where Should We Go after the Last Frontiers":[29]
The Case of Palestine

The story of Aliyah in Susan Muaddi Darraj's short-story collection *The Inheritance of Exile* (2007) incorporates an insightful account of a return journey to the West Bank. Having grown up with her parents' potent and lingering stories about their Palestinian background, Aliyah, one of the collection's four female narrators, embarks on a summer visit to her ancestral homeland.[30] But rather than embodying a tangible version of her parents' memories, this Arab homeland comes to represent for Aliyah her family's traumatic and scarred history of loss and tragedy. Her mothers' parents, for one, had been forced to immigrate in the early

1960s to the US (when their daughter was still a young girl), where they could only dream of a return to their Palestinian homeland. Aliyah's paternal grandparents had to move to the town of Ramallah in the West Bank after their land outside Jerusalem was confiscated to build Jewish settlements. In this way, Aliyah's return visit immerses her in a space pervaded by loss rather than discovery or reclamation. She says, "So I wasn't going to the home Baba had been born in. I never could return to that because it had been replaced by a walled-in city to which my dark skin and last name denied me access" (70). The systemic measures that bar Aliyah, despite her American passport, from fulfilling a veritable homecoming to her father's place of birth are furthermore accentuated by what she perceives as the lack of space available to her among her Palestinian friends and family within Ramallah.

In contrast to Khadra, Kaldas, or even Gigi, to whom the empty spaces left behind in the Arab homeland by immigrants and their families are tangible and visible within Syria and Egypt, Aliyah increasingly feels that there is no space for her within the Palestine she encounters on her visit. The critical self-awareness brought about by her return journey to Palestine and her rearrival in the US generates a reassessment of both her rootedness in Palestine, instilled in her since childhood, and her unmistakable American identity. She confesses to her friend Nadia how bothered she was about being branded as an American while in Ramallah. Nadia retorts, "I know. . . . We're different, and that's it. They [also] tell us [here] we're not Americans and, sure, we listen to the music and drink the coffee. . . . We're just different, and that's OK" (74).

This splitting of Arab-American identities into separate spheres, however, is countered by the sense of easy belonging that overcomes Aliyah while sitting inside the Dome of the Rock, which she had previously only seen "*crowning pictures of Jerusalem.*" "*Sitting quietly and breathing in the scent of musk*" upon being invited by a Muslim Palestinian woman to enter the mosque, Aliyah feels that she is "*finally inside the picture*" (72). Her mental replay of this experience when back in the US relays a particularly significant moment of rearrival for Aliyah. This particular experience directly interrogates and problematizes the inseparable link often made in the US between national and cultural belonging on the one hand and religious identity on the other hand, by which Arab equals Muslim equals non-American.[31] In fact, Aliyah grew up in a Christian family in South Philadelphia's small Palestinian community. Religious as well as class divisions are poignantly visible within this community, despite her mother's mantra, "Our [Arabs'/Palestinians'] religion doesn't matter here.... In America, our water comes in from the same pipe and our sewage exits from the same pipe—here we are all the same" (58). Through Aliyah's observation of and reflection on the Muslim women praying inside Jerusalem's Dome of the Rock mosque, she is able to disengage herself from the class- and religion-based forms of identification that shape her Arab-American community's connections to Palestine. "Remembering that day in the mosque, the orderliness of the service and the unison of female prayer" becomes a key moment in Aliyah's reformulation of her Palestinian-American identity beyond the binary constructs of mononational identity (72). Her revisionary perspective toward what she had traditionally understood as constituting home and homeland, as defined primarily by a Christian Palestinian-American household, is altered within the actual space of Palestine, specifically in Jerusalem. Aliyah states, "There was a power there [in the Dome of the Rock] that I identified with—it had been the first time I felt comfortable in Palestine" (72).

This broader understanding of self and identity in relation to religious affiliation is reminiscent of Khadra's moment of clarity in the Syrian orchard, which, despite its sharp contrast to Mecca as Islam's official place of worship, provides the appropriate setting for Khadra's transformative act of spiritual illumination. Like Khadra, Aliyah realizes through her visit that her Arab cultural identity goes well beyond the religious mores she had grown up with in the US. This fact is made particularly evident by the space of Jerusalem itself, with its rich and contentious historical and religious significance. Like Khadra's trip to Syria, Aliyah's trip to Palestine helps her develop a revisionary outlook toward her US-based religious and cultural upbringing. Her mother's insistence that "we [Palestinian Christians and Palestinian Muslims] are all the same" in the US in fact asserts and echoes hegemonic understandings of Arab-American identities as a monolithic and homogeneous entity (58). But instead of delineating differences among various religious and cultural iterations of Arab-American, and specifically Palestinian-American, identities to further distinguish and separate Arab from American identities, Aliyah's return journey to Palestine and rearrival in the US enable her to formulate a more fluid, complex, and transnational enactment of the two seemingly incompatible parts of her Arab-American identity.

While Kahf, Serageldin, and Kaldas portray the Arab world as the primary setting for the development of this transnational enactment of their Arab-American identities, Muaddi Darraj privileges the US space as an important venue for fully developing such transnational belonging.

Aliyah's negotiation of space and identity nevertheless expands on the duality of the US-versus-Arab-world framework to incorporate the complexities of space within Palestine/Israel. These complexities bring into focus variances in the experiences of Palestinians in the West Bank and Gaza, for instance, in comparison to the experiences of those living inside Israel (often referred to as the 48ers). In spite of such variances, however, all Palestinians within historical Palestine witness and directly suffer from the increased diminishing of the physical space available to them within the West Bank, Gaza, East Jerusalem, and Israel, let alone the space available to returnees from the diaspora.[32] In other words, given the intense debate around the issue of the Palestinian right of return (or *Haq Al-'Awda*)[33] and its pivotal role in the protracted Israeli-Palestinian peace negotiations, including the Oslo Accords, it is important to delineate the significance of undertaking discursive returns. This is especially significant for Palestinians living in the West, specifically in the US, whose access to a foreign passport provides them with the relative luxury of accessing occupied Palestine, albeit with great difficulty.[34]

Despite these difficulties, many Palestinian and Palestinian-American writers have insisted on pursuing actual and imaginative returns to historical Palestine in order to address this pressing humanitarian crisis in the history of their people. Even if relegated to the imaginative, the theme of return has been a lingering refrain that has appealed to these writers' need to satisfy an emotional lack that they often cannot fulfill through a physical return to the Palestinian homeland. When they do enact a physical return, their visits are for the most part temporary.[35] Even though some of these texts are written from the perspective of a female returnee, the male perspective is still a dominant one.[36] While this male perspective is quite insightful in delineating the role of gender in projects that reconstitute the Palestinian homeland (physically as well as imaginatively), it nevertheless falls short of integrating a full discussion of the female returnee's role in narratives of Palestinian repatriation. With this chapter focusing on female returnees' revised understandings of Arab-American identities through the concept of rearrival, I seek to supplement my literary focus by delineating other artistic venues that capture the variety of struggles involved in enacting Palestinian women's return journeys. To this end, I use the remainder of the chapter to analyze Annemarie Jacir's film *Salt of This Sea* and Emily Jacir's visual art, delineating in the process some of the intricate tensions of return in a variety of artistic works featuring the Palestinian homeland.

Moreover, these visual texts provide an important platform for discussing the role of women in the ongoing struggle to reclaim a sense of home and belonging within the harsh context of military occupation and dispossession. In contrast to Palestinian-American films that focus on the journey of a male returnee,[37] Annemarie Jacir's and Emily Jacir's work, by privileging a female perspective, provides an important framework for analyzing the intersection of feminist and anticolonialist struggles in transnational Palestinian-American artistic discourse. Such a framework captures some discursive responses to Israeli occupation as lived, experienced, and understood by Palestinians in Gaza and the West Bank, as well as those living inside Israel and in the diaspora. At the same time, these responses problematize the US support of Israeli occupation of Palestinian land as well as the hegemonic clout that both the US and Israel flaunt within the international community.

Salt of This Sea (2008), written and directed by Annemarie Jacir and starring poet and performer Suheir Hammad, has been hailed as the first feature film from Palestine by a female director.[38] Garnering several awards, including the International Critics Award, the film follows the US-born Palestinian-American Soraya on her return journey to her grandparents' Palestine, where she seeks to reclaim her grandfather's life savings from a bank account that was frozen and confiscated by the new Israeli state in 1948. When her claim is turned down, she devises and executes the plan of holding up the bank at gunpoint with the help of her Palestinian friends Emad and Marwan, retrieving by force her grandfather's savings (in addition to an extra sum she deems to cover some of the interest owed). Beyond this action-packed narrative and the developing love story between Soraya and Emad (who is struggling to permanently leave the West Bank to study in Canada),[39] the crux of the film lies in Soraya's discovery of her lost homeland. Her travels in Ramallah, Jerusalem, and Jaffa renew her love for historical Palestine, a love to which she had remained true throughout her life in the US. In other words, the intriguing love story between returnee and homeland featured in the film, rather than suggesting the heady passion of a new love, is in fact the chronicle of a rediscovered love for a place that Soraya had grown up knowing intimately by way of her parents' stories (which they themselves had inherited from their own parents) in their Brooklyn exile.

Toward the beginning of the movie, when Soraya is asked by a fellow Palestinian why a "pretty girl like her would want to return to Palestine," she replies, "They won't give us the right of return, so I took it," thus linking her return journey to the larger Palestinian demand for the

FIGURE 2.1. Annemarie Jacir's *Salt of this Sea* (2008). (Courtesy of Annemarie Jacir)

right of return, consistently denied since 1948 and constituting one of the major stumbling blocks in the protracted peace process. But her US passport provides Soraya neither complete nor indefinite access to historical Palestine. With Soraya admitting to the security officers at the Ben Gurion Airport that Ramallah is her final destination, she is only given a two-week visa. The irony is that many of the Palestinians she encounters within the Palestinian territories, like the man who asks her why she would want to return, do not understand her zeal for returning to what they deem to be miserable circumstances compared to the supposedly easy life in the West. For Soraya, life in the US contains neither ease nor luxury. In many ways, it is not very different from life in the Lebanese refugee camp into which both her parents were born after the Nakba in 1948, before they immigrated to the US.[40] In fact, Soraya sees her exilic life in the US as a mere replacement of one refugee camp with another (thus a temporary abode, while she awaits a rightful return). Responding to an older Palestinian woman's comment that Soraya is "a girl of the refugee camps," the latter agrees, adding that she is a "girl of the American camps" too.

The considerable shift in perspective between exiled Palestinian returnees and those who remained behind after 1948 and 1967 is captured most effectively in an exchange between Soraya and Emad during their rendezvous on top of a hill in Ramallah with a view that extends all the way to Tel Aviv. With their conversation turning to the past, as well as their present lives, it becomes evident that a future together is inevitably impossible for them. For while Emad plans to leave Palestine for good so he will not have to see another "soldier in [his] life," Soraya, adamant about finding a way to stay in her ancestral Palestinian homeland, states, "All my life, I've dreamed of coming here. There is no going back." The tenacity of Soraya's dream of return is nurtured by the stories and memories about her grandparents' life in Palestine before the Nakba, stories and memories with which she had grown up and that are so intricately and beautifully detailed that they become part of Soraya's own reality. Speaking of Jaffa, traditionally known as "the bride of the sea" due to its location on the Mediterranean, Soraya, from her perched position on top of the hill, recites her intimate knowledge of the city despite the fact that she has never visited it:

> My grandfather swam in that sea every morning, then he'd walk on Al Helwa Street to reach Al Tawfiqiya library, then on to Al Nuzha Street. Cars weren't allowed on Al Nuzha. The orange traders—Jaffa

oranges—met at Al Salahi market. My grandfather always talked about the Al Madfa Café. Umm Kulthum sang there, and Farid al-Atrash. My grandmother really loved Farid. Sometimes, my grandparents went to the cinema. The Hamra cinema. When they were broke, they'd wait by the side door and the doorman would sneak everyone in.

This narrative map of her grandparents' Jaffa helps Soraya link her life to a history that she feels she has missed, by force rather than by choice. "We had something here," she tells Emad. "We had lives. We were robbed." Emad's response to Soraya's secondhand reminiscences is anger. His subjection to regular and random strip searches by Israeli patrol troops, to a strangled economy in the West Bank, and to a restrictive identity card that relegates him to the bounded and closely monitored West Bank leaves him bitter and rebellious. As opposed to Soraya, whose understanding of Palestine is based on the preoccupation version of her grandparents' days, Emad lives and experiences Palestine via occupation. In other words, he does not or rather cannot imagine, reminisce, and construct versions of the Palestinian homeland that are based on ancestral memories and stories. He in fact reprimands Soraya for what he regards as her naive nostalgia, saying, "You think Palestine is just oranges? Jaffa oranges? What a fantasy!" And he is right. Soraya is quite naive.[41] The gendered stereotypes of the dreamy and flighty female versus the grounded and strong male, however, are quickly overturned by Soraya, who rebuffs Emad's scorn, stating, "I'm not some foreign chick who'll kiss your ass and say you're special because you're Palestinian. I don't need a lecture on Palestine! Don't tell me what Palestine is! I know what it is!" Her response challenges Emad's attempt to override her understanding of Palestine, by which she asserts her identity as a Palestinian woman whose knowledge is as valid as his, even if this knowledge is not rooted in lived experience. Instead, she validates her knowledge of a slowly eroding Palestine by rooting it in stories about her grandparents' lives there, in their stories of the land as "lived geography" (Jayyusi L. 124).[42]

A crucial question posed in *Salt of This Sea*, however, is one that investigates the degree to which Soraya is able to act out or reenact, in the present, her grandparents' past "lived geography." Even though she successfully retrieves from the British Palestine Bank in Ramallah the money she sees as rightfully belonging to her family, she accomplishes the more essential retrieval of her ancestral rights to a Palestinian locale

FIGURE 2.2. Soraya (Suheir Hammad) and Emad (Saleh Bakri) in Annemarie Jacir's *Salt of this Sea* (2008). (Courtesy of Annemarie Jacir)

by returning to her grandparents' house in Jaffa. Soraya, Emad, and Marwan cross into Israel by disguising themselves as Jewish tourists. They first giddily roam the streets of Jerusalem, eating oranges off its trees and finding the traces of a Palestinian presence etched beneath the city's Israeli façade.[43] Upon reaching the coast, they rush to the sea, ecstatic that they can finally touch the water that they had previously only heard of or dreamt about. But their delight in swimming in the Mediterranean is overshadowed by reminders of their illegal presence in Israel, captured by shots of the suspicious glances of other (presumably Israeli) beachgoers, the ever-present Israeli military helicopters flying overhead, and the Israeli flag planted among the rocks along the shore.

Arriving at her grandparents' house in Jaffa, Soraya, still accompanied by Emad and Marwan, is welcomed in by the house's current Jewish Israeli resident, who, upon being told about Soraya's connection to the place, invites them to stay as long as they want. With the camera panning across the inside of the house, lingering over the intricate floor tiles that Soraya's grandfather had laid out himself, as well as the tall arched windows overlooking the Mediterranean, we get to see the place through Soraya's eyes. Although she is seeing it for the first time, she nevertheless still situates it within the familiar setting of her grandparents' stories. In this way, the house itself becomes the embodiment of her grandparents', her parents', and her own missed futures. Inquiring about the original furniture that was left behind by her grandparents, Soraya finds out that the current resident's family had most probably thrown it out or discarded it. This piece of information triggers an intense bodily reaction in Soraya, with the next scene showing her throwing up on the beach. Her visceral response, similar to how one might react upon coming across a dead being, indicates Soraya's realization that the past she had claimed to know is in fact gone forever. But rather than merely accepting that loss as a permanent death, Soraya goes out in search of some remnants of this past that she might salvage, finding them in what looks like the city's pawnshops and secondhand-furniture stores, as well as in the city's garbage dump.

Documenting Jaffa's Palestinian remnants in one of the film's most powerful scenes, the camera visually retrieves a forgotten history. This history is embodied in discarded everyday Palestinian objects, such as a oud, a fez, a silver urn with Arabic calligraphy carved on it, and chairs and tables stripped down to the wood, all tucked away and forgotten in dusty Jaffa shops. This history also includes pieces of broken tile similar to that found in Soraya's family house, thrown out in the garbage dump. These "memory-objects," to use Lena Jayyusi's term, embody the materiality of the past as retold to Soraya by her grandparents and parents, enabling her to grasp at their past lives among the detritus of the immediate present (122).[44] Accompanying the shots of these objects is the famous song "Emta Ha Teraf," in which the Arab diva Asmahan sings of unrequited and hidden love, which "lives in her imagination like a ghostly presence." What this scene makes obvious is that the object of love here is not a person per se but historical Palestine itself, a thematic refrain running through the whole movie.

Capturing the ghostly presence of a Palestinian cultural history through the objects featured in the aforementioned scene is not only meant to remind viewers of the past. It also becomes a way to document the systematic erasure of a Palestinian material presence within the state of Israel. It is in this way, then, that the inclusion of these "memory-objects" within the present landscape of Jaffa, rather than intending to only pay homage to a bygone past, becomes a strategy to change dominant understandings of Israel's present (and future) landscapes. Rejecting the version of Israeli-Palestinian histories upheld by the Israeli woman living in Soraya's ancestral house (in which Palestinians such as Soraya's grandparents chose to leave their homes), and refusing to relegate Palestinian dispossession to a historical past that has no immediate relevance to the present, Soraya asserts her agency and her role in shaping the unfolding narratives of place and belonging. Addressing the woman who currently lives in her grandparents' house, Soraya states, "Your past is my every day. My right now. This is not your home. You can stay if you admit all of this is stolen. Recognize it."

The demand for such recognition is further explored through Soraya and Emad's search for the latter's ancestral village of Dawayima, where they find refuge among the abandoned ruins. But the lovers quickly realize that their demand for the acknowledgment of Palestinian loss is intensely circumscribed. Their dream of rearranging the reality of the present in order to build a home for themselves among the ruins of Emad's village is irrevocably threatened by the arrival of an Israeli teacher on a field trip with his students. When the teacher stumbles on their hideout, Soraya, in order to deter the risk of his notifying the Israeli police about them, assures him that they are Jewish-American tourists on a hiking adventure. The teacher informs Soraya of his goal to "teach them [his students] history. . . . They can climb here in these ancient ruins, . . . learn about their roots, . . . how to turn this biblical land into life again." Such a statement empties the landscape of its Palestinian history, turning it into a present that hinges on a particular biblical, albeit selective, reading of the past, one in which Palestinian roots and identities have no place or role.

Soraya and Emad's dream of return to their ancestral Palestinian homes is cut short when they are picked up by the patrolling Israeli police in Haifa. We as viewers are not privy to Emad's fate at the end of the movie, but his options include deportation to the West Bank, where he will be arrested for robbing a bank, or imprisonment within Israel. In contrast, Soraya, by virtue of her passport, faces the prospect of being deported back to the US. That is to say, unlike Emad, whose Palestinian body is constituted as a threat in both the West Bank and Israel, Soraya is subjected to other policing measures by virtue of her gender and, more importantly, her US citizenship. Contradicting the information recorded on her passport, Soraya answers her interrogators' questions regarding her country of birth and the duration of her Israel/Palestine visit with the following: "I'm from here. . . . I've been here all my life. I was born here . . . [in] Jaffa, [on] Nuzha Street." In an interesting twist to hegemonic readings of US citizenship, Soraya confuses her interlocutors by telling them that the US passport they have in their hands is in fact her Palestinian passport. In doing so, she inserts her Palestinian identity into the pages of her US passport, rewriting the logics of single-nation allegiance inherent in dominant performances of US citizenship and belonging.

Moreover, the US passport becomes the means through which Soraya claims her right of return to Palestine in the absence of the implementation of UN Resolution 194. Soraya's statement that her US passport is in fact her Palestinian passport widens the scope of US identities to include a dissenting, antihegemonic, and transnational conceptualization of US citizenship and belonging that acknowledges and encompasses Palestinian trauma and dispossession. In this way, equating US citizenship (represented by the passport) with Palestinian citizenship disrupts the typical power imbalance between American and Palestinian identities by pushing viewers to reconsider the consequences of collapsing the rigid and normalized boundaries between the two categories. Even more significant is the way in which the placement of the American and Palestinian identities within the same citizenship rubric renders the US responsible toward its Palestinian communities for its unilateral support of the Israeli state. In this way, the Israeli-Palestinian conflict is no longer a conflict perceived as happening "over there," removed from the everydayness of American lives, but becomes in fact part and parcel of US history and everyday reality. In this way, Soraya's claim that her US passport is in fact her Palestinian passport fully captures the simultaneity of belonging to transnational spheres and cultures as enacted by Arab-American identities.

Such disruptions of the privileges afforded by a US passport and the ease of travel and movement that it provides underscores the following question, which becomes even more pertinent and acute in the context of narrative returns to historical Palestine: Are such returns easily accessible to everyone? Who is excluded from such return projects? How do the restrictions on Palestinians' movement as monitored by the Israeli state (and of course aided by its Western as well as Arab allies) affect transnational Palestinian articulations? To address such questions, I conclude this chapter by discussing some of the works of leading contemporary artist and Palestinian-American Emily Jacir, whose art pushes against dominant and unquestioned narratives of wars, dispossession, travel, and identity, especially as pertaining to the Israeli-Palestinian conflict.[45]

Jacir places the question of transnational Palestinian return and movement at the center of one of her more well-known installation pieces, titled *Where We Come From* (2001–3). In doing so, she emphasizes many Palestinians' perspective on the limitations and prohibitions placed on their dream to return to their ancestral homeland. But instead of using grand political proclamations as a starting point for addressing the question of forbidden returns, Jacir turns to personal, albeit also political, stories of Palestinian exiles living in places such as the West Bank, Gaza, Israel, Lebanon, Syria, and the US to excavate a powerful narrative of loss, one that is often forgotten and overlooked in the larger international debates over the Israeli-Palestinian conflict. For the piece, Jacir asks thirty Palestinians (living both inside and outside Palestine and Israel) what they wish her to accomplish within the parts of historical Palestine that they themselves cannot access, given the relative ease of movement provided by her US passport.

The project is then premised on the following question asked by the artist: "If I could do anything for you, anywhere in Palestine, what would it be?" (qtd. in Demos 69). The result is an intimate and moving chronicle of these individuals' yearning for what Edward Said, commenting on Jacir's piece, calls the "simple gestures" provided by coveted homecomings ("Emily Jacir" 49). Such gestures include a visit and a hug given to a much-missed mother in Gaza, requested by her son Jihad, who lives in Ramallah and is not allowed to return to his Gazan home; a walk in the streets of Nazareth, requested by George, whose Palestinian passport and West Bank ID bar him from entering Israeli territories; a game of soccer with the first boy Jacir encounters in Haifa, requested by Hana, born in Lebanon to Palestinian parents and residing in Houston, Texas (where she awaits her US passport); and a visit to Gaza to eat *sayadiyeh* (a fish and rice dish), requested by Sonia, who, as a Palestinian with Israeli citizenship, cannot enter Gaza. The installation piece itself shows a typed transcript of each request, in both Arabic and English, accompanied by the identity of the person making the request and the reason he or she cannot fulfill it, along with a colored snapshot chronicling the outcome of Jacir's performance of each request. More than addressing the challenge posed by national borders as faced by many members of the Palestinian diaspora, Jacir's piece also captures the internal boundaries cutting off Palestinians living within historical Palestine from each other. As she notes, it was "just as hard to get to Jerusalem for someone in Syria as it was for a Palestinian living only eight kilometers away in Bayt Jalla" (qtd. in A. Moore 38).[46]

When Jacir was asked about the political statements conceived and enacted through her art, she stated, "I'm not trying to teach people about Palestine. My audience is Palestinian, and we're talking to each other" (qtd. in A. Moore 39). Despite such a claim, however, one still senses that

FIGURE 2.3. *Where We Come From,* 2001–3, detail (*Jihad*) *American passport*, 30 texts, 32 c-prints and 1 video. (Photo: Bill Orcutt, © Emily Jacir, courtesy of Alexander and Bonin, New York)

Jacir is invested in bringing her perspective on the Palestinian plight to a larger Western audience, as exemplified, for instance, in her project *Sexy Semite* (2000–2002). Coupling seemingly harmless romantic rhetoric with a politically charged message, she fills the pages of the *Village Voice* (in three issues, over a period of three years) with fake ads allegedly placed by Palestinians seeking Israeli mates. The implicit purpose of these ads is for Palestinians to enact a return to Palestine through the implementation of Israel's law of return for all Jews around the world. One ad, for instance, reads, "Shalom baby! Hot Palestinian Semite gal Hoping to find my perfect Israeli man. Let's stroll the beaches of Akka & live and love in Jerusalem. No Fatties" (qtd. in Demos 75). More than underscoring the flagrant discrepancies of the law of return when applied to Palestinians versus Jews, these ads mock current Israeli state policies that criminalize and forbid mixed marriages, thus questioning the representation of Israel as a democracy.[47] Another ad reads, "Palestinian Semite in search of Jewish soul mate. Do you love milk & honey? I'm ready to start a big family in Israel. Still have house keys. Waiting for you" (Jacir, "Stella Rollig" 15).[48] This tongue-in-cheek approach, however, by underscoring what can

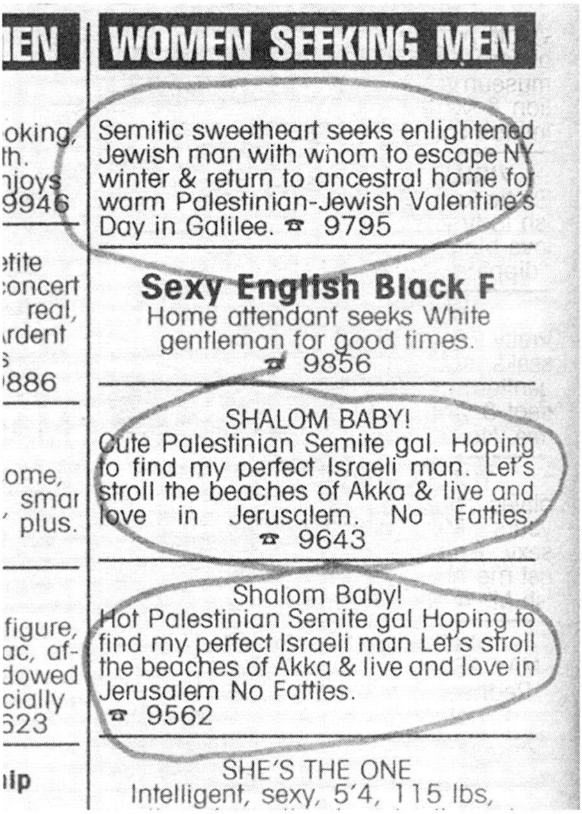

FIGURE 2.4. *SEXY SEMITE*, 2000–2002, Documentation of an intervention. Personal ads placed in the newspaper *The Village Voice*. The artist asked 60 Palestinians to place personal ads seeking Jewish mates in order to return home utilizing Israel's "Law of Return." (© Emily Jacir, courtesy of Alexander and Bonin, New York)

be described as the ironic absurdity defining many Palestinian lives, both within the Palestinian territories and in exile, relays a strong disruptive message that challenges the impossibility of procuring promising futures for Palestinians. In other words, more than bringing to light the futility and absurdity involved in navigating international as well as internal borders for many Palestinians, the return journeys referenced in Annemarie Jacir's and Emily Jacir's work signal an urgent need to change the existing status quo, a dismal one for Palestinians.

One strategy for doing so, as indicated by both artists, is to pay closer attention to the links connecting Palestinian, and more broadly Arab, experiences and identities to US ones, which in the case of the more than 3.6 million Arab-Americans in the US are one and the same. Forging such links does not only underscore the geopolitical and legal privileges afforded to US citizens against the limitations faced by Palestinians (within Palestine as well as those living in refugee camps). It also implicates mainstream US citizens and the role they play through their political engagements (or lack thereof) in either propagating or dissenting against injustices carried out in their name (whether they are of Arab background or not). The consistent US support of Israel's occupation of the Palestinian territories over the past half century or so, as well as the ongoing US military interventions in the Arab world, render a separation of the US and the Arab geographical spheres, and by extension the people who inhabit them, an untenable reality. In such a context, the articulation of transnational Arab-American citizenship and belonging becomes even more urgent and necessary.

The emphasis placed in Annemarie Jacir's and Emily Jacir's visual texts on producing revisionary notions of US belonging and citizenship in relation to the Palestinian struggle is similar to the interrogative stances taken up by the narrative texts by Kahf, Serageldin, Kaldas, and Muaddi Darraj. Whether depicted directly or indirectly, all these texts exemplify how return journeys to ancestral Arab homelands ultimately lead to US rearrivals that interrogate and revise inherited as well as hegemonic understandings of Arab-American identities. In turn, the transnational consciousness at the heart of the Arab-American rearrivals portrayed in these texts overturns the assimilative demands that govern dominant US citizenship and belonging. In doing so, such transnational consciousness questions the social, cultural, religious, and political uniformity at the heart of such hegemonic formulations.

Moreover, the enactments of transnational returns and rearrivals depicted in these texts change conceptions of US citizenship (Arab-American and otherwise) by revising the ways in which connections to the Arab world can be imagined and lived both by an Arab-American minority and by a US mainstream. Such revisions produce a language of transnational belonging that crosses ever-shifting blockades within and across the US and the Arab world. It is through such potent language that these Arab-American literary and artistic works create transformative spaces that are elemental for social and political justice.

3 / Translocal Connections between the US and the Arab World

From around the mid-twentieth century onward, emigration from the Arab world has been largely instigated by multiple wars and conflicts that have plagued the region, starting with the establishment of Israel in 1948, the Six-Day War between Israel and the Arab states in 1967, the Lebanese civil war (1975–90) and its ongoing repercussions, the First Gulf War in the early nineties, up until the US-led invasion of Iraq in 2003 and its aftermath. With hundreds of thousands of refugees, immigrants, and exiles arriving in the US during this period to escape the horrors of war and dispossession in their Arab homelands, the formation and articulation of Arab-American citizenship and belonging cannot be conceived of in isolation of these loaded histories and spaces that continue to haunt Arab-Americans in the US. Such hauntings are perpetuated with every new invasion, military intervention, and bombing carried out in an Arab country under the aegis of the US imperial vision in the region. The two key conflicts that inform the texts discussed in this chapter are the Lebanese civil war and the ongoing Palestinian Nakba.[1] My focus on thematic representations of these two specific conflicts is informed by their dominance in Arab-American literature, with many novels, poems, short stories, and essays consistently turning to explore these conflicts' disastrous effects on Arab identities, both in the Arab world and in the US. Such explorations produce transnational interconnections that trouble simplistic spatial and temporal divisions between the Arab world and the US. They also superimpose the war traumas embedded in Arab localities onto a US cultural and social landscape that is oblivious or at best indifferent to such traumas, let alone to the US role in instigating or perpetuating them.

The literary texts discussed in this chapter further diversify the range of strategies employed by Arab-American writers in their discursive articulations of transnational citizenship and belonging. The enactment of this transnational type of citizenship and belonging differs in this chapter from the ones discussed earlier. For while the first two chapters focus on revisions of nostalgic depictions of an ancestral homeland (chapter 1) and on return visits to these homelands (chapter 2), this chapter's analysis of transnational Arab-American identities is based on texts whose characters had lived in the Arab world for an extended period of time before immigrating to the US.[2] Hence, by positioning Arab landscapes as the geographical and psychological points of origin for many Arab-Americans, these texts shift the focus from mononational understandings of US citizenship and belonging. In doing so, they allow other national sites, and the complex histories embedded in these sites, to become an elemental part not only of Arab-American identity-making but of broader conceptualizations of US identity as a whole.

The narratives discussed in this chapter and the book as a whole attest to the importance of analyzing Arab-American literature within a transnational framework. They highlight the need to ground this framework in the specificity and uniqueness of particular place-based experiences that are primarily shaped within the Arab world and are then transported through immigration or exile into the multifarious US landscape. A generalized transnational framework that does not take into account the specificities of place, however, risks disregarding the internal differences and nuanced backgrounds within the Arab world and the US, which extend to ethnicity, dialect, religion, race, and political history. My analysis in this chapter focuses on the concept of translocality to further develop this transnational specificity. I use translocality to examine how immigrant and exilic rootedness in and production of translocal spaces alter binary understandings of home, homeland, and belonging in the US. The production of translocal spaces is evident in many of the texts discussed in this book, in which we find Arab-Americans straddling, connecting, or reimagining two or more seemingly disparate locales. In doing so, they reformulate Orientalist binaries dictating hegemonic conceptualizations of place, identity, and belonging. The articulation of translocal spaces takes on specific significance in this chapter given the ways in which the particularities of place in many Arab-American texts are embedded within specific traumatic histories that straddle and connect Arab and American locales.

In formulating my analysis of translocality in these texts, I draw on Arjun Appadurai's belief in the power of certain "moving groups and individuals" (including tourists, immigrants, refugees, exiles, and guest workers) to change the landscapes of national and international dynamics (33). I build on Appadurai's theorization by placing special emphasis on the fact that the formation of such groups and their cultural production is rooted in specific local contexts. Such localities continually shape individual and collective consciousness as people of a particular group move and travel to, as well as between and among, various locales. Rather than adhering to "[deterritorialized] landscapes of group identity" (Appadurai 48), an awareness of identities spanning and laying claim to multiple but clearly identifiable and territorialized spaces becomes a crucial component of complex forms of knowledge production about Arab-American lives in the US. As Khachig Tölölyan reminds us in his formative discussions of transnationalism, the emphasis on deterritorialization and mobility in diaspora studies (as in the case of Appadurai's and James Clifford's work) should not lead us to disregard the fact that "contemporary transnational diasporas require settled diasporic nodes in which a public sphere and civil society *peculiar to them* develop" ("Contemporary Discourse," 654; emphasis mine).[3]

Conceptualizing Arab-American cultural production within a transnational, or particularly a translocal, framework releases its subjects from the dangers of ghettoization or marginalization within the US or its categorization as merely an extension of Arab artistic and cultural forms. My engagement with the translocal in the analysis of Arab-American literary texts, however, is not so much focused on discursive explorations of the topographic features of a specific city or locale, whether it is Beirut or Detroit, for instance. Instead, it is engaged in analyzing characters' experiences and remembrances of an Arab locale within a specific social and political US location from which such experiences are overwhelmingly absent and/or occluded. Moreover, the focus on the translocal in these texts is not meant to isolate the spatial representations of an Arab homeland (or more specifically Beirut, the West Bank, or Baghdad) from the US space (whether it is New York City, San Francisco, or Syracuse, for instance). Instead, these spaces, as remembered and reconstructed in the narratives discussed here, come to echo and even bleed into each other, evoking a contrapuntal reading of the writers' and characters' experience of these locales.[4]

The first part of my analysis in this chapter elucidates the lingering effects of the Lebanese war on the lives of Arab-American immigrants and exiles. I focus primarily on Patricia Sarrafian Ward's novel *The Bullet Collection* and Haas Mroue's poetry collection *Beirut Seizures*, as well as Rabih Alameddine's *I, the Divine* and Etel Adnan's *In the Heart of the Heart of Another Country*. The characters/speakers in these works, by inserting their traumatic memories of the Lebanese war into the isolating and homogenizing space of the US, develop what I call translocal consciousness, one that imbues the Arab-American experience with empowering spatiogeographical specificities of an original homeland.[5] To further develop and contextualize my analysis of the role that translocal consciousness plays in Arab-American subject formations, I move on to analyze how Arab-American lives are often shaped by patterns of physical mobility that surpass a typical immigrant's western-bound, unidirectional itinerary. Such mobility can encompass multiple sites of displacement marking the contemporary immigrant's journey, as exemplified in Edward Said's memoir *Out of Place*, as well as Laila Halaby's and Randa Jarrar's novels *West of the Jordan* and *A Map of Home*, respectively, all of which widen singular notions of homes and homelands in Arab, Arab-American, and mainstream US formulations of citizenship and belonging.[6]

Re-membering, Rerooting, and Rerouting Traumas of the Lebanese War

The much-touted statement "We are a nation of immigrants" is often used to assert seemingly equalizing claims to US citizenship and belonging. Such effusive proclamations, however, still do not address the gaping disparities among immigrant groups in the US, with race, nationality, and religion being key factors in facilitating some immigrants' access to US cultural citizenship while barring others from it.[7] Immigrants arriving from impoverished or conflict-ridden countries, what are often disparagingly referred to as Third World countries, have an especially hard time integrating their national histories of trauma into US memoryscapes. That is largely due to the ways in which these alternative histories threaten to overturn the dominant narrative depicting the US as a nation of equality and opportunity, a narrative that occludes US colonialist practices at home and imperial ambitions abroad. As Rebecca Saunders and Kamran Aghaie remind us, these alternative histories become extremely important to explore the ways in which "sites of traumatic memory in South Asia, Africa, and the Middle East (dis)confirm, challenge or revise dominant Western conceptions of trauma and memory." Looking at how "experiences, narratives, and concepts . . . cross national and regional borders" enables us to study such revisions "not from the uncluttered comfort of abstract theory and essentializing axiom but from the intractable complexity of local detail, irreducible specificity, and contestatory cultural and personal perspectives" (16).

In drawing out such complexities, Saunders and Aghaie refer to Ruth Leys's statement that "the experience of trauma, fixed or frozen in time, refuses to be represented as past, but is perpetually re-experienced in a painful, dissociated, traumatic present" (qtd. in Saunders and Aghaie 17). The study of such a past as experienced and situated in the present takes on unique and complex aspects in Arab-American articulations of immigrant and exilic war trauma, as exemplified in the works of Patricia Sarrafian Ward and Haas Mroue. For one, the temporal gap between the past and the present in both works is concomitant with a spatial gap between the initial place of trauma (in this case Lebanon) and the US. In other words, the spatial rupture produced by leaving the homeland, whether willingly or unwillingly, problematizes the reenactment of trauma "as past . . . in a painful, dissociated, traumatic present" because this present has an inherently different commemorative structure that precludes the recognition of these traumas. Given the absence within the US of any material or imaginative spaces that recognize the effects of the Lebanese war, these texts become a way to reenact and mentally revisit, through memory, Lebanese-American sites of trauma.[8] In doing so, they challenge the seemingly unpassable gap between a Lebanese past fraught with war and conflict and a US present oblivious to or at best limited in its acknowledgment of such traumatic histories.[9] In this way, the immigrants' battle to maintain the memory of Arab homelands in the US incorporates the struggle to integrate such memories into the wider commemorative structure of the US.[10] In addition to bridging temporal and spatial gaps between the past and the present, as well as between the Arab world and the US, narratives such as those discussed here also collapse the boundaries separating Arab-American memoryscapes from those of the wider US public. In doing so, they show how complex transnational, and specifically translocal, Arab-American subjectivities become key actors in revisionary projects that alter dominant US landscapes of memory, history, citizenship, and belonging.

In Ward's novel *The Bullet Collection* (2003), the young Marianna remembers her past experiences growing up in Lebanon during the civil war from the present vantage point of an unidentified town in New England. To escape the war, she had left Lebanon with her family in the late 1980s as a seventeen-year-old for the safer shores of the US (but not before witnessing her fair share of the war). She arrives in the US accompanied by her American father, Stephen (who had lived in Lebanon for a long time teaching history at the American University of Beirut); her mother, Ani (a Lebanese-born Beiruti of Egyptian and Armenian ancestry); and her sister, Alaine (short for Magdalaine).[11] Once in the US, Marianna is confronted with the "amputation of exile" (Sobelle), which compels her to obsessively re-member and re-collect the past in order to seemingly avoid, but in actuality to survive, the present. She states, "It is as if there is a hidden law created in moving from one country to another, a law against remembering, and I am breaking it" (Ward 10).

Even though the novel is marked by its dark portrayal of depression and mental illness (driving both sisters to attempt suicide at different points of the book's convoluted narrative), it nevertheless underscores the redeeming and necessary power of memory in confronting war trauma, specifically as remembered and consequently relived in exile. Marianna compellingly negotiates the cultural and political gaps that inhibit her from adequately translating her traumatic experience from a Lebanese past to an alienating US present. In reviving the past, however fragmented the result, Marianna in fact confronts the silence of exile, often characterized as the lack of real and metaphorical spaces within the US from which the specificities of Middle Eastern war traumas can be disseminated. In fact, what Ward's novel ultimately asserts is how literary and cultural production can become or can be claimed as a commemorative discursive repertoire that revises hegemonic, selective, and uniform US national understandings of what is often construed as "the mess over there," in the Arab world.[12] This revisionary role is especially pertinent in the case of conflicts with unresolved outcomes, as evinced in Lebanon's postwar promulgation of a general amnesty and the adoption of the *la ghalib wala maghloub*, or "no victor, no vanquished" formula, which "became the official justification for . . . [the] transition from war into peace" in the 1990s (Haugbolle, "Public and Private Memory" 193).[13]

Central to my analysis here of Arab-American formations of translocal consciousness are the ways in which Ward's novel portrays the marked, albeit slow, transformation of the exilic space by virtue of Marianna's dis-membering and re-membering the past from within the immediate vantage point of the present. Reading the novel involves an intense process of piecing together discrepant and variant memories that are riddled with gaps, absences, and horrific images. Describing the jolting discrepancies between the temporal and spatial locales of a past Lebanese setting and a present US one, Marianna ironically flips the referents usually attached to war zones on the one hand and safe havens on the other. She represents the latter as the locus of tainted, claustrophobic encounters and the former as the embodiment of spatial purity and freedom. She states, "The air is different inside a stone house in the mountains [of Lebanon]. In summer the doors stand open, and a breeze brushes along cool surfaces, and stone melds with pine, earth, our bodies breathing stone-pure air. Here [in the US], the air surfaces from porous, warm wood that's rotting away from damp, warped from years of heat to cold to heat. We breathe the air of all the people who ever lived here" (67).[14]

Rather than signaling a continuity of lived experience, such shared air ultimately underscores the vast differences in outlooks separating Marianna and her family (including her American father) from the previous residents of what she describes as their shabby and run-down house in the US. Her descriptions of this house include the following: "Where the linoleum meets the walls and the shower stall in the bathroom, it curls away, a narrow nest for grit and damp dust balls, an old toothpaste cap, bobby pins. This at first appalled me, but now I recognize it as a necessary facet of our new life, a sign of all we have lost" (10). Such material details bring crashing home what Marianna portrays as "the utter foreignness of where we are" (10). In the face of such foreignness, Marianna obsesses over, even yearns for, the war she left behind. This war is embodied in her memory by scattered images such as the death of Ziad, a family friend on whom she had a crush; her sister's war collection of shrapnel, bullets, a hand grenade, and a corpse she claims to have found and buried on a Lebanese mountainside (71); the kidnapping and murder of her father's American friend Uncle Bernie; and the resounding Israeli jets breaking the sound barrier and circling the air above Beirut ahead of the 1982 Israeli invasion of Lebanon (137–39).

These images, to which Marianna turns and returns obsessively throughout her fragmented narrative, rather than emphasizing the gap between here and there (the US and Lebanon), point to the harmful and dangerous effects of maintaining such a mental separation. Despite her family's unified and anxious resolve to get over the anguish of their war-torn past by adhering to that amnesiac separation characteristic of many immigrant lives, Marianna insists on preserving that past. Claiming to be "the ghost of everything we [her family] lost" (92), Marianna even goes to the extent of reenacting, once in the US, her sister's failed suicide attempt carried out when the family was still in Lebanon.[15] Moreover, at one point, she takes her haunting embodiments quite literally by dressing up as a ghost for Halloween, reluctantly partaking in the family's feeble efforts to achieve normalcy in the US. More than being a literal allusion to her "ghost[ly]" presence, her costume is linked to a disturbing image she has retained from the war of a man described as a "traitor who [bundled up in a white sheet] was shot on television just a few months before [the family] left Lebanon; he didn't even have eyeholes" (179). By donning the ghost costume and associating it with the executed man, Marianna literally takes on the role of a traitor. Her obsessive memories about the war and her unwillingness either to assent to the constructed normalcy of her war-free present or to succumb to the ease of forgetfulness so coveted by her family (and demanded by the larger US public) become seemingly antithetical to survival. Unlike the traitor, however, Marianna grants herself the power of vision (reconceived as the power of remembering) by cutting out eyeholes in the sheet she uses for a Halloween ghost costume.

Marianna's description of the man inside as a "white bundle tied with rope to a mound" "turning his head from side to side" but with "no sound [coming from the TV], only static" (179) nevertheless differs from her own embodiment of this victim/ghost. Resisting his silence, she brings him into the space of the US; she refuses to excise him from familial and US public memory. Rather, she states, "I am the ghost of the man who was executed. I move up the sidewalk, showing him America, the glowing faces lighting stairwells, the children squealing as they run. This is insane, the man whispers. *I know, I comfort him*" (179–80). In this way, Marianna creates for herself a co-conspirator to alleviate and challenge the isolation of the immigrant and exilic condition.[16] By doing so, she reforms mandatory immigrant forgetting as dictated by a dominant US discourse into regenerative remembrance, one that transforms the rigid ideological and material isolation of the exilic space to encompass the unknown, the strange, and the haunted.[17] Such a testimonial, however, is not meant to affirm the alleged freedom offered by the exilic space but emphasizes instead its equally discomforting aspects. In collapsing the imposed segregation of immigrant war trauma from historical, public, and political discourse in the US, Marianna's testimonial changes the landscapes of US history and memory, even if only on the metaphorical or personal levels. For this change occurs neither seismically nor swiftly but slowly develops out of a potent and urgent need to enact a transnational, and more specifically translocal, type of belonging that hinges neither on amnesia nor on nostalgia.

Marianna captures the contradictions and conundrums embedded in such belongings when she wonders,

> What is this magic, this country [Lebanon] that insists on being remembered even after forcing us to leave? . . . There is hatred for feeling and remembering and hatred for not feeling and not remembering, for language that has no strength, its innocence on a page that can be torn, crumpled, its susceptibility to violence, for language at all, that it exists, only to hold my tongue, to twist it, to cut it out. (271, 302)

The strength of Marianna's regenerative translocal consciousness, then, lies not only in the act of remembering the past but also in the act of telling it in the present. The story that she is telling and scripting, despite its fragmented structure, conveys a first-person point of view that flies in the face of forgetting or burying war trauma for the sake of a fresh start in the diaspora.

The effects of this reclamatory, albeit critical, translocal consciousness is evident at the end of the novel, with Marianna reaching out to Walter (who works at the nearby gas station and, for her, represents the "outside world" [62]), thanking him for his role in getting her to the hospital in time after she had tried to kill herself by overdosing on aspirin. She also opens up to her father, acknowledging his grief over losing his friend Bernie, who was kidnapped and killed in Beirut. By doing so, Marianna succeeds in partly overturning the isolating effects of holding on to her war-laden memories in the amnesiac landscape of the US. This turn is elucidated in the book's closing section, in which she imagines the real possibility of bridging the spatiotemporal gap between the past and the present so that "the two times of [her] life would meet" (307). Even though such a possibility is frightening to her, she finds solace in the prospect of such a recuperative possibility. Echoing her metaphorical rescuing of the traitor/victim whom she saw being killed on Lebanese TV, she carries out on the novel's last page another form of imaginative recovery that embodies translocal survival.

Instead of the image of the dead traitor/victim, she evokes the image of Saisaban,[18] a mythical winged horse whose transgressive and magical powers she had daydreamed about in Beirut. To escape the "rows of blazing tires block[ing] the street," the "black smoke," and "the soldiers lounging on the sidewalks" in Beirut, Marianna would imagine Saisaban carrying her to the Beqaa Valley, which the war had rendered unreachable. While there, she would pick "poppies and daisies and lavender and violets" and then would ride back to Beirut on Saisaban's back (28). This image of Saisaban brings Marianna equal solace in the US. But instead of conjuring up the mythical horse as a way to escape her immediate exilic surroundings, Marianna's act of reimagining Saisaban is meant to draw strength from this horse's powers. This strength is what would allow Marianna to continue remembering *and* recounting war trauma within the US space, but without the pain that usually accompanies such recuperative acts.

> In the silence of this snowfall, so surprising and clean that it hurts, it might be possible to listen carefully, to stare into the whiteness of this late night, and perhaps in the distance on the slope of this foreign road the wings of Saisaban will spread open like milk spilling from a ewer, and his eyes, black as *mazoot* [diesel oil], will gaze with forgiveness on my remembering, and his hooves, sharp as bullets, will pierce the frozen air as he gallops towards me. (307)

Even though the end of the novel does not fully assert a more positive and less painful future for Marianna, it still holds the promise of such a future in the US. In this way, the novel affirms how the analgesic role of remembering broadens and even alters the scope of US national memory to include the marginal and the occluded. Rather than dulling or mainstreaming the poignancy of traumatic memories, the act of inserting them into US memory-scapes enables a wider range of transnational enactments of US citizenship and belonging.

Transnational formulations of Arab-American citizenship and belonging that insist on retaining the memories of Lebanese war traumas within the context of the US are also vividly captured in the poetry of Lebanese-American Haas Mroue.[19] In his poems "Beirut Survivors Anonymous" and "Beirut Survivors Anonymous II," both included in his poetry collection *Beirut Seizures* (1993), the speaker, like Marianna, juxtaposes his stark memories of the Lebanese war against an indifferent and mundane US space that, unlike the unnamed US setting of *The Bullet Collection*, is reflected in specific US cities and localities:

> In Beirut on good
> nights I watch rockets fly
> over rooftops until my eyes hurt.
> I listen for names of the dead
> on the radio, putting faces to names,
> scars to bodies, burns to flesh.

> I remove my contacts by candlelight
> and flush my eyes with Dettol.
> . . . .
> My generation drives BMWs
> down streets in Los Angeles or Long Island
> popping ecstasy pills hoping to be artistic,
> chanting for Hare Hare Krishna on the corner
> of College and 13th, wishing for a flying roadblock,
> Howitzers, snipers, anything
> to replace the monotony of oceans
> for the rhythm of the Mediterranean.
> . . . .
> We drink *arak* in Oriental restaurants
> in Denver or Burbank or Fort Lauderdale.
> We watch belly-dancers and vomit hummous
> with no garlic, hummous as thick as coffee
> at the aub milkbar. We live in a daze
> longing for green plums and salt,
> the ecstasy of Howitzers on a school night.
> . . . .
> We are experiencing post-traumatic stress
> somewhere in Massachusetts, Colorado.
> ("Beirut Survivors Anonymous" lines 1–8, 28–35, 41–47, 53–54)

What this poem makes clear is that the silencing of traumatic Arab histories within the US is directly related to, or better yet hinges on, the production of faux stand-ins and stylized versions of Arab cultures, complete with "Oriental restaurants," "belly-dancers," and "hummous / with no garlic." Such stereotypes, compared to the speaker's stark and disturbing spatiotemporal memories of a war-torn Lebanon, become symptomatic of the US's selective and Orientalist knowledge about the Arab world. "Experiencing post-traumatic stress" in specific US localities such as Los Angeles, Long Island, Denver, Burbank, or Fort Lauderdale underscores the geographical and temporal gaps that render any attempt to describe such traumatic experiences difficult, if not impossible, for the speaker. Yet Mroue's poems insist on addressing such difficulties by articulating memories of the Lebanese war as a way to defy the lack of knowledge about the Arab world within mainstream America. In addition to manifesting itself through common Orientalist stereotypes, this lack of knowledge is also evident in the lumping together (in the

American mind) of complex Middle Eastern histories, resulting in what is often referred to in mainstream discourse as "the mess over there in the Middle East." *Beirut Seizures* gives geographical and historical specificity to such vague and muddled US knowledge, grounding it in concrete and lived details of particular localities and conflicts, in this case the Lebanese war. These details, including "nights of unrelenting shelling," "neighbors / boiling coffee until dawn," and "gunpowder seeping / through shut windows," give a specific shape and sound to the so-called mess over there, overturning such monolithic discourse in the process ("Beirut Survivors Anonymous" lines 37–39).

The enumeration of these details as they pertain to a Lebanese, specifically Beiruti, locality does not merely intimate the speaker's yearning for a troubled spatiotemporal past. It also points to his disconnection from a US present that repeatedly defines his Arab background through stereotypes and erasures. The speaker states, "We lived a war with no name / and escaped. We now belong to a culture / that has no name" ("Beirut Survivors Anonymous" lines 25–27). What these lines make clear is that within the US, the intimacy wrought from living through a war at close range is lost, pushing the survivors of this war to resist not only dominant US discourse but also their own and each other's forgetfulness. Such resistance takes shape in *Beirut Seizures* through the formation of collectives such as the Beirut Survivors Anonymous, which is also the title of the first and last poems included in the book. Rather than these collectives furthering the anonymity of their members' memories and backgrounds, they in fact overturn prevalent silences and omissions that define Arab, particularly here Lebanese, lives in the US. Moreover, instead of relegating the act of remembering to one point of view or one perspective, these collectives potentially hold multiple viewpoints about the war that would complicate any tendency to simplify the convoluted history of the Lebanese civil war.[20] These multiple viewpoints, however, are not only restricted to a Lebanese context but encompass a wider understanding of loss and mourning pervading the US landscape. For in addition to "the woman who lost her son / on the museum crossing" in Beirut, the Beirut Survivors Anonymous meeting is attended by "a wife of a POW / missing somewhere in Laos" and "two HIV positive men" as well as "others, many others" ("Beirut Survivors Anonymous II" lines 18–19, 14–15, 17, 23). In this way, other painful and silenced US narratives such as the Vietnam War and the HIV epidemic also become part of the speaker's efforts to commemorate traumatic memories of the Lebanese war.

Despite the comfort of recognizing shared and lived trauma, the ultimate purpose of such commemorative efforts is to challenge the anonymity of wars and human loss as brought about by the Lebanese war, as well as other struggles. Such purposes also include overturning the erroneous representation of the cultures to whose histories those wars belong as their memories travel into new spaces and localities. This type of acknowledgment then broadens and even revises the selective and exclusionary nature of mainstream US histories in order to recuperate voiceless or unheard identities that are in danger of belonging only, as Mroue points out, in "the baggage of memories / baggage mislabeled, lost in handling / and heading to destinations unknown" ("Beirut Survivors Anonymous II" lines 74–76). In this way, Ward's and Mroue's explorations of the translocal consciousness wrought from an intimate albeit painful knowledge of specific localities (New England, Beirut, Los Angeles, etc.) enables them to link together these seemingly disparate places (even if only imaginatively). In doing so, they challenge simplistic separations of the cultures and histories attached to these places. By offering narrative reconfigurations of personal and collective Arab-American histories, then, these texts not only imbue the narrator or speaker with a revised vision of self and home but also present a US public with alternative historical and political memories that are typically misconstrued or even completely absent from dominant spheres of knowledge.

Echoing such complex spatial and emotional reconfigurations of US belonging is Rabih Alameddine's second novel *I, the Divine* (2001).[21] Like the two other texts discussed in this section, this novel also stresses a translocal enactment of Lebanese-American identity that alters dominant US memory-scapes. Unlike Ward's and Mroue's works, in which a return to the Lebanese homeland remains physically inaccessible to the exiled characters, *I, the Divine* depicts a specific type of translocal consciousness that retains physical mobility between Lebanon and the US as one of its central tenets.[22] The novel repeatedly retells and revisits the past from the first-person perspective of the elusive and infinitely complex Sarah Nour el-Din, ultimately comprising this protagonist's fragmented and botched attempts at writing her memoir. This memoir seemingly never ventures beyond a repeated drafting of the first chapter—hence the subtitle of the book, "A Novel in First Chapters."[23] Born and raised in Beirut to a Lebanese father and an American mother, Sarah lives in Lebanon through part of the Lebanese civil war, eloping with her boyfriend, Omar, to New York in 1980 at the age of twenty. Even after choosing to stay in the US after Omar's return to Beirut, she constantly shuttles back and forth between the US (specifically New York and San Francisco) and Lebanon (specifically Beirut). In doing so, she enacts translocal negotiations of both cultures that are nevertheless informed by an antinostalgic, critical perspective that extends to both sides of her hyphenated identity.[24]

Sarah's awareness of the conundrums as well as the appeal of traveling identities becomes clear when it occurs to her that "home is never where she is, but where she is not" (99). Whether accessed through actual travel, email, or telephone, the presence of Lebanon is always palpable and immediate in Sarah's life in the US. This presence ultimately invades her coveted American individuality and freedom and even dominates the larger portion of her memoir. In fact, the abundance of details about her memories of and ties to Lebanon saturates her fragmented narrative and leaves a great deal unsaid about her life in the US, which pales in comparison to Sarah's vibrant memories of home (including but not exclusive to war memories). Moving from New York to San Francisco after her second divorce "to see the sun set in water," Sarah (like the speaker in the poem "Beirut Survivors Anonymous") quickly realizes that the Pacific is not the Mediterranean, and San Francisco is not Beirut, "for the sunset" in San Francisco, among a list of other things, "was wrong. The sun disappeared into oblivion at strange angles and with the wrong colors." Thus, for Sarah, watching the sunset on a San Francisco beach comes in sharp contrast to, and disappointingly pales against, what, for her, is the unparalleled experience of sitting "on a real beach [in Beirut], under a *real* sun" (57).

This foregrounding of Beirut in Sarah's memoir challenges the centrality of the US space in dominant understandings of Arab-American lives. Moreover, similar to the representation of the Lebanese war landscape in the texts by Ward and Mroue discussed earlier, Sarah's memoir revises the systematic erasures and omissions of the difficult histories attached to ancestral homelands typical of dominant narratives of US citizenship and belonging. Despite the centrality of Beirut in Sarah's narrative and her alleged homesickness for Lebanon, she only returns home for short periods,[25] constantly deferring a permanent return to Lebanon. As Sarah tells her sister Amal, "Beirut holds terrible memories for me." Her homesickness, then, encompasses her sickness "*for* home" as well as her sickness "*of* home" (Friedman 191). In reality, Sarah's intensely traumatic memories of Beirut go beyond the horrors of huddling during bombings in the "stairwell, [which] seemed the safest place," enduring the "banal and clichéd" smell of "cordite, . . . garbage, urine, and decaying flesh," and having her half sister Rana killed by an infatuated Syrian soldier (38–39). Her memories extend to rape, which she endures at the age of sixteen at the hands of two armed men who in turn force a young adolescent boy, accidentally coming on the scene, to also rape her. In the expanse of one hour during a hot Beiruti summer evening, Sarah remembers how "her life had come to an end. In only one hour, she thought bitterly, she had become a woman" (199).

Even when Sarah finds out that she is pregnant as a result of the rape, the shame of the experience inhibits her from seeking out her family's support. With the help of her best friend, Dina, she gets an abortion and deeply buries her trauma. Metamorphosing into the embodiment of her traumatic experiences, Beirut gradually engenders a love/hate relationship in Sarah, whose longing incorporates a simultaneous sickness "*for*" and a sickness "*of*" this city and all the personal and communal traumas that it represents.[26] Nevertheless, it is her literal and metaphorical occupation of translocal spaces that enables Sarah to transgress the either/or, over there / over here binaries inherent in hegemonic understandings of Arab-American as well as mainstream US belonging. "Throughout my life," she says, "these contradictory [Lebanese and American] parts battled endlessly, clashed, never coming to a satisfactory conclusion. I shuffled ad nauseam between the need to assert my individuality [represented by the US] and the need to belong to my clan [located in Lebanon], being terrified of loneliness and terrorized of losing myself in relationships" (229). Rather than resolving such a locus-based dilemma by succumbing to one side of the hyphen or to one locality and forgoing the other, Sarah finds release in a translocality that maintains a critique of both locales and the identities attached to them. The vigilant interrogative stance defining such translocal positionings replaces secure and unproblematic national belongings. Thus, it creates a space of transnational, and more specifically translocal, negotiation, which constantly revises assimilative forms of citizenship and belonging that conform to hegemonic visions of the US nation-state.

It is from such a seemingly unhinged and multiple position that Sarah can better pinpoint a revised sense of home that enables her to develop what bell hooks defines as "new ways of seeing reality" that do not hinge on forgetting (148). Sarah's struggles to find this kind of home initially involve attempts to escape her own self rather than the past embedded in her memories of Beirut.[27] Nevertheless, it swiftly becomes apparent that movement, particularly translocal movement and its emphasis on Arab locales in negotiations of US citizenship and belonging, can be a means to understand the self instead of merely escaping it. Sarah comes to realize the validity of such self-knowledge through the act of writing her memoir/memories of Beirut. By looking at herself "on paper," she gradually accepts the fact that her US location is in fact an extension and not a replacement of the Lebanese space from which she has been so desperately trying to escape. Thus, her translocal perspective gives her the self-perception she needs to transform ambivalent in-betweenness into a revisionary positionality that reconstructs the over there, or the Arab world, so that it becomes a central rather than a peripheral or occluded aspect of the US cultural landscape.[28] At the end of her memoir, Sarah comes to a conclusion about what she needs to do in order for her readers to access her story:

> I have to explain how the individual participated in
> the larger organism, to show how I fit into this larger whole. So instead of
> telling the reader come meet me, I have to say something else.
> Come meet my family.
> Come meet my friends.
> Come here, I say.
> Come meet my pride (308)

By confirming the importance of Sarah's family and friends, she arrives at the ultimate realization that she not only was deluding the reader (who might not have been so easily deluded as she thought) but was in fact all along deceiving herself by seeking to be separate from her clan. Sarah's call to the reader at the end of her memoir to "come meet my pride" should not be regarded as an unproblematic resolution of her struggle or as a way to celebrate an uncomplicated, group-based representation of her Arab-American self. It can be better understood as a rearticulation of Arab-American identities that embrace rather than forget a specificity of place and history, an elemental aspect of translocal consciousness. Such specificity ultimately yields personal and collective cartographies of identity that produce complex forms of knowledge about the Arab world in the US. This knowledge in turn reconfigures strict formulations of US citizenship and belonging that insist on uncomplicated performances and articulations of mononational allegiances.

By focusing in this section on localities that mainly straddle two national spheres, my exploration of translocal consciousness leads to questions pertaining to translocalities that cut across multiple national terrains. But before turning to some depictions of multinational localities informing discursive depictions of Arab-American transnationalism, I will further investigate the extent to which a translocal consciousness of place and space opens up connective links among Arab-Americans of different national backgrounds. In other words, in addition to focusing on nation-specific translocal sensibilities to study particular sections of the Arab-American community, I also analyze how an understanding of war in one national context helps configure a deeper understanding of another conflict pervading other Arab landscapes. One question would be, for instance, how does the experience of war trauma in the specific Lebanese context change/affect understandings of Palestinian dispossession? Or how are war traumas (whether in the Lebanese case or otherwise) repeatedly reactivated with new and recurring wars (such as the war in Iraq)?

To pursue such a line of inquiry, I turn to Lebanese-American Etel Adnan's experimental memoir *In the Heart of the Heart of Another Country* (2005). By emphasizing a translocal approach to the ludicrous, traumatizing, and banal aspects of war, this text collapses not only temporal and spatial boundaries between the Arab world and the US but also the self-same boundaries constructed within each of these landscapes.[29] In response to writer William Gass's short story of the same name (made up of a series of repetitively structured paragraphs that depict life in an Indiana town referred to as "B."), Adnan offers her own fragmented depiction of a place close to her heart that also starts with a *B*, namely Beirut. Her portrayal of Beirut, her place of birth, is informed by a translocal perspective that straddles different places, including Lebanon and the US (specifically Beirut and California). In this way, *In the Heart* captures the writer's life as it unfolds across multiple continents, countries, and cities. Made up of seven sections written from the 1970s onward, the book might at first glance seem rigid in its strict paragraph divisions that (except for two of the essays) feature repeating titles such as "Place," "Weather," "My House," "A Person," "Wires," "Vital Data," "Education," "Politics." Such structured divisions, however, belie their content. Adnan's free-flowing discursive reflections defy chronological or linear depictions, incorporating "the past mixing with the present, each distorting the other, opening into the tensions of repetition" (Adnan xiv).[30]

The book's last essay, titled "To Be in a Time of War," is particularly relevant to my discussion here.[31] Exposing Adnan's anguish over the start of the Iraq War in 2003, it demonstrates how war traumas embodied by Arab-Americans from various national backgrounds are remobilized with every new and ongoing imperialist war project in the Arab world, regardless of whether it is one's own home country that is being targeted. In this way, translocal perspectives move beyond the specificities of a fixed Arab locality to incorporate larger conceptualizations of an Arab space that extends beyond the national boundaries of an original homeland. Such outlooks and perspectives ultimately ascribe a pan-Arab designation to Arab-American identities that surpasses allegiances to individual Arab nations or homelands.

Marking the beginning of the US-led invasion of Iraq in 2003, "To Be in a Time of War" is made up of phrases that all start with the infinitive *to*. These phrases focus on the daily acts and rituals performed by Adnan in her home in California (and while she is visiting New York City). Despite their simple structure, they effectively capture a powerful sense of disempowerment and futility caused by yet another power-ridden war narrative in Iraq:

> To listen to the radio, to put it off, to walk a bit, to think, to give up thinking, to look for the key, to wonder, to do nothing. . . . To rise early, to hurry down to the driveway, to look for the paper, take it out of its yellow bag, to read on the front-page WAR. . . . To have lunch. To ask for a beer. To give one's order. To drink, eat, and pay. . . . To hear a war from far away, for others. To bomb, eliminate a country, blow up a civilization, destroy the living. (99, 101)

The mundane, everyday acts conveyed in these and other phrases in the section (such as preparing meals, eating, buying gas, taking out the garbage, listening to the radio, and reading the newspaper) ground the Iraq War in an immediate temporal and spatial US present. The war is not merely over there, disconnected from a US landscape, but is evoked in every act performed by the speaker, even the most mundane ones. For as Adnan reminds us in the book's introduction, "Contrary to what is usually believed, it is not general ideas and grandiose unfolding of great events that impress the mind during times of heightened historic upheavals, but rather the uninterrupted flow of little experiences, observations, disturbances, small ecstasies, or barely perceptible discouragements that make up day-to-day living" (xii).

In this way, the immediate present of the US space is always and forever shadowed by another present (or other presents), by other locales, by other realities, and most effectively here for Adnan, by other wars in the Arab world that echo the Lebanese civil war she had experienced. Focusing on the predictability and mundaneness of life in the US, whether in

California, New York, or somewhere else, only serves to further accentuate the disruptive and grotesque effects of war for traumatized Arab-Americans. For this war, even though occurring thousands of miles away, still seeps into every aspect of Adnan's surroundings and inevitably becomes a haunting presence coloring the minute details of her everyday actions. She writes in the same essay, "To sweep the living room in order to disperse all the cluttering angels. . . . To release into the air a vision of Baghdad disappeared. . . . To encapsulate the present" (111). Such an acute awareness of an Iraqi space shadowing the speaker's US present is in stark contrast with the ways in which many Americans' everyday lives are completely disconnected from wars and conflicts overseas, specifically those wars and conflicts that their government has a direct hand in. Adnan's translocal consciousness dismantles the privilege inherent in disconnecting oneself from the atrociousness of a war being waged beyond the US, albeit in the name of American freedom. The phrase "To release into the air a vision of Baghdad" signals a break in the monotony of Adnan's mundane and repetitive everyday actions. These phrases and the breaks they connote consequently disrupt the secure predictability of everyday life that Arab-Americans allegedly find in the US.

In this way, instead of safeguarding the distance separating the safe from the dangerous, the familiar from the horrific, Adnan mixes them up so much that she creates a palimpsest reality.[32] In this reality, a deadly Iraqi war is palpably present under the veneer of US normalcy, threatening its comforting and comfortable façade. Collapsing rigid spatial boundaries (imagined and real) among various spatialities in the Arab world and the US ultimately leads to a discursive reformulation of geographic and cultural distance that challenges a collective mainstream's ambivalence about Arab histories and realities.[33] Dominant understandings of US national belongings and citizenships are transformed in the process, taking on transnational and translocal aspects. Such discursive reformulations, while shedding light on the distinct histories that make up Arab-American backgrounds, also instigate pan-Arab connections that extend beyond allegiances to specific Arab homelands.

Adnan's contrapuntal reading of Iraqi, American, and in the larger framework of the book, Lebanese realities widens the sphere of translocal consciousness I discussed earlier. It encompasses a broader conceptualization of war trauma that might exceed the geographical boundaries of an Arab-American's original Arab homeland. Such consciousness, even though it might be informed by a debilitating sense of guilt or helplessness, nevertheless offers a type of knowledge that defies limited or at best compartmentalized conceptualizations of Arab-American identities. In this way, including a pan-Arab reading of home and homeland produces a specific consciousness of space and temporality that constructs "critical maps of knowledge . . . fundamental in a transnational age typified by the global 'travel' of images, sounds, goods, and populations" (Shohat, "Gendered Cartographies" 2). Such "critical maps of knowledge," even while challenging neat spatial and temporal divisions, still signal the importance and specificity of place as grounded in interconnected geopolitical and historical contexts. For as Shohat also reminds us, "The challenge . . . is to produce knowledge within a kaleidoscopic framework of communities *in relation* without ever suggesting that all the positionings are identical" ("Gendered Cartographies" 3; emphasis mine). In fact, as mentioned earlier, the focus in this chapter on depicting transnational localities between the Arab world and the US and also within the Arab world is not meant to blur or homogenize the distinctive aspects of these heterogeneous entities. It instead breaks down a hegemonic approach that regulates and relegates minorities, in this case Arab-Americans, to the realm of the Other or the foreign by virtue of their connections to and their memories of Arab homelands.

Reconfiguring Imaginative Geographies of Home through Multinational Displacement

Foundational to our critical understanding of reductive formulations of Arabs as Other is Edward Said's *Orientalism* (1978), in which he discusses the crucial formation of what he calls the "imaginative geographies" of the Near East. These "imaginative geographies" have played a major role in constructing and consolidating colonial and neocolonial identities starting in the nineteenth century and continuing into the current geopolitical moment. Discussing their power in producing knowledge about Muslims and Arabs, Said writes, "For there is no doubt that imaginative geography and history help the mind to intensify its own sense of itself by dramatizing *the distance and difference* between what is close to it and what is far away" (*Orientalism* 55; emphasis mine). Such a geographically mediated formulation of the Arab as Other is relevant to my discussion here particularly in the way this formulation employs clearly demarcated notions of space and place in constructing identities of difference in the US national unconscious. In turning to discuss Arab-American literary texts that delineate multiple localities of displacement (specifically Palestinian displacement) across the Arab world and the US,

I deploy Said's term "imaginative geographies" to show how the formula of difference in (and difference as) distance embedded in Orientalist discourse is challenged and revised in the narratives under study. These narratives enact the important yet challenging task of turning "imaginative geographies into geographical imaginations that can enlarge and enhance our sense of the world" (Gregory, *Colonial Present* 262).[34]

Geographical imaginations lie at the heart of the transnational mobility depicted in many of the texts discussed in this book. More than focusing on returns to an original homeland (like the literary works discussed in chapter 2) or immigrations from a war-torn country to an amnesiac US landscape (as exemplified by the texts discussed earlier in this chapter), texts such as Said's *Out of Place*, Laila Halaby's *West of the Jordan*, and Randa Jarrar's *A Map of Home* employ the thematic of multilocal mobility to produce a spatial understanding of US citizenship and belonging. Such an understanding collapses the simplistic difference-in-distance formula propagated by neo-Orientalist and imperialist discourses. Such discursive reconfigurations of home and homeland "rethink geography" (Said et al. 21) and renegotiate rigid ideological boundaries separating the US from Arab countries.[35] Rethinking geography takes on varying forms in the texts discussed in this section. They are nevertheless connected by a common transnational, and more specifically translocal, vision that draws on multiple understandings and experiences of home, displacement, and US belonging. This vision redraws hegemonic configurations of geography and citizenship to reinvent, demythologize, and at the same time complicate both Arab and US landscapes, as well as Arab-Americans' positionality within each of them.

Said's memoir *Out of Place* (1999) moves across multiple locations, including Cairo, Jerusalem, Dhour El Shweir (a town in the mountains of Lebanon), and finally Massachusetts and New York. In doing so, the memoir paradoxically grounds the autobiographical delineation of an identity that is "out of place" in a study of the self-same places that form and inform Said's physical and metaphorical displacement. "Each of the places I lived in," Said writes, "has a complicated, dense web of valences that was very much a part of growing up, gaining an identity, forming my consciousness of myself and others" (xii).

The experience of multiple dislocations, which triggers the feeling of being "permanently out of place," manifests itself early on in Said's life, represented in his family's Christian Palestinian expatriate status in Cairo, with the family's strong links to Lebanon, Palestine, and Syria. Said himself was born in West Jerusalem in 1935 and up till the age of twelve spent his time between Talbiyeh and Cairo (*Out of Place* 19). His description of his parents as "two Palestinians with dramatically different backgrounds and temperaments living in colonial Cairo as members of a Christian minority within a large pond of minorities" encapsulates the weight of the contradictory nature of his inherited identity (19).[36] Augmenting such contradictions is the fact that he had inherited US citizenship from his father, Wadie. To avoid being conscripted into the Ottoman army, Wadie had left Jerusalem and immigrated to the US as a young man. He became a citizen and fought on the US side during World War I before returning permanently to the Arab world. For Said's father, this US citizenship is not only a nominal one. He uses it to fashion his lifestyle and demeanor as a Palestinian-American exile living in Cairo, self-creating his own identity in the process. Said's father's insistence on claiming a US identity, even though both he and his wife were born in Palestine,[37] is also imposed on Said and his sisters. It elicits what Said describes as awkward and embarrassing questions about his background from his schoolmates: "What are you?"; "But Said is an Arab name, and you've never been to America"; "You don't look American!" (5).

Said's initial access to US citizenship therefore occurs, as he points out, "without [him] ever having been to the US" (*Selves and Others*). The burden of inheriting a US citizenship leaves an indelible mark on the young Said, especially since he was expected to be "an American businessman's son, ... [but he] hadn't the slightest feeling of being American" (*Out of Place* 80).[38] Thus, a split occurs early on in Said's identity between his self-representation (on his father's insistence) as an American on the one hand and the way in which others, specifically his British teachers, perceive him first and foremost as an Arab.[39]

Even after Said is sent to study in the US at the age of fifteen following his expulsion from Victoria College (due to what the teachers perceive as his unruly behavior), he understandably cannot easily fit into what is forever referred to by his father as his country. His arrival in 1951 as a student at Mount Hermon School in Massachusetts marks a rude awakening for Said. Deeply affected by the lack of any intellectual or cultural space in which his knowledge and experience of the Arab world can be shared and articulated, he feels constricted by what he calls "the extraordinary homogenizing power of American life ... in which memory has no role": "I felt myself to be encumberingly full of memories.... I had spent all my life in two rich, teeming, historically dense metropolises, Jerusalem and Cairo, and now I was totally bereft of anything except the pristine woods, apple orchards, and the Connecticut river valley and hills *stripped of their history*" (*Out of Place* 233–35; emphasis mine). Said is then conscious early on of the gaps and ironies produced by the suppression of his intimate knowledge of Palestinian dispossession within a landscape that is emptied of its history of indigeneity and colonial violence. Such budding consciousness develops into a full-blown intellectual stance that is very much informed by what I refer to as translocal consciousness. This type of consciousness ultimately alters homogeneous landscapes of US memory and reconfigures the enactment of citizenship and belonging within those landscapes. For Said, the crux of this translocal vision and the citizenship it engenders is political in nature. Upon his arrival in the US, he quickly realizes that laying claim to a transplanted and inherited US citizenship is further delayed when placed against the backdrop of the political and historical events in the Arab world. Even as a student at Princeton a few years later, his anxieties and concerns about the Middle East, especially Gamal Adel Nasser's influence in Egypt, "had no outlet" except for his conversations with a few other Arab students, and he only broached the topic of the 1956 Suez invasion with a couple of Jewish students (278).[40]

Reflecting on such disconnections, Said acknowledges the huge relearning process that his move to the US instigated. He states, "The sheer gravity of my coming to the United States in 1951 amazes me even today. . . . I do know that I was beginning again in the United States, unlearning to some extent what I had learned before, relearning things from scratch, improvising, self-inventing, trying and failing, experimenting, canceling, and restarting in surprising and frequently painful ways" (*Out of Place* 222). Such acts of self-invention and relearning become crucial for the development of Said's interrogative translocal consciousness, one that places special emphasis on Palestinian dispossession. It is within the landscape of the US, then, that Said's antihegemonic and anticolonial intellectual stances come into full fruition.

The memoir, however, does not fully explore Said's life narrative in the US, thus ending with another beginning (Khoury xiii). References to Said's US beginnings might be found in some of the numerous interviews conducted with him, such as the one featured in the documentary *Selves and Others*, shot right before his death in September 2003. In one of the scenes, Said recalls in detail how, as a young assistant professor at Columbia University during the summer of 1967, he would often see people with transistor radios standing in the doorways in New York City listening to the news of the Six-Day War:

Very often I would hear people say, "How are we doing?" They were Americans. . . . I felt as an Arab not only embarrassed, but I wished I would disappear. Even when I became politically active, it became more difficult. The narrative in the popular [US] mind was that Israel and the Jews were democratic (white people like us), whereas the Arabs were fanatical and violent. To give the perspective of the other side is always difficult.

But Said was quite informed about the detrimental effects of Palestinian dispossession well before 1967. The scattering effects of the 1948 Nakba were devastating on his extended family in Palestine, and he was familiar, by way of his aunt's humanitarian work in Cairo, with the conditions of many Palestinian refugees. However, experiencing the Six-Day War of 1967 from his US positionality becomes a turning point in the full-blown assertion of his translocal consciousness. For it is at this point that he fully recognizes the difficulties inherent in "giv[ing] the perspective of the other side." Informed by this translocal consciousness, such difficulties and omissions are constantly challenged throughout his memoir (as well as in his other critical work) in ways that disrupt explicit and implicit articulations of a uniform and hegemonic American "we" or "us."

It is from a translocal vantage point, then, that Said is able to critically engage with a past that is rooted in multiple Arab locales, unearthing in the process an underlying narrative of Palestinian exile and dispossession with which he comes to strongly identify and be identified. This state of translocality is the necessary condition not only for achieving a newfound commitment to the Palestinian struggle but also for weaving an interrogative, counterhegemonic, and transnational Arab-American identity. This type of citizenship and belonging creates complex political and historical narratives that alter US knowledge about the Arab world. Said addresses the challenges inherent in such revisionary projects by calling attention to the vulnerabilities of Arab, specifically Palestinian, identities in the US. He states in the same film interview, "I feel marked as a Palestinian [in the US]. . . . There is a battle for space."[41] Such spatial claims include physical and literal aspects but also extend to the metaphorical to evoke an empowering space of articulation distinct from token inclusions.[42] For Said, such a battle for space and for accurate representation is often developed at the expense of achieving a lifelong sense of belonging, whether it is in the US or in the Arab world.[43]

In an interview originally published in *Ha'aretz*, Said explains such transnational belonging by saying, "My fate is to remain in New York.

On a constantly shifting ground, where relationships are not inherited, but created. Where there is no solidity of home" ("My Right of Return" 457).[44] Rather than "solidity" signifying a rooted and secure sense of place, I read it here as a fixity of/in place that limits the fluidity engendered by transnational belonging. This "constantly shifting ground," however, where belonging is never taken for granted but constantly negotiated, is ultimately a favorable position for the Arab-American to be in. It equips him or her with a revisionary perspective that opposes an uncritical and unquestioned attachment to a nation or a collective (whether in the US or in the Arab world).[45] In fact, Said describes such a perspective as the impetus to locate and claim "a new kind of wakefulness" or the healing role of "conscious recollection and articulation that have been a substitute for sleep" during his long struggle with leukemia (*Out of Place* 217). This "new kind of wakefulness" can also be read as a collective Arab/Palestinian-American consciousness that is transnational and translocal in nature, one that inevitably challenges the binarism, divisiveness, and occlusions inherent in hegemonic narratives of US belonging and citizenship.

Similar challenges brought about by multiple Palestinian displacements are also evident in Laila Halaby's first novel, *West of the Jordan* (2003).[46] Its narrative encompasses a variety of stories and viewpoints that undercut and question spatial and temporal binaries separating the past from the present, the Arab homeland from the US diaspora. Consisting of a series of short chapters written from the rotating perspective of four young cousins (Hala, Khadija, Soraya, and Mawal), the book's narrative straddles multiple locales, both in the US and in the Arab world. Mawal describes her life in the small Palestinian village of Nawara, Khadija and Soraya negotiate Arab-American identity and their parents' immigrant life in California, and Hala adjusts to life in Jordan, to which she returns for a short visit while living in Arizona with her uncle Hamdi and his American wife, Fay. The stories of these four cousins crisscross and overlap, holding at their center the locality of Palestine both as imagined in its pre-1948, predispossession dimensions and as concretely represented by the Palestinian village of Nawara, to which all four characters claim an attachment.[47] Even though this small village, located in the occupied West Bank, is relatively peaceful and can be reached through Jordan (albeit with military permission) by the novel's characters (who often visit for various occasions),[48] it is still susceptible to the rules of occupation and dispossession. "Nawara," explains Mawal, "sits at the top of the West Bank, just west of the Jordan River, east of

Jenin and far enough away from both of these places to be a peaceful village that only every so often releases an avalanche of stones and fire. This is something that happens more often as the Israelis take parts of our village to build their settlements" (Halaby, *West of the Jordan* 15).

In mapping out a concept of home that is heavily informed by multinational and multilocal mobility, Halaby's characters carry out complex mappings of transnational belonging. Crucial to the novel's cartographic layout of multiple diasporic locations is not only its emphasis on the characters' disconnection from Palestine but the way they transform this disconnection or deterritorialization into a form of reterritorialization (Gregory, "Imaginative Geographies" 448).⁴⁹ It is this emphasis on territoriality and on specific Arab spatialities that forms the crux of my theoretical framing of translocality. But with the loss of historical Palestinian land on the one hand and the Israeli occupation of the West Bank and Gaza on the other hand, tangible access to such territoriality is less and less possible for many Palestinians (whether in its pre-1948 or post-1967 form).⁵⁰ Reterritorialization, then, becomes the means to enact such translocality, by which versions, memories, and fragments of Palestine are regrounded in other locales to give Palestinian transnational belonging much-needed tangible spatialities.

Hala is one of the main characters in *West of the Jordan* who offers reterritorialized understandings of Palestine, as well as of Jordan. Her transnational mobility encompasses the Jordan of her father, in which she grew up; the village of Nawara, from which her mother was exiled in marriage; and the US (specifically, in her case, Arizona and California).⁵¹ The open-ended version of home and homeland generated by such transnational mobility stands in direct contrast to the concept of an unchanged and unattainable Palestine as imagined by the novel's older generation of Palestinian exiles, even those living in Arab countries such as Jordan. Such a fixed view is represented by the character of Sharif, Hala's older cousin on her mother's side, who lives in Amman and also hails from the village of Nawara. During Hala's visit to Jordan, she reacquaints herself with Sharif and falls in love with him, but ultimately her return to the US and to her studies trumps any chance of marrying him and staying in Jordan (this choice, however, is ultimately made by Sharif and not by Hala).

In an interesting passage, Hala recounts her memory of an afternoon from her childhood (when she was "five or six") spent with her family on the Aqaba beach (south of Jordan). Sharif, "nineteen or twenty" at the time, looks across the water to what he describes as home, to Palestine, convincing the young Hala that they can paddle across the border that he sees as starting somewhere in the middle of the body of water between Aqaba and, in his mind, Palestine. While listening to Sharif, Hala sees "a small shell under the water, but when [she] go[es] to grab it, the water moves and it vanishes" (124). This shell, like Palestine itself (or at least the version that Sharif has created in his mind) remains physically inaccessible. The more intently Sharif talks about reaching home/Palestine across the water, the more blurry the water becomes until Hala cannot see the shell anymore. Knowing fully well that the Israeli soldiers will not let them cross into Israel, Sharif reluctantly abandons his plan of returning to this homeland of his imagination and is led back to the Aqaba shore by the Jordanian coast guard.

Sharif's dogged belief in clearly bounded, pre-1948, traceable contours of his imagined version of Palestine reemerges decades later, when he places in Hala's hand an envelope with "a gold charm of Palestine" in it (204).[52] On the plane back to the US, she puts the charm on her necklace and "run[s] [her] fingers along [its] edges" thinking of Sharif and his plans to marry his cousin's niece (204). Hala, however, has her own version of a portable (in quite the literal sense) symbol of Palestine, namely her mother's *roza* (Palestinian dress) made by her grandmother for her daughter's trousseau. Even though Hala's father deems it inappropriate, she insists on wearing it on the flight back to the US, stating, "My mother wore mostly western clothes—skirts and shirts or western dresses—but at home she liked *dishdashes* and this *roza*. I remember her wearing it and being happy. It is not a fancy one, but the pattern is clever and it suits me" (203). In her appropriation of her mother's *roza*, Hala is not merely replicating someone else's version of Palestinian identity. She refashions it in new ways to "suit" her. Not only does she choose not to wear the usual "T-shirt and *shalwar* pants [that] her mother would [typically] wear" under the *roza* (204), but she also relinquishes the belt around her waist. In this way, she creates a more fluid, free-flowing, and amorphous version of the *roza*[53] and its representation of Palestine and of Palestinian identity than the one Sharif hands her, with its clearly demarcated borders.[54] It is my contention here that it is Hala's physical enactment of a translocal traveling identity that helps her achieve a constant reconceptualization or reterritorialization of Palestinian, and by extension Arab, subjectivity in the US.[55] For it is her ability to travel between and across the multiple locales of Palestinian diaspora (Amman, Irbid, Arizona, California) and her exposure to the multiple (and often contradictory) versions of an imagined and actual Palestine within them that allows

Hala to shift away from a deterritorialized Palestinian identity to one that is reterritorialized and rooted in transnational US space.

Hala's insistence on remembering intimate details of her life in Nawara and Amman is integral to her struggle to find a place for herself in the US in spite of displacement.[56] Just like in the context of the Lebanese civil war discussed earlier, remembering becomes the key for surviving in the assimilative US landscape that insists on immigrant amnesia. Hala's uncle's house embodies such a threat for her, with its stark empty walls representing "high-class American blah, [with] no soul, no colors, only outside walls that wandered in and stayed" (*West of the Jordan*, 216). Hala rebels against such whitening erasures, first projecting her memories of an Arab home onto these white walls and then physically installing a collage of photographs featuring her family and friends. Most importantly, these imaginative and literal projections hold the memory of Palestine at their center. This memory nevertheless surpasses nostalgic remembrances of Palestinian trees, land, and home and is instead shaped by the painful and arduous aspects of Palestinian lives within occupied Palestine and other Arab countries, as well as within the US. The hardships of multiple displacements, then, inform Hala's articulation of transnational belonging and become an elemental part of reterritorializing Palestinian memory in the US. In countering the white empty walls, Hala demands of herself,

> Remember the stories of Nawara: everything, including the tragedies. . . . Remember the ones who left, who fled, whose memories are vague and lives are changed. Remember the young men in their prime, who work twelve-hour days, driving taxis, running grocery stores, selling merchandise door to door. Remember all those women lost in different ways, with no tomorrows. Remember the young ones, who came here as babies, but who cannot remember what they have not seen and therefore have no reason to behave. (219)

The incorporation of a multinational and multilocal sense of home place within the US domain (in this case represented within Hala's domestic sphere) challenges the difference-in-distance formula embedded in Orientalist and neo-Orientalist discourse by importing intimate and collective notions of other homelands into the US landscape. Rather than forgetting, or latching on to a temporally fixed memory of the homeland (typical of the type of immigrant memory I refer to in chapter 1), Hala insists on a type of reterritorialization that prioritizes regenerative remembering and invention.[57] Hala reminds herself of her deceased mother's words, which become a comfort as well as a way to reconceive her sense of identity and citizenship in the US: "Remember to make your day new and old, but be sure to think of something you never thought of before. If you don't, your life will be like having your foot stuck in a mouse hole, looks small and harmless, but holds on tight and won't let you go until something comes along to change the landscape" (218). Refusing to get emotionally and physically stuck in the past and unwilling to passively wait for something to come along and enact change in the present, Hala is able to invent her Palestinian identity in the US while retaining a transformative awareness of multiple localities. Such a perspective ultimately alters US hegemonic knowledge about the Arab world, more specifically here about the history of Palestinian dispossession. In doing so, it alters US landscapes of memory and knowledge, yielding in the process more politically engaged Arab-Americans and more politically informed US citizens.

Reimagining and reinventing Palestinian identities, then, as made evident in Said's memoir and Halaby's novel, require first and foremost an intimate knowledge of Palestinian histories of displacement and struggle. Both Said and Hala consolidate such knowledge within the US sphere and in doing so transform dominant conceptualizations of citizenship and belonging. Yet in many cases, with the US often being the final leg of multiple Palestinian dislocations, such knowledge can also be developed within the Arab world. As Juliane Hammer notes in her book *Palestinians Born in Exile*, "the majority (80 percent) of Palestinian refugees [which comprised at least 726,000 Arabs in 1948] live within a hundred miles of the border of historical Palestine," as made evident in the large Palestinian populations in Jordan, Syria, Lebanon, Egypt, and several Arab Gulf countries (11).[58]

The setting of Randa Jarrar's coming-of-age novel *A Map of Home* (2008), for one, exemplifies the development of its protagonist's Palestinian consciousness within multiple Arab locales, including Kuwait, Alexandria, and Jenin (with the novel featuring Houston, Texas, as the final site of immigration).[59] More importantly, it is not these cities and towns in and of themselves that instill in the main character, Nidali Ammar, an awareness of the geopolitical factors at the heart of regional and international conflicts (including the Israeli-Palestinian conflict). It is rather the constant negotiation and transgression of these locales' constructed political borders that characterize the protagonist's attempts at mapping her own as well as broader understandings of home. Contrary to the novel's title, however, such attempts turn into plural and multilocal mappings of home, which take on multiple geopolitical and personal significances.

Nidali's background itself is made up of a dizzying mix of Arab and US affiliations. Born in Boston to an exiled Palestinian father (Waheed) and an Egyptian-Greek mother (Fairuza), Nidali moves with her parents at a very young age to Kuwait, from which they subsequently flee when Saddam Hussein invades the country in 1990, heading first to Alexandria and then to Texas. With her family's status shifting from expatriates in Kuwait (where her architect father works at an engineering firm) to refugees in Alexandria, Egypt (her mother's home city), and finally to immigrants in the US, Nidali starts out with very limited geopolitical knowledge of her complex and intersecting backgrounds. Alongside the permeating presence of multiple Arab locales and her family's status within them, Palestine retains a central position in the development of Nidali's political and transnational consciousness.

Initially, Palestine is for Nidali for the most part a blurry and mythical entity. Her firsthand memory of it is restricted to the humiliating treatment she and her family receive at the hands of the Israeli soldiers at the Allenby Bridge when traveling from Alexandria via Jordan into the West Bank to attend her grandfather's funeral in Jenin.[60] But slowly, over the course of the novel, Nidali (which means "my struggle" in Arabic)[61] comes to articulate an understanding of place and belonging that encompasses a transnational and translocal "struggle over geography" (Said, *Culture and Imperialism* 7). This struggle is primarily focused on the inescapable Israeli-Palestinian conflict revolving around territory, sovereignty, and identity, as well as the different perspectives on the homeland prevalent among various Palestinian and Arab generations (both inside and outside the Arab world), depending on their class and citizenship status.

Nidali's developing understanding and negotiation of this struggle slowly but surely leads her, just like the young Said in *Out of Place*, to "rethink [this] geography" and its significance in the formulation of multiple and shifting conceptualizations of home (Said et al. 21). Toward the beginning of the novel, Nidali responds to her father, Baba, a self-described failed poet who left his native Jenin to study architecture in Egypt and was not allowed back after the 1967 Arab-Israeli war. Listening to his diatribe about growing up writing about "our homeland, about Palestine," and how he "grew tired of writing about war . . . and how sad we were after '67," she reveals her disconnection from and ignorance of

Palestinian/Arab history by asking, "What is '67?" (*Map of Home* 66). After a vitriolic rant bemoaning his daughter's colonialist education, Baba promptly gives her a detailed history lesson and leads her to the page in a blue book titled "PALESTINE IS MY COUNTRY" with "the *real* map of Palestine on it and ma[kes] [her] trace the map and draw it over and over again." After several attempts, Nidali proclaims, "Baba checked my last map, the map of home, he called it, and let me go, saying I drew the Galilee perfectly, like the water violin that it is" (68).[62]

But Nidali quickly realizes that cartographic representations, specifically here in the case of Palestine, are not what they seem to be, for in actuality they often involve great levels of geopolitical restriction and maneuvering. Such restrictions become apparent to Nidali on the plane from Egypt to Jordan, the first leg of the geographically convoluted trip to the West Bank that the family takes to attend her grandfather's funeral in Jenin. During the short plane trip, Nidali finds a map clearly showing Palestine as "the country stuck to Egypt," prompting her to ask her father, "Why can't we just drive there [Palestine], or take a plane straight there?" (95). This question marks a crucial moment at which Nidali comes to situate herself directly within the context of geopolitical struggle. The discrepancies between topographic mappings and geopolitical actualities push Nidali to confront the factors that determine and monitor the movement of certain peoples, specifically here Palestinians, across international borders.[63] Needless to say, such factors are linked to the national, religious, political, and ancestral makeup of these traveling identities. By juxtaposing such visual and physical negotiations of borders, Jarrar's novel becomes itself an alternative map for tracing multiple Arab localities and the transnational identities inhabiting them, specifically here Palestinian ones. Such remappings release Nidali from restricted and bounded cartographies of home and homeland, stressing instead the ways in which understandings of original homelands and the sense of belonging they convey can be developed and revised outside their bounded geographic spheres. Furthermore, the ways they are carried into multiple spaces redefine them and at the same time transform the new landscapes they travel into.

Nidali's redeployments of Palestinian and Arab landscapes are shaped by the geographic knowledge she gains not only through her own travel and movement but also through the lessons conveyed to her by her Egyptian grandfather. Listening to him reminisce about his involvement in World War II and the Free Officers revolution in Egypt, Nidali comes to understand the role of power and perspective in shaping spatial and historical knowledge. "Political power," he states, "is the knowledge and command of space.... You should learn that when it comes to maps, accuracy is always a question of where you stand" (188–89).[64] Such advice is further consolidated by her Palestinian father, who is specifically keen on developing Nidali's knowledge about Palestine, albeit one that is constantly shifting and changing in relation to the political landscape. Upon seeing Nidali reproduce "the *real* map of Palestine" that he had initially taught her to draw, he admits to the instability of cartographic representation. "That map is from a certain year," he tells her. "The maps that came earlier looked different. And the ones that come after, even more different.... There's no telling where home starts and where it ends" (193). Upon hearing this pronouncement, Nidali actively rethinks geography by revising the "perfect ... map of home" with which she had first started out under her father's tutelage. Applying her grandfather's advice, she not only acknowledges but also privileges her subjective position within/on this map:

> I took the map [of Palestine] I drew to my room, flipped my pencil and brought the eraser's tip to the page. I erased the western border, the northern border. I erased the southern and eastern border. I surveyed what remained: a blank page, save for Galilee. I stared at the whiteness of the page blended with the whiteness of my sheets. "You are here," I thought as I looked at the page and all around me. And oddly, I felt free. (193)

With the revised borderless map of home (representing an over there) blending into the physicality of Nidali's temporary bedroom in Alexandria, to which her family has fled during the First Gulf War, Nidali remaps the connection between identity and homeland to such an extent that a feeling of belonging to an original or ancestral homeland does not hinge on one's physical presence within its boundaries. Nidali's stance has as its central trope a transnational and translocal awareness of the challenges of defining national, religious, and political identities within the entrenched, secure, and well-defined geographic boundaries of a single homeland. In other words, by reshaping fixed mappings of home, whether it is Palestine or otherwise, Nidali is in fact reshaping predetermined definitions of identity, thus breaking constructed, artificial, and unilocal or mononational understandings of home, redefining belongingness in the process. This type of transnational belonging retains translocal mobility at its central aspect, with the locality of this mobility switching from an Arab to a US, specifically Texan, sphere in the last section of the novel.

Just as in Said's memoir and Ward's novel discussed earlier, the type of belonging that Nidali develops in the US is shaped by and articulated through a translocal consciousness that incorporates her experience and memory of Kuwait, Egypt, and Palestine. In fact, her move to the US with her family at the age of fourteen enables her to reterritorialize, and hence revise, her inherited Arab identities. Despite the fact that she was born in the US, Nidali realizes that citizenship does not automatically confer belonging: "I was terrified of never fitting in, of that new place that was my birthplace, that place I belong to only on paper, in the confines of my short blue passport" (201). Moreover, experiencing the immediate locality of the US interestingly enough breaks down the imaginative geography that Nidali had unconsciously constructed around it while in the Arab world, primarily through her exposure to Western pop culture and media. Arriving at the airport in the US, Nidali immediately notices the gap between her imagined version of the place and its actual reality: "Nowhere were the blonde bimbettes or the brunette foxes I'd seen on vintage soaps. The men at the airport didn't yell to their wives, 'This isn't the last you'll see of me!' then disappear into season-long comas. They helped them with their luggage and bitched and moaned like the rest of us" (214). In this way, Nidali's translocal perspective redraws imagined as well as actual cartographies of struggle and conflict. It does so by collapsing, by way of travel and mobility, the difference in the distance separating various spheres and locales of knowledge and identity.

By rethinking imaginative geographies of the Arab world, and turning them into alternate geographical imaginations, literary texts such as those by Said, Halaby, and Jarrar serve two main demythologizing purposes: first, they portray the Palestinian diaspora as it exists across multiple Arab and US settings. In doing so, they contextualize the experience of dispossession and displacement by highlighting the contours of specific national geographies as well as the tensions that exist between and among these geographies. Second, these texts enlarge and challenge the constructed political and ideological boundaries separating localities of belonging, thus undercutting single and uniform definitions of homes and homelands. Such a stance is corroborated in the texts by Ward, Mroue, Alameddine, and Adnan discussed in the first section of the chapter. All of these texts insist on transforming the Arab-American as well as mainstream US landscapes by highlighting multiple nodes of experience and memory, particularly the lingering pain and war trauma that are lived and relived within the US space. In this way, the representation of Arab-Americans' experiences of translocal mobility as discussed in this chapter restructures stable and unchanging concepts of home, citizenship, and belonging. They point to the political uncertainties and the racialized treatments that continue to plague Arab-Americans both in the Arab world and in the US. Such uncertainties and racializations, as I show in the next chapter, become even more flagrant in light of the events of September 11. For with the persistent Islamophobia and anti-Arab racism pervading the US, complex Arab-American religious and national affiliations are further simplified, framing this minority as a suspicious and dangerous presence in the US.

4 / Representing Arabs and Muslims in the US after 9/11: Gender, Religion, and Citizenship

In the short story "Alone and All Together" (2002) by Lebanese-American writer Joseph Geha, the teenage protagonist, Libby (an Americanized version of the Arabic name Labibeh), is watching the events of September 11 unfold on television in her suburban Chicago home while talking on the phone with her sister, Sally (originally Salma), in New York. Distraught by the "strip at the bottom of the screen" indicating "that everything points to the hijackers being Middle-Eastern extremists," Libby declares, "I just wish they wouldn't say it's us . . . until they're, like, *sure*." On hearing this, Sally fires back, "Us? . . . What us? . . . We were born here, and so were Mom and Dad, right here in Chicago, Illinois, U.S.A. . . . What I want to know . . . is when 'us' stops meaning *ibn Arab* [son of Arabs] and starts meaning American!" (53). More than merely pointing to some of the debates within Arab-American communities pertaining to the adoption of the Arab-American label,[1] Sally's and Libby's respective espousal and disavowal of a Middle Eastern, or more specifically Arab, identity become symptomatic of a divisive rhetoric that quickly dominated post-9/11 national discourse. This rhetoric separates the American from the un-American, the patriotic from the unpatriotic, with Arab and Muslim subjectivities being squarely cast in the latter category.

This chapter addresses a range of Arab-American literary and cultural texts that respond to the post-9/11 political and social terrain in the US. They capture and challenge homogenized depictions of Arab-Americans, forging in the process what can be identified as revisionary or counterhegemonic spaces that redefine exclusionary conceptualizations of US citizenship and belonging. In addition to problematizing simplistic types of post-9/11 patriotism that demand a unilateral type of US national identity, the creation of these revisionary spaces responds to racial stereotyping, blanket labeling, and discriminatory profiling by insisting on complex representations of Arab-Americans. The focus on literary and cultural texts is meant to highlight the role of Arab-American creative production in shaping discussions of national belonging and citizenship in the US, particularly following such an intense and traumatic crisis in the history of the nation as the 9/11 attacks.[2]

The attacks of 9/11, however, do not mark the first or the only event that has fomented reductive perceptions about Arab-Americans in the US. They are in fact a recent installment in a long history of national and international crises and conflicts that have repeatedly and consistently underlined the provisional nature of US citizenship and belonging for Arab-Americans. These crises include the Six-Day War in 1967, the 1973 oil embargo, the First Gulf War, and the attacks on the World Trade Center in 1993. Such events position the formation and development of Arab-American identities within well-cemented racialized structures that hold the political relations between the US and the Arab world at their center. These relations are dominated by US political and military hegemony. Domestic and foreign US policies underwent intense changes in the months and years after September 11 (including, for instance, the USA PATRIOT Act, the National Security Entry-Exit Registration System, and the establishment of the Department of Homeland Security).[3] These changes, as well as the mobilization of extreme US military operations in Afghanistan and Iraq, make evident that it is political rather than so-called civilizational or cultural factors that inform demonizing depictions of Arab identities, as they exist in the Arab world as well as in the US.[4] Such political factors render 9/11, as pointed out by Nadine Naber and others, "a turning point, as opposed to the starting point, of histories of anti-Arab racism in the United States . . . in that representations of 'terrorism' and 'Islamic fundamentalism' have increasingly replaced other representations (that is, the rich Arab oil sheikh, bellydancers, and harem girls) and have become more fervently deployed in anti-Arab state policies and everyday patterns of engagement than ever before" ("Introduction" 4). But more than being a "turning point," and notwithstanding obvious continuities in anti-Arab forms of discrimination that precede 9/11, I would argue that 9/11 constitutes a formative moment in self-iterations (literary and otherwise) that insist on portraying Arab-Americans through a transnational and anti-homogeneous lens. This formative moment has mobilized more vocal, assertive, and unapologetic claims to transnational enactments of Arab-American identities that problematize the assimilative pressures inherent in dominant performances of US citizenship and belonging.[5]

In this way, the questions and issues raised by the texts discussed in this chapter assert the need to acknowledge and make space for transnational and critical types of US citizenship and belonging in order to acknowledge the multiple connections to and remembrances of trauma that 9/11 evokes, specifically here as it applies to Arab-Americans. Such questions include the following: Did 9/11 have uniform US national and collective repercussions? Whose experiences does such an overarching narrative exclude? How would the acknowledgment of such narrative exclusions change the US national perspective on 9/11? How do US reactions to 9/11 promote an exclusionary narrative of national trauma that misidentifies Arab- and Muslim-Americans as a threat and at the same time overshadows other traumatic and violent conflicts in other countries, specifically in the Arab world?

In addressing such questions, the texts analyzed in this chapter articulate transnational Arab-American assemblages that overturn exclusionary conceptualizations of US citizenship and undercut the us-versus-them binary still pervading national discussions of 9/11. At the same time, they problematize the divisive rhetoric identifying the good Arab from the bad Arab, terms that I examine in more detail in this chapter. The texts analyzed in this first section include the short stories "Alone and All Together" and "The Spiced Chicken Queen of Mickaweaquah, Iowa" by Joseph Geha and Mohja Kahf, respectively, as well as the novel *Once in a Promised Land* by Laila Halaby. Pointing out other discursive strategies that challenge the historical exceptionalism dominating US national rhetoric post-9/11, I analyze in the second section of the chapter the ways in which Arab-American literary texts position the events of 9/11 along a transnational, transpolitical, transhistorical, and transgeographical continuum of aggression, violence, loss of civilian life, and conflicts that continue to plague the Arab world. The texts discussed in this section include the poems "first writing since" and "america" by Suheir Hammad and Dima Hilal, respectively, as well as the nonfictional essay "Where Is Home? Fragmented Lives, Border Crossings, and the Politics of Exile" by Rabab Abdulhadi. In depicting US and Arab lives within a transnational framework, these works debunk dominant representations of the events of 9/11 as an inexplicable attack on US freedom.

Rather than condoning the 9/11 attacks, however, the push to overturn an emphasis on US innocence undercuts US historical amnesia by placing the role of a militaristic US foreign policy in the Arab world at the forefront of dominant discussions of 9/11 trauma.[6]

After addressing such issues, the chapter turns in its third and last section to examine the ways in which gender and sexual stereotypes are embedded in the us-versus-them, good-Arab-versus-bad-Arab binaries. This last section focuses specifically on how texts such as Yussef El Guindi's play *Back of the Throat* and Wafaa Bilal's performative and installation art interrogate the intersection of gendered, religious, racialized, and sexualized violence in the construction of a hegemonic narrative of US national security and citizenship post-9/11. By contextualizing the 9/11 attacks within a complex framework that privileges transnational perspectives, works such as the ones discussed in this chapter move national responses to 9/11 beyond the simplistic narratives of "you're either with us or with the terrorists" touted by George W. Bush and his administration. They also complicate rationalizations such as "they are jealous of our freedom" formulated in response to an uninformed public's bewildered "Why do they hate us?" question.

The Homogenization of US Citizenships after 9/11: Arab-American Diversity in Crisis

A persistent and insidious aspect of the us-versus-them binary prevalent after 9/11 is an acknowledgment (albeit a shortsighted one) of the porous nature of transnational identities, by which the Arab and Muslim Other (as conceived and constructed by so-called patriotic agendas) is no longer exclusively located outside the realm of the US nation-state. Instead, the difference allocated to a "them," positioned as backward and uncivil Arabs "over there," in the Arab and Muslim world, is simultaneously inscribed on the racialized bodies of Arab- and Muslim-Americans "over here," in the US. Such logic yields a culture of suspicion and paranoia that uses religious and racial markers as yardsticks for determining the "American" from the "un-American," regardless of citizenship status. Such constructions of exclusionary citizenships and belongings produce what M. Jacqui Alexander describes as the "citizen-patriot," distinguished by appearance and patriotic intent from what is construed as the foreign Other (211). As Alexander states, "Not just (any)*body* can be a patriot at a time of empire building. Some bodies have been marked by the neoimperial state as unpatriotic, with the capacity to destabilize a newly imagined homeland, threatening national sovereignty, and otherwise imperiling the U.S. nation" (207–8). The use of racialized religious, ethnic, and gendered body markings (including skin color, the hijab, skullcaps, and beards) to gauge true patriotism and national allegiance inevitably ends up conflating widely varied minority groups within the US (Arabs and South Asians, for instance) or even subgroups within one minority group (Christian Arabs and Muslim Arabs, for example). Such identification strategies reduce these minorities to supposedly recognizable subjects that need to be monitored, controlled, and contained.[7]

Not only does the prevalence of such reductive strategies used by the state for safeguarding national security through the containment of its citizenry precede 9/11, but these strategies have in fact been repeatedly used to pinpoint and identify the "enemy" during periods of historical crises in the US. Such crises include the internment of Japanese during World War II and the McCarthyism of the 1940s and 1950s. In the context of 9/11, strategies of containment (including the establishment of the Department of Homeland Security, the National Security Entry-Exit Registration System, and the USA PATRIOT Act) have drastically undermined the development of complex understandings of Arab-American identities. In addition to stigmatizing the term *Arab* itself, the result of which has been the disavowal or the whitewashing of the Arab-American label even by many members of this diverse collective, such politics of containment have served with some success to isolate Arab-Americans from each other as well as from other minorities in the US. Such isolation occurs largely through a pervasive guilt-by-association logic that frames the post-9/11 mandate of vigilant citizenship.

More than complicating the us-versus-them binary defining limited forms of national belonging, the texts discussed here also undercut what I identify, building on Mahmoud Mamdani's and Sunaina Maira's work, as the divisive formula of the good Arab versus the bad Arab.[8] According to this binary logic shaped by post 9/11's "citizen-patriot" dictum (Alexander 211), the good Arabs are those who successfully and consistently distance themselves politically, religiously, and often even physically from the bad Arabs, or those bodies (both in the Arab world and in the US) purportedly bearing the neo-Orientalist designations of fundamentalism, terrorism, and cultural stagnation. In analyzing how such a binary formulation is reexamined in Arab-American literary texts written after 9/11, I broaden Mamdani's and Maira's focus on the religious facets of the good-Muslim-versus-bad-Muslim formula to study how these texts' insistence on capturing the multiplicity of national, class, educational, and religious Arab-American backgrounds destabilizes good-versus-bad formulations of Arab-American identities. In doing so, these texts place this minority group within a complex rubric of US citizenship and belonging that defies the pervasiveness of hegemonic patriotic performances. However, as will be elucidated in my analysis to follow, these texts also point to the limits of enacting such a diverse form of US citizenship and belonging in the post-9/11 landscape, in which any kind of Arab label is suspect.

The overpowering sense of isolation triggered by the relentless, state-imposed scrutiny of Arab-Americans after 9/11 is reflected in the title of Geha's short story "Alone and All Together." Relaying a firsthand account of the sense of vulnerability sweeping over Arab-American communities in the days following 9/11, the story captures the anxieties and dangers inherent in being of Arab descent or background within this homogenized construct of US citizenship. The story's opening exchange between the two sisters mentioned earlier examines the extent to which their Arab roots should determine formulations of Arab-American belonging in the US, with the sisters initially differing in their claim to such roots. For while Libby embraces a transnational, pan-Arab understanding of a collective "us," Sally chooses to position herself squarely among the ranks of a US hegemonic center, claiming her family's multigenerational presence in the US as proof of her entitlement to an unambiguous type of US citizenship. Such binaries point to the continuation of pre-9/11 racializations of ethnic and religious markers that are to a large extent internalized and replicated by many Arab-Americans.

Even before the attacks, the preponderant practice of using physical features to determine national authentication or true US belonging is implemented by none other than the girls' father, who jokes that Libby, with blue eyes and "almost blonde" hair, is his American daughter, while Sally, with her "black, curly" hair, is his Arab daughter (Geha, "Alone and All Together" 56).[9] However, despite "appearances," it is actually Sally who manifests early on an interest in her Arab background by helping her grandmother "cook *loubyeh* [green beans] and *kusa* [zucchini] and *beitenjan mihshee* [stuffed eggplant]" and by going to the local mosque with her friend Jamila "to learn to read and write Arabic" (57). Nevertheless, despite Libby's engagement in and espousal of a collective Arab "us" that the short story opens with, the events of 9/11 bring about a debilitating challenge to her budding self-awareness as an Arab-American. On the Monday after the attacks, stopping at a red light while in the car with her mother, Libby is relieved by the following thought about the people crossing the street in front of them: "They don't know us, what we are," for which, she states, "I'm glad" (58). Libby quickly realizes that terms such as "we" and "us" that she uses to signal an Arab-American collective with strong familial and cultural connections to the Arab world have become a liability in the volatile atmosphere of post-9/11. Even though she feels guilty for passing for white due to her light complexion, she nevertheless gets over her guilt when she remembers the "incidents" of the past week in and around Bridgeview, where "a lot of the *ibn Arab*" live. The incidents included "three hundred people waving American flags and chanting 'USA! USA!' [who] tried to march on the Mosque foundation . . . [and had] kids gathered outside [one] high school waving flags and shouting anti-Arab insults at passing cars" (58).[10]

In fact, these incidents initially create in Libby an urge to pass as a mainstream white American,[11] or at least to distance herself from any perceivable racial or racialized Arab markers that would connote difference. This racial trope of passing constitutes an unmistakable cross-ethnic reference to the histories of other minoritarian racial formations in the US, including the African-American one.[12] Implicitly adhering to the binary logic inherent in Sally's question ("What us?"), Libby starts out by participating in a hegemonic discourse of identity by intuitively drawing a line between a different us-versus-them binary: the good and the bad Arab-Americans. Seeking metaphorical refuge in her fair complexion and her Christian, specifically Melkite religious background, she fully asserts herself as the good Arab-American by designating her Muslim friend Jamila, who wears the hijab, as her reverse doppelganger. In doing so, Libby sees in Jamila all the markings of racial and religious Otherness that purportedly denote her friend as the "enemy." Looking at Jamila sitting next to her in class, Libby thinks to herself, "I wish she would take off that thing [the hijab]. Okay. She was born in Egypt, and she's a Muslim, but she's an American, too. She's in honors classes with me and her English is just about perfect" (58). Such a statement points to Libby's deeply conflicted state of mind. She recognizes her friend's right to her Arab *and* Muslim heritage, but at the same time she wants Jamila to neutralize this heritage by taking off her hijab, a reminder of Islam's alleged incompatibility with mainstream American identity. Libby, then, believes that Jamila, by removing her hijab, would be visually asserting an unhyphenated, a non-Arab, and hence an unproblematic type of American identity.

Despite Libby's ability to pass and her initial inclination to adopt the good Arab-American designation by distancing herself from Jamila, she is still hyperconscious of her Arab identity, which she sees as being deeply ingrained within her. She states, "Even though I don't look like her [Jamila], I still keep getting this creepy sense that people passing by are turning and noticing me, as if they can detect Arabic in my brain, or something" (60). Libby's denial of her Arab identity in the name of self-preservation, however, is short-lived. While hanging out with her "American" friend Erin in Hyde Park a few days later (60), she witnesses Jamila's older brother Ahmed, whom she calls "*dib*" (Arabic for "bear") due to his height and gait, being harassed by three guys in "ball caps turned backwards . . . and shiny tight muscle shirts" (61). One of the guys keeps asking Ahmed, "So are you or aren't you?" (60). Looking at Ahmed's "olive skin, . . . brown eyes and dark curly hair, . . . [d]arker even than [Sally's]," Libby knows what they are asking him. On hearing the word "Raghead" flung at Ahmed (61), Libby's fear and acquiescence dissolve, transforming into rage. She steps in, and with the support of adult passersby, prevents Ahmed from being physically hurt.

Libby's newfound courage fortifies in Libby a fierce reconsideration of the racial, national, and religious lines separating different segments of Arab-Americans from each other. This reconsideration in turn revises exclusionary and narrowly defined notions of US belonging. Going back home after the harassment incident, Libby looks over at the Sears Tower, which she describes this way: "Lit against the dark sky, its high beacons point right to Chicago, to us." Rather than referencing a fragmented and alienated Arab-American minority or an exclusionary US identity, this "us" imagines a connective national alliance that cuts across race, ethnicity, and religion, envisioning in the process inclusive and multi-layered participations in national trauma. Despite the sharp contrast between such idealistic forms of US belonging and the grim actualities after 9/11, specifically pertaining to the treatment of Arab- and Muslim-Americans, Libby herself remains convinced of the potential powers of such inclusive yet antihegemonic collectivities, notwithstanding the possibility of other attacks that might target Chicago's Sears Tower, for instance. "Yes, it could happen here next time," she admits to herself. "And yet people are up there again, working. People are in airplanes, too, flying again. Being afraid is catching, but so is being brave" (62).

This sense of togetherness, or a vision of national unity that hinges on the acknowledgment and acceptance of difference, is shared by Libby's sister, Sally, albeit as she experiences it from her vantage point in New York City. On the phone with the girls' mother, Sally describes the candlelight vigil she attended in the city in honor of the 9/11 victims:

"There were all nationalities. Muslim women. There were Asians. Lots of people with their children. . . . We walked to the Promenade. People were praying. They held candles and pictures. Then everyone went quiet. . . . Every one of us. . . . I was alone, and we were all together" (63). This pervading sense of solidarity-in-difference comes as a culmination of the two sisters' individual struggles with conceptualizing their place in both an Arab-American and a larger US collective. It empowers them to articulate a complex form of US citizenship and belonging that resists the homogenizing forces of post-9/11 narratives of patriotism by cutting across racial, ethnic, religious, and national boundaries.

"Alone and All Together" is the only story I know of to date that offers an optimistic conclusion and a positive outlook on Arab-American futures in the post-9/11 landscape. As will become clear in the rest of my analysis, many of the Arab-American texts written after 9/11, despite their discursive insistence on destabilizing homogenized conceptualizations of US citizenship and belonging, still point to the limits of such radical enactments in the context of the Islamophobia and anti-Arab racism currently sweeping over the country.[13]

The discursive destabilization of homogeneous depictions of Arab-Americans and uniform performances of US citizenship is also evident in a short story by the Syrian-American Mohja Kahf, titled "The Spiced Chicken Queen of Mickaweaquah, Iowa" (2004). Like Geha's story, this narrative also problematizes and underscores the tenacity of a polemical good-Arab/bad-Arab rhetoric defining the Arab presence in the US. If "Alone and All Together" portrays some of the religious distinctions separating Christians from Muslims among Arab-Americans, "Spiced Chicken Queen" offers the reader a sample of the diversity of Muslim identities among Arabs. This diversity is not restricted to the religious per se but encompasses wider cultural, national, and socioeconomic referents. Opening a few weeks before the attacks of 9/11, the story portrays the travails of the battered Omani immigrant Mzayyan, who, after taking refuge at her local women's shelter to escape her husband's abuse, is offered the voluntary translation services of Dr. Rana Rashid, a physicist of Syrian descent who works at the local nuclear-energy plant. Separated by the circumstantial gulf of education, class, and family status, the two women could not be more different. Against "Dr. Rana Rashid with her well-cut hair and tailored Talbot's skirt-suit ensemble in navy and taupe . . . [stood] the darker, squat woman [Mzayyan] in a voluminous embroidered caftan, sweaty black curls escaping from under her black head kerchief" (138). Such physical differences are accompanied by a socioeconomic and educational gulf separating the two women's backgrounds, described by Kahf with a generous amount of humor and irony. Both Rana and her husband, Emad, a successful cardiologist, come from upper-class Syrian-American families who inculcated Arab culture in their children by enforcing Arabic private lessons, yearly visits to Syria, and an inescapable expectation that their children only marry fellow Syrians, the fairer-skinned the better. Mzayyan, on the other hand, hails from a close-knit, conservative Omani community in Philadelphia described condescendingly by Rana's husband as "positively tribal" (141).

These depictions, in addition to capturing the national, religious, ethnic, and racial heterogeneity of Arab-Americans, also point to the complex web of attitudes and assumptions that typically exists among Arabs of different nationalities both inside and outside the US. Such attitudes in many ways underscore the exclusionary (and often internalized) constructions of US citizenship and belonging that deem certain Arab racial and religious characteristics (read: light skin, Christian identity) more compatible than others with US assimilation politics. When Emad hears that his wife is involved in the case of an Omani woman at the shelter, he states, "Oman, huh? . . . And the prize for 'most remote and backward part of the Arab world' goes to . . . I don't even know where Oman is" (141). In this way, internal nuances among Arab-Americans, aside from being deployed to construct a discourse of solidarity-in-difference, can also become a way to mobilize and enact a type of assimilative politics that compels some Arab-Americans to distinguish themselves from other, less assimilated, and therefore more suspect Arabs in the US. Echoing Libby's and Sally's initial reluctance to identify themselves with a more visible form of Arabness in Geha's "Alone and All Together," Kahf's description of Emad and Rana informs the reader that, despite their knowledge of Arabic and their Arab activism (one that is nevertheless restricted to signing online petitions), "they weren't Arab. They were Arab-American. The hyphen said that they had been here a while. They were not the huddled masses of the Greater Jersey City Mosque, reeking of incense and henna and wearing their *jubbas* [robes] everywhere, and jabbing their fingers at the waiter and asking, 'Is there pig in this dish? Is there pig in that dish?'" (137).

Despite such differences characterizing the Arab-American label, in the larger framework of vigilant patriotism and homeland security post-9/11, such differences, whether flagrant or nuanced, self-imposed or mandated, become secondary, if not altogether insignificant. In other words, the post-9/11 backlash against Arabs and Muslims in the US ultimately erases internal differences within the Arab-American community. It depicts all Arabs in the US (whether they are recent immigrants, second-, third-, or fourth-generation Arab-Americans, residents, or students and regardless of their varying political and religious beliefs) as the enemy or at least as a potential enemy. With Emad's brother interrogated for naming his baby son Osama ("as if it hadn't been a perfectly respectable Arab name for two thousand years") and a friend of the Rashids "roughed up and held nine hours for questioning in Virginia after being stopped for a traffic ticket" (153), Rana and Emad are confronted with the ways in which 9/11 enforces the dissolution of the socioeconomic, educational, or generational buffer zone separating them from their more identifiable Arab and Muslim counterparts in the US.

In fact, the hegemonic strategy of dissolving internal nuances among Arab-Americans after 9/11 extends to the erasure of the distinctions among Arab-Americans and members of other minority groups including South Asian Muslims, Sikhs, and Hindus, who, by virtue of their skin color, religious or cultural dress, or accent, come to embody, in presumably recognizable ways, the elusive threat of terror that the nation is waging war against. Such a conflation of ethnic, racial, and religious difference is captured quite evocatively in Suheir Hammad's poem "first writing since" (2001), in which the speaker, bemoaning the shortsighted assumptions inherent in hastily drawn-up portrayals of the enemy, states,

> more than ever, i believe there is no difference.
> the most privileged nation, most americans do not know the
>   difference
> between indians, afghanis, syrians, muslims, sikhs, hindus.
> more than ever, there is no difference. (lines 23–26)

The speaker's espousal in the first line of a solidarity-in-difference that is formulated across racial, ethnic, religious, and national boundaries is stifled and rendered powerless in the post-9/11 landscape by homogeneous categorizations that point to dangerous misinformation about, if not downright ignorance of, the complex and distinct histories of minoritarian identities in the US. By lumping together various ethnic, religious, and national affiliations under the banner of the enemy, such homogenizations strip Arab-Americans of their right to belong in the US, resulting in what I am identifying as an Arab-American citizenship in crisis.[14] My use of the term *citizenship* extends to both its legal and its cultural dimensions, with cultural citizenship being an integral part of the everyday interactions and experiences of immigrant, ethnic, diasporic, and transnational subjects, extending beyond legal rights and duties.[15] While the racialization of minorities who do not fit into a Eurocentric understanding of US identity plays a major role in determining who *can* become a legal US citizen, such racialization becomes even more intense in determining who is eligible for cultural inclusion into the "American way of life," notwithstanding legal citizenship.[16]

In light of the steady erosion of Arab-Americans' legal rights after 9/11 and the ongoing depiction of their religious and cultural affiliations as being antithetical to US values, issues of social class and upward mobility come to play a major role in this group's position within constructions of US citizenship and belonging, specifically pertaining to the pursuit of the so-called American Dream. For even when Arab-Americans are equipped with the economic means to fully participate in what Inderpal Grewal refers to as consumer citizenship (a type of citizenship referenced, for instance, in George W. Bush's post-9/11 call for Americans to go shopping), their racialized and gendered bodies inevitably flag them as chronic Others.[17]

In Laila Halaby's *Once in a Promised Land* (2007), Arab-American belonging and citizenship (both legal and cultural) are recurrently depicted through the characters' economic success and their purported attainment of the American Dream, which nevertheless turns out to be short-lived and inauthentic. Just like Emad and Rana Rashid in Kahf's "Spiced Chicken Queen," the protagonists in *Once in a Promised Land*, Jassim and Salwa Haddad, are well-to-do and successful Muslim Arab-Americans, living in Tucson, Arizona. But unlike the American-born Rashids, who retain a hint of Arab political activism (albeit of the armchair variety) by signing online petitions and listening to Marcel Khalife,[18] the Haddads' immersion in the consumerist comfort of upper-middle-class American life overpowers any lingering transnational political engagement linking them to the Jordan they have left behind. The demands of such an immersion limit the enactment of transnational Arab-American belongings by challenging the maintenance of strong and varied connections to Arab homelands. Salwa herself was born in the US, while her parents tried their hand, unsuccessfully, at achieving the American Dream. Back in Jordan, she meets Jassim at her university in Amman, where he is visiting from the US and giving a guest lecture on the role of water in the regional politics of the Arab world. They consequently marry and settle in Tucson, Arizona, where their lucrative jobs postpone any permanent return to Jordan. Jassim's thriving career as a hydrologist for the Tucson water company and Salwa's job as a banker and real estate agent provide them with the material luxuries that seemingly mark their attainment of the American Dream.

But appearances prove to be deceiving, for happiness remains elusive for the couple in their "predictable, well-ordered American life" (Homsi Vinson). This happiness becomes permanently out of reach when their lives take a sharp turn for the worse after a series of escalating events (triggered in part by 9/11) leaves them physically and spiritually broken and estranged from each other. For, against a post-9/11 backdrop that compels them to become deeply self-conscious of their Arab identities, Salwa lies to her husband about her pregnancy and miscarriage and has an affair with a young co-worker. At the same time, Jassim not only fails to tell his wife that he has killed a boy in a car accident but also neglects to inform her that he has been fired from his job after falling victim to a post-9/11 witch hunt. The culprit behind these lies and betrayals, according to Salwa, is the alleged Promised Land, America. As she sees it, her errors of judgment would have never gone unchecked "back home" in Jordan: "Here in America . . . [n]o one tiptoed into the dark rooms of other people's homes with their buckets of judgment and said what they really thought. There were no intrusive neighbors or blunt aunties to announce what they knew and say, *You'd better not, or else*" (Halaby, *Once in a Promised Land* 181).

Through such constant comparisons between the Arab homeland and the US host land, the novel characterizes the latter as a *ghula* (Arabic for "female monster/sorceress") that tricks immigrants and their children into believing in the American Dream. In doing so, this *ghula* leads them to abandon their values, culture, language, and religion and to relinquish any attempt at a permanent return home. Even though Halaby's pronouncements about this America can often sound didactic and overly generalized, they still successfully capture the effects of having one's US citizenship readily stripped away and rendered suspect (if not altogether invalid) by virtue of place of birth or binational (or even multinational) affiliations.[19] I would argue, however, that it is not merely Salwa and Jassim's unquestioned embrace of an easy and comfortable American lifestyle (or their enactment of a consumer citizenship) that deludes them into a false sense of US belonging. It is in fact the concomitant choice (whether conscious or unconscious) to abandon the political beliefs that they grew up with in Jordan that makes their post-9/11 loss of a sense of belonging in the US even more pertinent and painful.

Even though the suspicion and downright racism meted out to the Haddads after the September 11 attacks awakens in them, particularly in Salwa, a sense of justice and outrage at being discriminated against as Arab Muslims, it becomes apparent that in their pursuit of material comforts, they had slowly relinquished all forms of transnational political engagement, building their image in implicit compliance with the assimilative criteria that guarantee the good Arab-American label. Such criteria mandate that the good Arab-American subject denounce, renounce, or at best neutralize his or her political and/or religious identity, thus conceding to the directive that the only acceptable iterations of Arab culture within the US are those that reify a bland, uncritical type of US multiculturalism. This type of US belonging celebrates diversity by strictly focusing on politically tame cultural fragments, extending for instance to culinary, musical, and folkloric traditions.

The state's demand for (as well as subjects' compliance with) normative religious and political acquiescence comes out in full evidence during the FBI's investigation of Jassim, who is flagged by one of his office secretaries playing the role of the hypervigilant "citizen-patriot." Before meeting with Jassim, the FBI agents first visit his boss, Marcus. Their questions about Jassim's "reaction to the war in Afghanistan, . . . [his opinion] about Jordan's leadership," and his political activities outside the office affirm the recurring confluence among political dissent, Muslim identity, and terrorism in national security (as well as public) rhetoric after 9/11. Marcus assures the FBI agents that Jassim is "as apolitical and unreligious a person" as he knows (224), thus confirming his employee's stout adherence to the good Arab-American category. Jassim's apoliticism, which enables him to participate for some time in the fiction of the American Dream, in fact renders him oblivious to the associations pegged onto his male, Muslim, and Arab (and hence suspect) status in a post-9/11 America. When Salwa tells him that their Lebanese-American friend Randa is worried about her children's safety after the attacks, he deems such worries unreasonable and extreme. Moreover, while wondering about the office staff's strange behavior toward him, he quickly dispels the notion that they might in any way be drawing a direct line between him and the hijackers. "He had as little connection to those men as they [the office staff] did, and there was no way he could accept that anyone would be able to believe him capable of sharing in their extremist philosophy," he tells himself (22). Even though such reasoning points to Jassim's focused, if not even rigid, character and his single-minded scientific obsession with the subject of water, it is not the outcome of an apolitical background. Jassim's childhood memories betray an acute political awareness developed while growing up in Jordan, an awareness that is slowly stifled and forgotten in the pursuit of material comforts in the so-called Promised Land.

In fact, Jassim's passion for studying water was instigated when he was a young boy by a comment made by his uncle Abu Jalal. Grounding the Israeli-Palestinian conflict in a political struggle over water, Abu-Jalal states, "All these fools, so worked up over land and rights and they don't see the greater picture. Water is what will decide things, not just for us but for every citizen of the world as well" (40). This political view on the role of water in the region becomes the seed that eventually sprouts into Jassim's full-fledged obsession with water management and rainwater harvesting. The impact of Abu Jalal's words comes into full effect during Jassim's early career as a hydrologist, when he is still unsure about whether he will settle down in the US or return to Jordan after finishing his degree. On one of his visits back home, he gives a talk at the University of Jordan, where he meets Salwa for the first time. During this talk, Jassim lectures passionately on the geopolitical and global implications of water shortage, putting special emphasis on water's often underrepresented role in shaping regional and international politics. Drawing a provoking parallel between early European settlers in America and the Israeli government, he states, "The 1967 war started because Israel was caught trying to divert the Jordan [River] away from the West Bank and Jordan. The result of that war was that Israel controlled—controls still—most of the headwaters of the Jordan, much of the Jordan itself, and is in partial or total control of all the aquifers" (244). Jassim adds to this political pronouncement another statement that shows his invested interest in promoting a larger understanding of social justice and human equity. He concludes his talk by saying, "Don't believe it is just the Israelis who divert water though. It is the Chinese, the Americans, the Egyptians. It is everyone. Water is life, technology is power, and humans are thieves" (245).

But with Jassim's decision to settle and work in the US, such political and humanistic zeal slowly starts waning and is eventually replaced by a complacent outlook that leaves Jassim feeling that he has been "eaten by the West . . . [and by] the easy American life" (278). He overwhelmingly feels that "he had walked away from the life he had planned," a life entrenched in the political role of water in the Middle East (219). The accusations hurled at him and many other Arabs and Muslims in the US after 9/11, compounded by the fact that he has accidentally killed a boy in a car accident, reveal to Jassim his delusional and false sense of citizenship and belonging in the US:

> It had taken killing a boy for his soul to awaken.... He saw that
> the past nine years (and even more than that) had been a sabbatical
> from real life, a rich man's escape from the real world.... In more
> than a decade of *good citizenship*, he had never for a minute imagined that his successes would be crossed out by a government censor's permanent marker, that his mission would be absorbed by his nationality, or that Homeland Security would have anything to do with him. Things like this aren't supposed to happen in America.
> (218, 299; emphasis added)

Despite Jassim's eye-opening realization that in his march toward "good [US] citizenship" (and his attainment of the illusory comforts accompanying the good Arab-American label) he has sacrificed the powerful potential of his political beliefs, the narrative insinuates that it is too late for him to rectify his shortsighted assimilative ambitions.

With exclusionary conceptualizations of US citizenship following the attacks of 9/11 defining good citizenship as docile citizenship,[20] it has been a challenge for Arab-Americans to overturn such definitions, especially with the loud and persistent demonization of Arabs and Muslims still fully operational on the national level.[21] In this way, in spite of the narrative's insistence on pointing the finger at America's promise of plenty as the cause for the moral emptiness (as well as physical danger) that Jassim and Salwa find themselves in by the end of the novel, such singular blame remains largely insufficient. It in fact has to be placed alongside the concomitant erasure of the characters' transnational, anti-imperial political identities and viewpoints (an erasure that is both self-willed and imposed by the pressures of assimilation and the promise of the American Dream). In light of such erasures, the causes of Jassim and Salwa's moral downfall and their implied shameful return home become complex and multiple.

Salwa self-identifies as a Palestinian from Jordan and is quick to deflect any disparaging comments about her background. Nevertheless, it becomes clear that her zeal for defending Palestinian refugee rights (her family included) in the diaspora is no match against her consumerist love for beautiful things, particularly sexy and silky lingerie, for which she is dubbed the Queen of Pajamas. While Salwa herself is never portrayed as being overly political, even when in Jordan, her decision to marry Jassim marks an attendant yet unstated decision to forgo a commitment to the Palestinian cause. For, by marrying Jassim, Salwa breaks her unspoken engagement to Hassan Shaheed, a Palestinian refugee boy she grew up with, whom, with his "handsome face, sense of humor, and political activism," Salwa regards "as a symbol of Palestine" (240).[22]

Even though Salwa admits that this American life "was the life she had chosen, but it was not the life she wanted," she is nevertheless unable to resist the illusory appeal of the American Dream (91). In this way, she becomes the antithesis of the folkloric figure Nus Nsays (which in Arabic means "half of a halving") that her grandmother used to tell her stories about. In one such story, Nus Nsays, using his cunning and resourcefulness, succeeds in escaping with his friend from the evil clutches of a wicked *ghula* that had held them hostage. Salwa, faced with her own *ghula* (America), is reminded of her grandmother's explanation that the small size of Nus Nsays is meant "to show that with determination and a clever wit, small characters can defeat larger evils. Every Palestinian has a bit of Nus Nsays within him. Or her" (98). Salwa's political acumen in the US, however, remain far from challenging any evils, real or metaphorical, other than her reprimanding of a teenage salesgirl at the local mall who sees Jassim's Arab features as suspect. Her privileging of a consumer citizenship in her pursuit of "good citizenship" inevitably leads to the silencing, if not complete demise, of the Nus Nsays within her, the emblem of her political Palestinian identity. Bloodied and disfigured after her lover, Jake, attacks her in his apartment in a drug-induced rage after she breaks up with him, Salwa is left at the end of the novel semiconscious at the hospital, with a still-unsuspecting Jassim sitting next to her. Although her actual return to Jordan is alluded to rather than included in the narrative, this promised final return takes on an ominous form, pointing to her shame and her failure in the Promised Land, which in turn comes to fully exhibit its less-than-promising dimensions. It is in this way, then, that at the novel's end, Salwa, "Palestinian by blood, Jordanian by residence, and American by citizenship" (70), retains no sense of true belonging to any country.[23]

Despite the immense revisionary and counterhegemonic potential of the texts discussed in this section, they reflect some of the challenges inherent in the performance of critical and transnational Arab-American citizenships and belongings. For one, such performances have to contend with a dominant insistence on polemical narratives of racial, ethnic, religious, and national identities prevalent in the post-9/11 US cultural and political landscape. Accompanied by the decree of "imperative patriotism" (Salaita, "Ethnic Identity" 154), post-9/11 hegemonic constructions of US identity demand the relinquishment of "suspect" affiliations altogether, with Arab and Muslim identities (or a conflation of the two) being the most suspect. In other words, the various counterhegemonic texts that I analyze here often strategically incorporate some of the self-same language of discrimination and occlusion they are seeking to undercut and refute. Such strategies, even while informing an antiessentialist and transnational Arab-American discourse, can run the risk of perpetuating a hegemonic binary structure even through disavowal. For even when offering multiple and alternative views, these texts, by virtue of engaging with the polemical narratives of us and them, good and bad Arab, in order to refute them, can indirectly end up affirming them. Some questions that have to be addressed, then, are the following: To what extent do these texts' rebuttal of simplistic labels and exclusionary US citizenship relegate them to a position of constant retaliation that limits innovative forms of aesthetic creation or thematic exploration? How can Arab-American artistic and cultural production transcend the pressures of representation in developing a transnational politics of dissent? Might these questions even be premature given the important demythologizing role that Arab-American literatures and cultures are playing during this crucial stage of identity reformulations?

In addressing such questions, *Once in a Promised Land* and other texts discussed here engage directly with the dangers inherent in the absence or censorship of a visible and vocal type of transnational political citizenship among Arab-Americans. At the basis of this citizenship lies an interrogative approach that complicates the post-9/11 construction of "a national [US] identity through discourses of political freedoms and liberties" (Grewal 205). It also demands difficult but necessary interrogations of US foreign policy as well as of the internal Islamophobia and anti-Arab racism pervading the US. One promising aspect of this type of political citizenship is an active commitment to defining Arab-American as well as US identity in general through the prism of transnational politics. According to this itinerary, Americans, of Arab background or otherwise, rather than succumbing to the numbing and silencing effects of homogeneous US patriotism, would instead practice a form of US citizenship that demands a critique of the racist and imperialist agendas imposed by the state, despite the threat of curtailment, imprisonment, or deportation.[24] As made apparent in the texts discussed in the next section, it is through the development and enactment of such transnational political awareness that both minority and mainstream US belongings are redefined and reimagined.

"Over There Is Over Here": Positioning 9/11 within a Transnational Political Framework

With the impact of violence and trauma arriving in full force at the shores of the US after 9/11, neat ideological and political separations between the Arab world and the US were immediately contested. Arab-Americans collectively and individually rushed to denounce the attacks of 9/11, vehemently defining them as the acts of a handful of nonrepresentative extremist individuals. The poems by Suheir Hammad and Dima Hilal discussed in this section, as well as the essay by Rabab Abdulhadi, contribute an additional and crucial layer to such condemnations by viewing the events of 9/11 through a transnational lens. In doing so, these writers connect the attacks of 9/11 to Arab-Americans' direct or indirect experiences of war and conflict in the Arab world. In this way, the antihegemonic and transnational type of political citizenship espoused and enacted in these texts becomes the antithesis of the apolitical acquiescence pervading the lives of some of the Arab-American characters discussed earlier in the chapter. It is in voicing such interrogative forms of dissent against imperial ventures overseas, then, that Arab-American literature not only imagines but also concretizes an antiamnesiac and transnational political landscape on the US domestic front, which in turn leads to transformed understandings of US citizenship and belonging.

One of the first Arab-American literary pieces to articulate this transnational, hybrid perspective is Hammad's poem "first writing since." Written a week after the attacks and widely distributed on the Internet, the poem came to the attention of Russell Simmons, who subsequently signed Hammad to a deal with HBO's widely successful *Def Poetry Jam*, with which she toured for two years.[25] In this poem, Hammad widens the sphere of trauma and catastrophe resulting from the 9/11 attacks by including the perspective of Arab- and Muslim-Americans. More than doing so, Hammad places the attacks within a larger rubric of conflict and loss that transcends US national boundaries. Noting that 9/11 should in fact be regarded as part of a chain of violence to which people across the globe are repeatedly subjected, the speaker evokes places such as Gaza and the West Bank, where Palestinians have to deal with the brutal reality of loss, disruptions, and ruptures on a daily basis due to the vicissitudes of the Israeli occupation:

> if there are any people on earth who understand how new york is
> feeling right now,they are in the west bank and the gaza strip. (lines
>   88–89)

This observation is followed by the speaker's jolting and powerful proclamation that "over there is over here" (line 121), a stark rebuttal of the neat geographical, national, and ideological categorizations (inherent in theories such as Samuel Huntington's clash of civilizations for instance) that ultimately enable facile constructions of the Other and his or her concomitant dehumanization. In doing so, Hammad enlarges the impact of the national catastrophe of 9/11 to incorporate more intricate and informed political, geographical, and human mappings of loss and trauma. By taking on a transnational approach to reading (or even reading into) 9/11, the poem overturns the markings of "true" US citizenship that distinguish between the grieving and the nongrieving or the patriotic and the unpatriotic. In this way, the claim that "over there is over here" ultimately points to the fact that 9/11 is not a starting point of suffering and trauma in contemporary US history or an inexplicable act of aggression against Americans but is in fact a continuation of worldwide acts of violence that the US is complicit in through its foreign policy and strategic relationships with international powers as well as local governments in the Arab world. The pain and suffering that have for decades characterized thousands of lives "over there," in the Arab world, are in the poem brought to the US, "over here," so much so that the language of trauma pervades both locales.[26] The recognition of this connectivity triggers a bittersweet sense of déjà vu for many Arab-Americans, one that brings back the memory of war and conflict in Arab homeland(s), while reminding them of their vulnerable and suspect status in their US home. What such a poetic articulation ascertains, then, is that the grafting of a similar traumatic pain onto both geographical domains ironically brings them into conversation with each other, thus challenging the neat separations between "here and there" and in turn between "us and them."

In addition to placing 9/11 within a transnational geopolitical rubric, the perspective offered in "first writing since" also challenges homogeneous conceptualizations of US citizenship by diversifying the narrative of fear propagated by the attacks, homing in on the specific fears of Arab- and Muslim-Americans. Upon hearing about the attacks, the speaker in the poem states,

> fire in the city air and I feared for my sister's life in a way never
> before. and then, and now, i fear for the rest of us.
> first, please god, let it be a mistake, the pilot's heart failed, the plane
> engine died.
> then, please god, let it be a nightmare, wake me now.

please god, after the second plane, please, don't let it be anyone
who looks like my brothers. (lines 10–16)

But with the realization that the pilots who drove planes into the World Trade Center and the Pentagon do look like her Arab brothers, the speaker, and by extension Arab- and Muslim-Americans generally, had to tackle and face the divisive rhetoric that pitted the two parts of their hyphenated identities against each other. They could not adequately grieve as Americans since their Arab racial and religious attributes and affiliations connected them with what quickly and simplistically became synonymous with evil or, simply, anti-American:

> 4. ricardo on the radio said in his accent thick as yuca, "i will
> feel so much better when the first bombs drop over there. and my
> friends feel the same way."
> . . . .
> if i can find through this exhaust people who were left behind to
> mourn and to resist mass murder, i might be all right.
> thank you to the woman who saw me breaking my cool and blinking
> back tears. she opened her arms before she asked "do you want a hug?"
> a big white woman, and her embrace was the kind only people with the
> warmth of flesh can offer. i wasn't about to say no to any comfort.
> "my brother's in the navy," i said. "and we're arabs." "wow, you
> got double trouble." word.
>
> 5. one more person ask me if i knew the hijackers.
> one more motherfucker ask me what navy my brother is in.
> one more person assume no arabs or muslims were killed.
> one more person assume they know me, or that i represent a people.
> or that a people represent an evil. or that evil is as simple as a
> flag and words on a page. (lines 50–52, 65–78)

The pain induced by having one's identity unquestionably lumped with desperate extremist actions inevitably leads to anger on the part of the speaker, especially since what she conceives of as not only her American or New Yorker but specifically her Brooklyn identity is readily stripped away so that she becomes a stranger in her own city. The paradox imposed on Arab-American identity post-9/11, succinctly and beautifully captured here in the words "double trouble" describing her brother's seemingly disparate roles as a Muslim and a navy man leads the speaker to vacillate between fear and anger: fear of the repercussions awaiting

Arabs and Muslims in the US and in the Arab world, and anger that presumptions and blanket assessments become the dominant means for posttraumatic recuperation. Moreover, the speaker's refusal to succumb to polarizing reactions to the attacks leads her to turn her anger against assessments of US political and historical culpability in the Arab region that leave her no room to grieve as an Arab-American who considers the US her home:

> yet when people sent emails saying, this was bound to happen, let's not forget u.s. transgressions, for half a second i felt resentful.
> hold up with that, cause I live here, these are my friends and fam, and it could have been me in those buildings, and we're not bad people, do not support america's bullying. can i just have a half second to feel bad? (lines 59–64)

The use of the word "we" in these lines is important, for it points to the speaker's refusal to participate in the polemics of national exclusivity propagated by the us-versus-them rhetoric. The word "we" is also a reminder that the speaker is American as much as she is Arab, with a need to mourn her "friends and fam" who died in the World Trade Center. However, this "we" that the speaker identifies with is not an uncritical collective but one that imbues US identity and citizenship with a dissenting strain that denounces "america's bullying." Acknowledging nuanced forms of citizenship and belonging necessitates a complex approach to notions of alterity and difference, an approach that maintains at its center a transnational awareness of place and experience that connects various spaces and geographies of knowledge.

The thematics exploring the transnational reach of conflict and war are also explored by Dima Hilal, another strong voice emerging from the contemporary collective of a younger generation of Arab-American poets. Hilal was born in Beirut, Lebanon, and like Hammad, moved with her family to the US at a young age. Echoing the historical and geopolitical continuities in narratives of war and aggression as explored in Hammad's "first writing since," Hilal's poem "america" captures the anguish of Arab-American immigrants who have left their war-torn homelands behind, only to be faced with violence and personal threats in their new home:

> we fade into the fabric of these united states
> pay our taxes, pledge our allegiance
> lose ourselves in its thick folds

success finds us and we find success
intoxicating

until a plane carves a path though steel and glass
smoke billowing from two wounded skyscrapers,
the aftermath all too familiar
. . . .

until the sudden sidelong glance,
the step back
wait, isn't that where you're from?
let's bomb them back to the stone age
those arabs
never should have let them into our country
those arabs
. . . .
we'll teach those turban-wearing, towel-headed,
dirty, motherfucking, camel loving, terrorists
a lesson they'll never forget
fractured skull, baseball bat,
crushed bones, clenched fists
battered bodies, a switchblade, crow bar
gun shot blast

it's us versus them
are you with us
are you with us
are you with us
or against us? (lines 11–18, 25–31, 37–48)

Here again, the speaker refutes the assumption that 9/11 constitutes the single, overarching, and transformative act of political aggression that mitigates all others in recent history, asserting instead that for many US citizens, specifically for Arabs, the attacks of 9/11 in fact are another devastating installment in the continuum of violence and oppression experienced on a daily level in the Arab world and beyond. With "the aftermath [being] all too familiar," the events of 9/11, notwithstanding the specificity of the circumstances or the political motives that brought them about, ultimately yield a disconcerting language of anguish and loss recognizable by all war-zone survivors intimately familiar with what the poem describes as "the endless sorrow / of life snatched without warning or reason" (lines 15–16). But rather than enabling many war-weary Arab-Americans to assert their US belonging and participate in collective national healing, this sense of déjà vu in many ways links them to violent histories that are then used as justifications for regarding Arabs and Muslims (regardless of citizenship rights) as a foreign and even downright dangerous presence in US society.

Demonstrating a dexterous use of poetic voice, Hilal's poem addresses the exclusionary dimensions of US citizenship as constructed and conceived after 9/11 by switching the identity of the collective evoked by the word "we" midway through the poem. She uses it first to designate an Arab immigrant collective intent on making the US its home and then changes its ascription later on in the poem to point to a suspicious and violent faction of US society intent on upholding its patriotic post-9/11 fervor by attacking "towel-headed . . . terrorists." With this switch in the groupings signified by the word "we," the repetition of the phrase "are you with us or against us" toward the end of the poem, more than merely undercutting, through redundancy, the rudimentary logic informing such a polemical stance, is in fact further problematized by Hilal's strategic destabilization of what or whom the two terms, "you" and "us," signify. In doing so, Hilal, like Hammad and the host of writers whose works are discussed in the first section of this chapter, embeds her work with transnational and revisionary articulations of US citizenship and belonging that reimagine homogeneity and hegemony by transforming "'the American way of life' into 'American ways of life'" (Salaita, "Ethnic Identity" 165).

The dogged insistence on underscoring the transnational links informing Arab-American citizenship as depicted in Hammad's and Hilal's work takes on more specific dimensions in the nonfictional piece by Abdulhadi, "Where Is Home? Fragmented Lives, Border Crossings, and the Politics of Exile." In this essay, Abdulhadi, currently a professor at San Francisco State University and originally from the city of Nablus in the West Bank, reflects on the thematic of Palestinian exile and the construction of individual and collective Palestinian identities in the US in light of 9/11. Creating two interconnected narratives, she describes in one narrative her attempts (as a Muslim Arab) to navigate and survive the closed-off boundaries of New York City in the hours and days following the 9/11 attacks. In another narrative, she replicates the same concerns from the geographical vantage point of the Israeli-controlled Palestinian territories. In both cases, Abdulhadi portrays Arabs and Muslims as a besieged and monitored group, even if the contexts of such positionings might seem divergent at first glance.

Trying to reach her home in upper Manhattan right after the planes hit the World Trade Center, Abdulhadi finds herself suddenly engulfed by a throng of policemen and checkpoints in an area that has quickly become akin to a war zone. Sensing the rising levels of fear and paranoia, she becomes increasingly conscious of her visibly Arab features and accent. In self-censoring her actions and speech in a taxi she is sharing with other New Yorkers trying to reach their homes (including a businessman she suspects to be Iranian),[27] she is reminded of similar restrictions faced every day by Palestinians in the West Bank and Jerusalem. These restrictions include checkpoints, unwieldy border crossings, and the overall debilitating effects of Israeli occupation on Palestinians. Using linguistic parallels to link the critical tropes of racial passing and border crossing, and pointing to the privileges and limitations entailed in both, Abdulhadi states, "My split lives are on a collision course again: I feel like such a traitor for *passing*. But wouldn't it be better to *pass* today? Do I want to identify with 'them' [meaning Arabs]? Do I want to escape the collective guilt-by-association, the fate of my fellow Arabs, Palestinians, and Muslims? Should I renege on my roots?" (74).

These questions and musings not only underscore the volatile and changeable nature of Arab-American citizenship and belonging in the US but also point to the forever-shifting qualities of homes and homelands. Speaking of a sense of Arab belonging in the US (which 9/11 made all the more fleeting and questionable), Abdulhadi draws on the collective experience of Palestinian dispossession, stating, "This *home* [the US or specifically New York City] is becoming so similar to what happens back *home* [in Palestine]" (76). Here again, as in Hammad's poem, the transnational political lens through which Abdulhadi negotiates the post-9/11 fear and panic "over here," in the US, incorporates dispossession and trauma as experienced "over there," specifically in the occupied Palestinian territories and the refugee camps in Lebanon.[28]

Such a perspective overturns exclusionary depictions of 9/11 that frame it as the single most defining moment of national or even international trauma. Instead, alternative models of historical and geopolitical continuities between seemingly disparate locations are placed at the forefront of 9/11 trauma, so much so that the events "over there" come to inform and bleed into crises "over here." This strategy, however, is not meant to conflate two such distinct geographical locales but is geared toward questioning the shortcomings involved in fixing identities in seemingly bounded places. Such a perspective transforms concepts and practices of homes and homelands, which, instead of being stable and solid entities, are always revised and evaluated to assess not only who is included but also who is excluded from dominant understandings of citizenship and belonging.

Further questioning the politics of containment that occlude Arab-Americans from discussions of national recuperation after 9/11, Abdulhadi asks, "Whose memories are valid? For whom memorials are built?" (82). Through such questions, what this essay and in fact many of the texts discussed in this chapter speak to is the need to acknowledge and make space for transnational articulations of US citizenship and belonging in order to acknowledge the multiple connections to and remembrances of loss and trauma that 9/11 evokes, specifically here as it applies to Arab-Americans. In doing so, these texts unveil a strong, informed, yet complex type of transnational political commitment that minimizes the ideological gulf separating "here" (the US) from "there" (the Arab world). In doing so, they challenge the state-sponsored politics of containment and the monitoring of racialized Arab and Muslim bodies, in turn discrediting racist and exclusionary articulations of US citizenship.

Rethinking the Mobilization of Gender and Sexuality in the National Security State

The mobilization of a transnational political framework (albeit of the imperialist, neo-Orientalist kind) has not been absent from the workings of the US security state since 9/11. In the name of securing the homeland, hypervigilant patriotism demands that the elusive threats of terrorism posed by a homogenized Muslim or Arab enemy "over there" be reinscribed on the racialized bodies of religious, ethnic, and diasporic minorities "over here." The containment of racialized bodies at home (in the US) through surveillance, incarceration, and deportation becomes an extension as well as a justification of the US wars abroad, all in the name of preserving (and disseminating) US freedoms. The rhetoric developing out of such a state-defined transnational political framework vastly differs from the one deployed in the counterhegemonic discourse evident in the Arab-American texts discussed in this book. Such difference becomes most obvious in the ways in which dominant US narratives eschew any acknowledgment of or responsibility for the violence, trauma, and loss of lives "over there" that are directly caused by so-called democracy or freedom projects such as Operation Enduring Freedom in Afghanistan and Operation Iraqi Freedom. A specific strategy of such hegemonic transnational deployments is devising the identifiable Arab and Muslim body within the US as the internal embodiment of the external threat posed by the distant Other. Following such logic, then, the security of the US homeland necessitates perpetuating the foreignness of Arab and Muslim bodies, with this foreignness always being a gendered one that pits the demasculinized, homosexualized, and even perverted figure of the Arab or Muslim man against a hypermasculine and heteronormative (or even homonormative) understanding of US nationalism and citizenship.[29]

Mainstream representations of Arabs and Arab-Americans after 9/11 have obsessively focused on what has been described as "the Faceless Veiled Woman" (Muaddi Darraj, "Personal and Political" 256).[30] Numerous feminist and postcolonial scholars have tackled the problematic simplification of complex political and religious identities that such stilted representations help produce. Yet in deconstructing the "saving brown women from brown men" narrative (Spivak 296), the figure of the Arab and Muslim man remains undertheorized. In the rest of this chapter, I delineate some discursive itineraries in Arab-American literary and cultural texts that respond to the fixing of Arab and Muslim men within the debilitating framework of racial, sexual, and religious stereotypes (terrorists, fundamentalists, uncivilized, perverted, etc.).

What is primarily perceived to be most insidious and threatening about Arab and Muslim men is their ability to "infiltrate" the US social fabric. Such a possibility places the US public in a policing position vis-à-vis difference and dissidence, which are then constructed at the interstices of religion, race, ethnicity, politics, and sexuality. One aspect of such positionings that is most pertinent to my discussion here is the ways in which homophobia, racism, and fear of the Arab and Muslim Other intersect in constructions of the male terrorist (suspect) as he is identified within the US. Such constructions interweave discriminatory descriptors such as "monster, terrorist, fag," which are lumped together to form a necessary prescriptive antidote in national productions of "docile patriots" (Puar and Rai 117, 130). Hence we find that the fight against terrorism both at home and abroad (over there and over here) necessitates not only military violence but also sexual violence that, as enacted on the male Arab and Muslim body, becomes a means to both reveal and punish its perverse identity (a rationale made evident by the torture tactics carried out at Abu Ghraib, Guantanamo Bay, and elsewhere).[31] Rather than pursue representative constructions of this "monster, terrorist, fag" figure in dominant US cultural discourse (ranging from television shows to the rhetoric circulating during the 2008 presidential election),[32] I focus on Arab-American authors' and artists' own negotiations of such imposed identity constructions in their work. I single out Yussef El Guindi's play *Back of the Throat* and Wafaa Bilal's installation art to exemplify performative destabilizations of public and governmental constructions of threatening Arab and Muslim masculinities post-9/11.

Back of the Throat was written by El Guindi and was performed in various cities across the US including San Francisco, Seattle, New York City, and Chicago since 2005. The play is about an American-born Muslim Egyptian writer, Khaled, who is visited in his apartment by two federal agents, Carl and Bartlett, in the period immediately following 9/11 (the whole play takes place inside his apartment). The two agents initially claim to be following a procedural investigation and even come equipped with evaluation forms for Khaled to fill out. Their "friendly" interrogation, however, hits a turning point toward the middle of the play when Khaled realizes that the agents have already determined him to be guilty of colluding with the 9/11 attackers. Representing these attackers is Asfoor (depicted as the mastermind behind the 9/11 attacks), who haunts the whole scene and makes ghostly appearances throughout the play. Asfoor's character in fact has interesting parallels to that of Mohammad Atta, the so-called leader of the nineteen 9/11 hijackers, parallels made evident by some of the details provided in the play that I will turn to shortly. The agents visiting Khaled start constructing the narrative of his guilt by examining his political beliefs in conjunction with his sexual leaning. Searching his apartment for "clues," they come across some porn magazines, one of which features a woman "draped over a cow" (16). The agents read these magazines not merely as kinkiness or sexual curiosity but as material evidence of what they eventually describe as Khaled's "unnormal" character (19). In fact, it is this same abnormality (which gets paired with religious and political difference) that they also see surfacing in the titles of the books he owns. For in addition to the Quran, a gift from his mother that Khaled cannot even access because of his inability to read or speak Arabic, these titles include *Getting Your Government's Attention through Unconventional Means*, *A Manual for the Oppressed*, *Covering Islam*, *Militant Islam*, and *Quotations from Chairman Mao Tsetung* (17).[33] These findings provide the agents with insurmountable evidence pointing to Khaled's questionable US identity, leading Bartlett to state,

> I am frankly amazed at just how abnormal everything is in your apartment. I have actually been growing quite alarmed by what we've been finding.... I mean we've already established you're a left-leaning subversive with Maoist tendencies who has a thing for bestiality and militant Islam. Throw in your research on guns and assassins and I could have you inside a jail cell reading about yourself on the front page of every newspaper before the week is out. (19–20, 21)

Such a pronouncement, which might seem an extreme threat, nevertheless captures the dangerous paranoia and random deductions that informed the rounding up of Arab and Muslim men by government officials right after 9/11, as well as the continued targeting and incarceration of Muslim men (many of whom are US citizens) in the name of state security.[34] Bartlett's statements, then, clearly delineate how Khaled's sexual, intellectual, religious, and political identities (or what is presented of them through the culled evidence) become incriminating links to, or evidence of, a threatening, antinormative type of US citizenship. Khaled's repeated and insistent reminder that he is a "citizen" throughout the "interrogation" inevitably begs the weighty but unstated question, but what *kind* of citizen is he? In fact, it becomes clear that such a question is not even a necessary or valid one, for the agents have already determined what kind of citizen Khaled is before they entered his apartment. Khaled's possessions then duly confirm to the agents that his is a type of citizenship that tears at the ideological fabric of US national identity, producing a questionable type of belonging that not only deters cultural inclusion but is a valid reason for its holder's prosecution.

In an interview with dramaturg Walter Bilderback, El Guindi presents his own self-reflexive fascination with issues of citizenship, shaped by his own immigrant story. Born in Egypt and having immigrated to London with his parents at the age of four, El Guindi eventually went back to Cairo for his undergraduate studies, after which he moved to the US, where he pursued a graduate degree in playwriting at Carnegie-Mellon University. He then took up a playwright-in-residence position at Duke University before moving to Seattle to work full-time on his plays. He acquired US citizenship in 1996, an experience he describes this way: "It brought together a bunch of amorphous elements and subterranean emotions that were in effect, but to which I just couldn't give a name to, or find a coherent story for, . . . a story [that] was the simple one of the immigrant journey. . . . Becoming a citizen plugged me into my own journey. Strangely. It allowed me to write about it" (El Guindi, "Interview").

In *Back of the Throat* (which incidentally refers to the advice that Khaled gives the agents on how to pronounce the first letter of his name in Arabic), Khaled's repeated insistence on asserting his US citizenship is his way of (naively) seeking out just treatment. But the agents' strategy of disassembling his behavioral normalcy leads to the erosion of his citizenship and the rights that it should convey. After all, in the post-9/11 national security state depicted in the play, the only citizenship allowed or deemed safe is of the hetero- and homonormative, compliant, and docile kind. The erosion of Khaled's rights reaches a crescendo in the second half of the play, in which the agents implicate him in the 9/11 plots by providing flimsy evidence that he was present at a strip club the same night that Asfoor was there. A shadowy picture and a pay stub prove to be enough for the agents to confirm that, on "August 21st, at around 10:05" o'clock, Khaled visited the "Eyefull Tower Club," where he met with Asfoor. "Ms. Jean Sommers, aka, Kelly Cupid, 'Dancer Extraordinaire and Stripper Artiste'" (45) is presented as the eye witness of this encounter. In fact, her testimony is preceded by that of two other female characters who are brought in as "witnesses" during the makeshift interrogation scene in Khaled's apartment. The first "witness" is a librarian who allegedly sees Asfoor approaching Khaled for the first time at the local library, and the second is Khaled's ex-girlfriend, Beth.[35] Kelly Cupid recounts how, after performing a lap dance on Khaled (or someone she is told was Khaled), she sees him follow Asfoor into the men's bathroom, where she "see[s] both of their legs under one of the stalls." She states, "they must have heard me, because Khaled comes shooting out and runs, just runs past me. And out saunters Mr. Creepy [Asfoor] after him. Calm as can be, like he'd just been holding a meeting in his office.... Might have been sucking each other off for all I know. Or shooting up. Who knows. At least one of them's dead" (in reference to Asfoor's suicide mission) (48). Khaled's purported disinterest in Kelly Cupid's lap-dance act (which frustrates her to the point that she breaks her professional code and makes him come), closely connects the charge of terrorism or terrorism plotting to Khaled's failed heterosexual desire. In fact, in some productions of the play, Kelly Cupid herself performs such an intermixture of heterosexuality and patriotism through her American-flag-inspired costume, which confirms the binary of healthy patriotic heterosexuality versus perverse homosexual terrorism.

Toward the end of the play, in a desperate last bid to collect "evidence," agent Bartlett subjects Khaled to a violent and invasive strip search in order to find out if Khaled has a tattoo on his penis, a discovery that he thinks would thereby certify Khaled's guilt. The tattoo clue is gleaned from an email fragment allegedly sent by Asfoor, in which he makes a vague reference to tattoos done "where the skin folds so you can hide it if you change your mind" (32). The agents interpret this reference as a way for sleeper-cell agents to recognize each other. What becomes clear in the second part of the play is that the basis of the agents' conviction of Khaled's guilt is intricately and closely related to what they perceive as his questionable nonnormative sexuality. Even though the strip search does not yield a confirmatory tattoo sighting, a guilty or innocent verdict vis-à-vis any terrorist act remains irreversibly connected to Khaled's sexuality. Bartlett,

FIGURE 4.1. Silk Road Rising production of *Back of the Throat—the agents interrogate Khaled*. (Photo by Johnny Knight; courtesy of Silk Road Rising)

confessing that he finds the strip search extremely unappealing, states, "It still leaves us wondering what you did all that time in the bathroom with one of the more hideous individuals [Asfoor] we've come across? Now would be the time to fess up to any deviant sexual inclinations. It might get you off" (49). The multiple meanings attached to the pronouncement "get you off" cements the link between Khaled's alleged sexual and terrorist acts. The end of the play does not yield any easy answers about Khaled's guilt or innocence, with the audience (or the reader of the play) being positioned as the ultimate judge of Khaled's character and actions.

Asfoor's closing address propagates such ambiguity. Stepping out of the closet after the two agents leave Khaled's apartment, Asfoor addresses Khaled (who remains crouching on the floor after his invasive interrogation). Asking him for English lessons, Asfoor tells Khaled, "I might even teach it.... I will teach language back. I will make them speak their own language differently. I will have them speak words they never spoke before.... And soon my language will also fall on their heads. Like theirs falls on ours. Exploding in our brains 'til we can't even dream in peace.... I can help you [Khaled] find your voice.... You've lost your way.... I can help.... I know how to inspire.... I know how to inspire" (50–51). I read such proclamations not merely as an anti-imperialist statement or as a harbinger of Khaled's possible radicalization as a result of his traumatic interrogation. They point to the inescapable branding of Khaled as a so-called terrorist at the hands of the agents so much so that he comes to embody that role, regardless of his innocence or guilt. I also read the play's open-endedness as a deliberate tactic aimed at engaging an audience (visually and discursively) in interrogations of citizenships. Such tactics, as deployed in Arab-American cultural and literary production, disrupt and defy normative models of nation and belonging by specifically underscoring the intersection of religion, sexuality, and nationality in racialized constructions of the terrorist figure. The end result of such revisionary deployments is the formation of counterpublic sites or spaces in which dissident and transnational forms of political citizenship could be imagined and enacted, which in turn pushes against (and transforms) the logic of normative and "docile" US citizenships.

Nevertheless, the various counterhegemonic articulations discussed in this chapter, in their response to simplistic and binary formulations of US citizenship after 9/11, often strategically incorporate some of the self-same oppressive language of racial, religious, and national discrimination they are seeking to undercut and refute. Such strategies, even while informing an antiessentialist and transnational Arab-American discourse, can run the risk of perpetuating a hegemonic binary structure even through disavowal. In other words, in the same way that George W. Bush's affirmation (following the 9/11 attacks) of Arab- and Muslim-Americans' "true" Americanness rendered their foreignness more vivid and immediate in the public's imagination (Salaita, "Ethnic Identity" 151), the question becomes, can these texts' engagement with questions of exclusionary US citizenship and belonging inadvertently reify the racialization of

FIGURE 4.2. Silk Road Rising production of *Back of the Throat—Khaled and Asfoor*. (Photo by Johnny Knight; courtesy of Silk Road Rising)

Arab- and Muslim-Americans in the US? To investigate the boundaries as well as the possibilities posed by such a question, I conclude my discussion of Arab-American literary responses to 9/11 by looking briefly at other forms of cultural interventions to seek out the various ways in which the limits of Arab-American self-representations after 9/11 can be reconfigured and renegotiated. To do so, I examine the work of Iraqi-American installation artist Wafaa Bilal, work that directly challenges and undercuts the normalization of the culture of surveillance and militarism in the US.

Ranging from photography to installation art and video, Bilal's work repeatedly defamiliarizes elements of war, combat, surveillance, and torture, all of which have become part and parcel of everyday social and cultural consciousness in the US. Uncovering the artificiality of the ideological apparatus that serves to rationalize war atrocities and violence to a desensitized Western audience, Bilal's work is ultimately meant to disrupt the neat separation between what he calls "the comfort zone" and "the conflict zone" as captured in what I referred to earlier as the binary of over here and over there (Bilal and Lydersen, *Shoot an Iraqi* 1). Some of his works that exemplify such a revisionary outlook include his 2007 month-long art installation titled *Domestic Tension*. In this installation project, performed by Bilal in a room of Chicago's FlatFile Galleries, the artist links his computer to a remote-controlled paintball gun and gives worldwide viewers free access to shoot at him around the clock with a press of a button on their computers. With very little reprieve, Bilal confined himself to that space, placing himself directly in the line of "fire" coming from his virtual shooters, resulting in eighty million hits and more than sixty-five thousand shots from 136 countries in thirty days (Becker xvi; Bilal and Lydersen, *Shoot an Iraqi* 2). He chronicles his performance in his book *Shoot an Iraqi: Art, Life and Resistance under the Gun* (2008), which integrates two parallel narratives. One narrative follows Bilal's life in Iraq under Saddam Hussein's regime, his survival in refugee camps in Kuwait and Saudi Arabia after the First Gulf War, and his arrival to the US in 1992 after being offered asylum. The other narrative provides a day-by-day chronicle of his *Domestic Tension* project.

Bilal's positioning of the body, specifically his male, Muslim Iraqi body, at the center of artistic investigations of national discourse constructions is also evident in another project, . . . *and Counting*, a twenty-four-hour live performance in which Bilal "turns his own body . . . into a canvas, his back tattooed with a borderless map of Iraq covered with one dot for each Iraqi and American casualty near the cities where they fell. The 5,000 dead American soldiers are represented by red dots (using permanent visible ink), and the 100,000 Iraqi casualties are represented by dots of green UV ink, seemingly invisible unless under black light. During the performance, people from all walks of life read off the names of the dead" (Bilal, ". . . and Counting").

In addition to framing a particularly antiessentialist claim to the male Muslim Arab, specifically Iraqi, body, what is particularly interesting about Bilal's work is the way in which the audience or the viewer becomes an integral part of the artistic piece. In . . . *and Counting*, for instance, one camera shows the tattoos being done on Bilal's back, and the other shows the audience, which at once becomes the viewer and the viewed. Unlike in El Guindi's play, where the spectator/reader is called on to impart a judgment on Khaled's guilt or innocence despite his or her physical disengagement or removal from the action of the play, Bilal's performative pieces integrate the viewer/spectator as a central and formative element of the counterpublic spaces that he creates. In this way, the audience becomes both spectator and participant, shaping the content and direction of such exploratory iterations.

Such panoptic methods of looking and being looked at are central to Bilal's yearlong project (which started in December 2010), called *3rdi*, for which he had a camera implanted in the back of his head, taking a snapshot every minute and transmitting it to a website where viewers can access the images.[36] With Bilal calling it a form of "anti-photography" ("3rdi"), capturing images that his body cannot see, the project provides a platform for commenting on the insidious methods of technological surveillance that have permeated our everyday lives to such an extent that we do not see them anymore. Bilal's invitation to resee and to reassess how we see and are seen again gives the viewer the power of choice, allowing him or her to manipulate/control the images through a browsing function that can be used to scroll through the images arranged by month, day, and hour (with sixty snapshots available for each hour). This project was commissioned by the Mathaf, Qatar's new Arab Museum of Modern Art, for its inaugurating exhibition "Told/Untold/Retold: 23 Stories of Journeys through Time and Place" on December 30, 2010. In fact, the *3rdi* installation at the exhibition underscores (in more immediate and obvious ways than the online version) the role of the viewer as a central factor in shaping the specific and shifting ways in which the images are displayed. As Bilal describes the museum exhibition on the *3rdi* project's website, the installation is divided into three connected rooms, with the middle room set up in such a way that the images shift in accordance with the viewer's movement through the space.

Other than some brief updates occasionally provided by Bilal on the webpage indicating the dates and destinations of his travel itinerary, no information accompanies the images, leaving it up to the viewer to

FIGURE 4.3. Wafaa Bilal, detail from *Domestic Tension*, 2007 performance. (Photo: Wafaa Bilal)

deduce Bilal's location by piecing together the narrative itinerary of the fragmented images. In fact, these images, while literally being projected through the movement of Bilal's body, become largely disengaged from him (or at least from this viewer's perspective), except for some fleeting ones that capture Bilal's back in a mirror or glass reflection or when the dark panels indicate that it is nighttime and that Bilal is sleeping. The fact that New York University, where Bilal teaches at the Tisch School of the Arts, made him place a cap on the camera's lens whenever he was on campus (to protect their students' privacy) underscores how such interrogative redeployments of surveillance methods denaturalize their pervasiveness and emphasize their invasive and dehumanizing policing aspects, especially when applied to NYU's normative student *body*. As Bilal states in some introductory reflections on the *3rdi* project, "My work to date has been concerned with the communication of public and private information to an audience so that it may be retold, distributed" ("3rdi"). It is, then, the retellings and redeployments of images and information through such counterpublic spaces that give rise to new sites of knowledge that extend

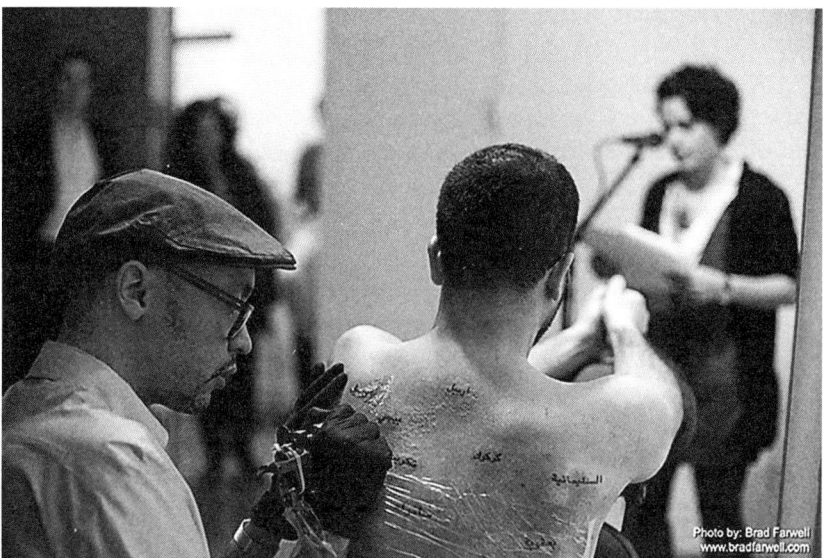

FIGURE 4.4. Wafaa Bilal, detail from ... and Counting, 2010. (Photo: Brad Farwell)

our understanding of identity constructions beyond imperialist projects' polemics of "us and them," "over there and over here."

Even twelve years after the attacks of 9/11, Islamophobia and Arabophobia are still widely prevalent in the US, as evident in the anti-Muslim rhetoric that circulated in the 2008 presidential elections, the Cordoba House or Ground Zero crisis in the summer of 2010, and the March 2011 congressional hearings conducted by Rep. Peter T. King, which sought to attack the so-called radicalization of Muslims in America.[37] The revised ways of seeing, defining, and representing Arab-American identities that inform the literary and cultural interventions discussed in this chapter engender radical reconceptualizations of the hegemonic gaze that currently shapes the depiction of Arab-American subjectivities as homogeneous Others. Moreover, it is through such projects that the normalization of masculinist and imperialist agendas are questioned and problematized. In espousing heterogeneous, multilayered, and transnational Arab-American belongings, these texts destabilize exclusionary forms of US citizenship (extending to the racial, political, religious, and sexual) by incorporating new spaces and horizons that give rise to complex knowledges of US identities while promulgating an important awareness of the power relations that continue to inform and shape the various segments of US society.

Now that we have come out of hiding,
Why would we live again in the tombs we'd made out of our souls?

    And the sundered bodies that we've reassembled with prayers
      and consolations,
What would their torn parts be other than flesh?

    Now that we have tasted hope
And dressed each other's wounds with the legends of our oneness
Would we not prefer to close our mouths forever shut on the wine
That swilled inside them?

    Having dreamed the same dream,
Having found the water that gushed behind a thousand mirages,
Why would we hide from the sun again
Or fear the night sky after we've reached the ends of darkness,
Live in death again after all the life our dead have given us?

    Listen to me Zow'ya, Beida, Ajdabya, Tobruk, Nalut, Derna,
      Musrata, Benghazi, Zintan,
Listen to me houses, alleys, courtyards, and streets that throng my
    veins,
Some day soon
In your freed light and in the shade of your proud trees,
Your excavated heroes will return to their thrones in your martyrs'
    squares,
Lovers will hold each other's hands.

    I need not look far to imagine the nerves dying rejecting the life
      that blood sends them.
I need not look deep into my past to seek a thousand hopeless vistas.
But now that I have tasted hope
I have fallen into the embrace of my own rugged innocence.

    How long were my ancient days?
I no longer care to count.
How high were the mountains in my ocean's fathoms?
I no longer care to measure.
How bitter was the bread of bitterness?
I no longer care to recall.
    Now that we have tasted hope,
Now that we have lived on this hard-earned crust,
We would sooner die than seek any other taste to life,
Any other way of being human.

                KHALED MATTAWA, "Now That We Have Tasted Hope"[1]

Conclusion: Transnational Solidarity and the Arab Uprisings

This book conceives homes and homelands as constantly changing and evolving entities that are configured and redrawn based on individual and communal positionalities and outlooks. In doing so, it broadens rigid parameters of US national, religious, ethnic, and racial belonging by placing such configurations within a wide transnational framework. Such a reconceptualization of space and perspective enables us to metaphorically collapse the distance, and the concomitant difference that is believed to accompany it, between Arab-Americans' original homelands and the new homes they claim for themselves and their children in the US. Contemporary Arab-American literature is a primary site for envisioning and delineating transnational reconfigurations of citizenship and belonging by virtue of its ability to transform social discourse and to shape subjectivities through the imaginative yet deeply effective tools of narrative and storytelling. The transnational lives described in many of the texts discussed in this book take on various forms and iterations, crucially expanding on ethnic and diasporic theoretical frameworks of citizenship and belonging. The ethnic framework on the one hand trains our sights on issues of communal representation, cultural enactments of tradition and heritage, and the negotiation of power within specific national structures. The diasporic framework on the other hand positions the original homeland(s) as the primary site(s) of engagement for displaced communities. Both fall short, however, of fully addressing the transnational aspects of multiple Arab-American belongings. The analysis I provide in this book enables us to trace discursive articulations of

Arab-American belongings and citizenships that defy the hegemonic classification of minority bodies in the US according to restrictive trajectories of national, ethnic, and racial inclusions and exclusions.

The phenomenon of the transnational, however, should not fall outside the scope of rigorous critique, for it also incorporates its own limitations and exclusions. For instance, even though the texts I discuss here point to the revisionary role of transnational consciousness in transforming singular and unilocal understandings of US citizenship and belonging, they also raise the important question of who gets to access and enact such transnational performances among Arab-Americans themselves. While the enactment of the transnational as I describe it here exceeds the scope of physical mobility and extends into the realm of imaginative connections to original homelands, it still highlights the disparities in the opportunities and experiences available to members of Arab-American communities as determined by factors such as class, education, and gender, for instance. Keeping such disparities in mind is important, yet they nevertheless should not deter us from recognizing the alternative frameworks of belonging made available through transnational Arab-American visions that are marked by their multiplicity and diversity.

Within the texts I discuss in this book, we find Arab-Americans such as the ones in the poems of Lawrence Joseph and Naomi Shihab Nye who have never visited, let alone lived in, their ancestral Arab homeland or any other Arab country. Their performance of Arab identity is informed by what they have learned from their parents, grandparents, aunts, and uncles or by what they have willed themselves to learn or relearn in light of their elders' insistence on willful forgetfulness and earnest immigrant assimilation. We also find Arab-Americans such as those featured in the works of Rabih Alameddine and Samia Serageldin who had spent most of their lives in the Arab world and had immigrated to the US as adults. Many of these characters spend most of their time on planes going back and forth between their Arab homeland and the US, not able to permanently settle in either location of displacement. Among the other characters that we encounter in these texts are the children of Arab immigrants, who came at a young age to the US, acquiring the 1.5-generation label but with enough memories of their Arab roots to keep their eyes intently, and often painfully, trained eastward. Such an outlook is captured most poignantly by Suheir Hammad and Mohja Kahf, whose works are shaped by strong Muslim and feminist perspectives.

Other configurations of Arab-American subjectivities featured prominently in this selection of texts include identities that are of mixed heritage. Several of the works discussed throughout the book portray characters with Arab fathers and Caucasian mothers. For someone like Sirine in Diana Abu-Jaber's novel *Crescent*, for instance, such mixed heritage takes on racial overtones, with her white complexion belying deep Arab roots that she reenacts through her cooking. Despite such heterogeneity of backgrounds, however, many of these characters are united by the pain and anger they experience through witnessing their Arab homelands constantly being plunged into military conflicts and wars that are abetted, if not outright instigated, by the self-same country, the US, that they equally claim as their home. Such contradictions, rather than compelling many of these characters to comply with the pressures of choosing one location over the other as a permanent home base, drive them instead to negotiate and maintain both belongings simultaneously. In doing so, they defy unilocal or mononational constructions of citizenship and belonging, thus changing national landscapes of membership and inclusion in the process.

In this way, the power of the transnational consciousness permeating contemporary Arab-American literature lies not merely in its ability to bridge two separate localities or nationalities deemed as separate and contradictory. The power of this transnational consciousness is rendered most potent and immediate in its potential to collapse and defy the alleged differences between these two entities, thus confirming Suheir Hammad's poetic statement that "over there" is in fact "over here," and vice versa. In my analysis of this transnational consciousness, I have paid close attention to the specificities of such outlooks given the variety of positions and backgrounds among Arab-Americans mentioned earlier. In addition to the thematic groupings that inform the book's structure, these specificities are reflected in particular modalities of transnational consciousness that I examine in the various chapters, including, for example, the concepts of rearrival and translocality as they pertain to the Arab-American experience.

Other important considerations to take into account in further analyses of the transnational consciousness prevalent in contemporary Arab-American literature include a close look at the circulation of these texts and the movement of their authors within transnational and translocal circuits. For in addition to positing the content of these works as evidence of the transnational enactment of Arab-American subjectivities, it would also be helpful to delineate the effect of Arab-American literature on the development of other forms of transnational connections between the US and the Arab world. In other words, it is important to investigate the role of Arab-American literary and cultural production in facilitating larger conceptualizations of transnational frameworks linking the US and the Arab world. Some questions that might be raised in such investigations include the following: How are these literary and cultural texts used in activist projects of anti-imperialism and antimilitarism across the US and the Arab world? What is the role of Arab-American literature within the classroom? How can we connect the classroom to other venues of knowledge production? How do Arab-American literary texts travel across the US and the Arab world? How does the circulation and reception of contemporary Arab-American literature and culture within various Arab countries affect literary and cultural spheres? What is the role of Arab-American literary and cultural texts in creative and activist formations of cross-ethnic and cross-racial coalitions within but also beyond the US?

Such questions raise additional issues that would further help us understand how the transnational aspects of Arab-American literature and culture alter various spaces of knowledge about minoritized identities across different spaces and temporalities. These multilayered aspects stand against the very real danger of having these texts be co-opted or perceived as iterations of an Arab-American literary niche with a predictable and didactic political agenda. In order to avoid such pitfalls, stressing the heterogeneity of this field and its range of thematic engagements is a central and ongoing concern for Arab-American writers and literary critics alike. Over the past few years, we have seen such heterogeneity become more entrenched and evident in Arab-American literary and cultural production. The more recent novels by Diana Abu-Jaber, including *Origin* (2008) and *Birds of Paradise* (2012) for instance, depart from the themes of Arab roots and cultural in-betweenness permeating Abu-Jaber's earlier novels. Writers such as Rabih Alameddine and Etel Adnan, whose work incorporates a radical experimentation with prose, are often described as Lebanese writers first and foremost. Alameddine himself prefers his identity as a writer to be more fluid and less restricted to the Arab-American label.[2]

More and more Arab-American writers are engaged in the important task of translating Arabic literary texts into English, as in the case of Khaled Mattawa's translation of the work of Syrian poet Adonis in the collection *Adonis: Selected Poems*. This collection won a 2011 PEN translation award and a 2011 Banipal Prize and was also shortlisted for the prestigious Griffin Poetry Prize.³ Other notable works of translation include Fady Joudah's translation of the final three collections of the late Palestinian poet Mahmoud Darwish's work in *The Butterfly's Burden* (2006), which was a finalist for the PEN Award for Poetry in Translation. *In the Presence of Absence* (2011) is Sinan Antoon's translation of the last prose book by Darwish, for which Antoon received the 2012 National Translation Award. Instead of regarding such variations on traditional Arab-American themes and projects as a form of disengagement or departure from Arab-American concerns, we should instead recognize them as evidence of a rapidly evolving and expanding literary field whose complexity mirrors that of the Arab-American communities.

The current expansion of the Arab-American literary and cultural scene includes an increase in the variety of genres being produced as well as in the number of intellectual, virtual, and physical spaces available for showcasing such work. Prominent presses and academic journals are increasingly featuring titles focusing on Arab-American studies, and more colleges are including Arab-American topics in their course offerings. The Center for Arab American Studies at the University of Michigan–Dearborn is the first of its kind, and Arab-American studies is a major component of the Department of American Culture at the University of Michigan–Ann Arbor. The inauguration of the Arab American National Museum in Dearborn, Michigan, in 2005 marks a culmination of various organizational efforts intent on formalizing the articulation and commemoration of Arab-American histories and cultures. The museum hosts conferences, workshops, screenings, and performances that focus on Arab-American arts and cultures, thus providing an important venue for local, national, and international Arab-American artistic and academic communities. Its biennial forum "DIWAN" attracts a wide range of Arab-American writers, artists, critics, and performers.

Other important outlets for the articulation of Arab-American literature and criticism include the magazine *Al-Jadid: A Review and Record of Arab Culture and Arts*, established in 1995 and edited by Elie Chelala, as well as *Mizna*, launched in 1999 as the first journal of Arab-American literature. Based in Minneapolis, *Mizna* publishes poetry, fiction, essays, and visual art focusing on Arab-American themes. Its annual Twin Cities Arab Film Festival and other events such as the "Mideast in the Midwest" attract speakers from all around the US and also from the Arab world, thus emphasizing the ways in which the transnational plays out in various artistic and cultural venues. The bilingual journal

Meena, based in New Orleans and Alexandria, Egypt, also exemplifies such transnational engagement. According to the journal's website, "The word 'meena' means port, or port-of-entry, in Arabic, and that is exactly what we would like *Meena* to be: a port between our cities, our countries, our languages, our cultures. 'We' are a group of writers and artists based in the port cities of New Orleans and Alexandria but from all over the United States and Egypt (and beyond) who want to share our work with each other and with you."[4]

The transnational concerns of such cultural and artistic venues simultaneously engaging both the US's and the Arab world's various forms of cultural production are also echoed in other Arab-American artistic outlets. For one, the rise of Arab-American stand-up comedy has marked another type of challenge to the discriminatory and racist treatment meted out to Arabs and Muslims in the US after 9/11. At the helm of such initiatives are stand-up comedians Ahmed Ahmed, Dean Obeidallah, and Maysoon Zayid. In 2003, Obeidallah and Zayid founded the Arab-American Comedy Festival in New York, which has become an annual event. Obeidallah and Ahmed have also collaborated with other stand-up comedians including Iranian-American Maz Jobrani and South Korean Won Ho Chung to produce the stand-up comedy show *Axis of Evil*, which has toured all over the Arab world and the US, forming another avenue through which antidiscriminatory representations of Arabs and Muslims can travel and circulate. Moreover, Arab-American and Middle Eastern theater collectives have been flourishing over the past decade. In addition to individual playwrights such as Betty Shamieh, Yussef El Guindi, Mona Mansour, Nathalie Handal, and Heather Raffo, various collectives such as Nibras, the Noor Theater, the Silk Road Rising, and Golden Thread Productions have been producing work to great critical acclaim.[5]

Transnational Arab-American musical venues, specifically hip hop, form another space in which discriminatory labels against Arabs and Muslims are challenged in full force. Even though Arab-Americans have been part of the hip hop scene starting from its early days, in the past few years more vocal and self-identified Arab-American and Arab-Canadian collectives of hip hop artists have emerged. They focus in particular on the political landscapes permeating the Arab world and its relationship with Western countries, rapping about military crackdowns, Israeli checkpoints, Islamophobia, and second-class citizenship. Some of these groups include The Philistines and The N.O.M.A.D.S., whose members have been able to accrue wide recognition both in the US and Canada, and in the Arab world.[6] Members of these groups include Syrian-American Omar Offendum (who forms half of the group N.O.M.A.D.S.), Iraqi-Canadian The Narcycist,[7] and Palestinian-American emcee Ragtop (from the Philistines). These three artists have formed the collective called the Arab Summit, which in 2007 released the CD *Fear of an Arab Planet*, a riff on Public Enemy's album *Fear of a Black Planet*. Collaborative work is at the heart of these artists' music, as made evident by the video "#Jan25," released in 2011 and featuring Omar Offendum, The Narcycist, and African-American artists Freeway and Amir Sulaiman (both Muslims), as well as Toronto-based female Palestinian singer Ayah. The song, dedicated to the Egyptian protestors at Tahrir Square, quickly went viral.

The collaborative video project was not the first one and was preceded by other similar work that resulted in the album *Free the P* (2005). This album, whose title stands for "Free the Palestinians," was coproduced by Omar Offendum and Ragtop and is a compilation of spoken word and hip hop featuring twenty-four different artists from the US, Canada, and the Middle East. The proceeds of the CD went into supporting the production of the documentary *Slingshot Hip Hop* (2008), directed by Jackie Salloum, which focuses on the day-to-day struggles of Palestinian hip hop artists living in Gaza, the West Bank, and inside Israel.

Despite this exciting flourishing of Arab-American artistic and cultural venues and the affirmation of the connections between Arab-Americans and their brethren in Arab countries, there still exist serious impediments to the flow and mobility of transnational enactments of identities. The alleged globalization of nations and communities and the swift circulation of products and ideas across the globe are in direct contrast to the increased militarization of countries and the vigilant policing of national and international borders. Such contradictions are more visible and effective in some cases than in others, with the political and military conflicts in the Middle East, for one, posing a huge impediment to Arab-Americans' easy access to Arab homelands. Such restrictions can extend to the lives of Arab-American writers themselves, as was the case for Palestinian-Egyptian-American writer Randa Jarrar. On a 2012 visit to the West Bank to see her sister in Ramallah, Jarrar was stopped at the Ben Gurion Airport in Tel Aviv. After being extensively questioned by the Israeli police about her Arab background, Jarrar was forbidden to pass through Israel and was sent back to the US.[8] This is but one example of the dangers and tribulations inherent in negotiating transnational lives and identities, which can have far-reaching consequences that we often never hear about.

Moreover, the seismic changes sweeping across numerous countries in the Arab world and the rising demands for social and class equality and justice in the US, embodied in what has been dubbed the Arab Spring and the Occupy movements, respectively, are a testament to the ways in which the concepts of homes, homelands, citizenship, and national belonging are constantly being interrogated, revised, and reformulated. Within the Arab world, specifically in countries such as Tunisia, Egypt, Libya, Syria, Yemen, and Bahrain, the will of the people, as individuals and as a collective, to demand and in some cases to succeed in enacting much-needed revolutionary reforms in government and political ruling have had a major effect on Arab diasporics' connections to their ancestral homelands. In the same vein, the various forms of solidarity emanating from numerous sectors of the Arab diaspora, ranging from community organizing and academic teach-ins to virtual participation through online social networks such as Facebook and Twitter have had a direct role in imbuing the uprisings in the Arab world with a vigorous and much-needed transnational facet. Such participation becomes acutely pertinent given that the experience of immigration for many Arab-Americans has been shaped by their own or their parents'/grandparents' violent and forceful uprooting from an ancestral homeland to avoid political and religious persecution, imprisonment, or even death at the hands of the same regimes that the current demonstrators have been rising up against.

But these diasporic engagements with an unfolding political and social scene in an Arab homeland do not necessarily lead to the easy or automatic privileging of original national ties at the expense of Arab-American groundings in a US locale. In other words, the overthrow of Zine El Abidine Ben Ali's, Hosni Mubarak's, or Muammar Qaddafi's dictatorial regimes and the efforts exacted through nonviolent means to build democratic and just governing bodies in their stead do not automatically open up or imply a clear-cut, unidirectional path of return for many Arab-Americans with roots in those countries. Such an assumption would only reinstate the myopic and erroneous claim that Arab-Americans are mere sojourners or an alien presence in the US awaiting return to their "true" home. We find in Arab-Americans' responses to the Arab uprisings a persistent questioning and outright rejection of passive and acquiescent articulations of citizenship under hegemonic rule, including a crucial problematizing of the role of the US itself in supporting despotic rulers or even in installing them in power in the first place. By participating in such a critical stance, Arab-Americans underscore their commitment to interrogating both sides of the hyphen, thus calling for more educated, informed, and radical citizen engagement both in the Arab world *and* in the US.

As happens with every crisis or, in this case, historical change occurring in the Arab world, Arab-Americans have, with the unfolding Arab uprisings, been once again interpellated within the US to speak of their experiences and knowledge of Arab identities and histories. This interpellation more often than not frames them as educators or as native informants charged with the responsibility of disseminating an insider's knowledge about events in Arab countries to a US public. Such positionings can be problematic in that they can reaffirm prevalent suspicions regarding Arab-Americans' allegiance to the US as a homeland. At the same time, when used strategically, this public platform affords Arab-Americans the empowering ability to assert complex articulations of Arab as well as US identities that do not comply with hegemonic and militant rule. By showing the continuities in popular struggles against oppression, discrimination, and misrepresentation across the Arab world and the US, Arab-Americans further transform rigid and binary constructs of national identity and create direct links and collations between "over there" and "over here," "us" and "them."

In supporting such revisionist approaches to constructions of Arab and US subjectivities, Arab-Americans are constantly rethinking and reshaping the ways in which dominant knowledge about Arabs is developed and circulated. Such strategies, as enacted by various Arab-American writers and thinkers, highlight the effect that the people's voices resonating in the streets of Tunisia, Egypt, Libya, Syria, Bahrain, and Yemen have on overturning derogatory depictions of Arabs worldwide. In the essay "Rewriting the Story," Randa Jarrar describes how the January 2011 uprising in Egypt has forced the West to rethink stereotypes of Arabs as "savage people that need the iron fist of a decades-long government for their own good; that they don't deserve dignity or freedom because they would squander it; that they are violent and infantile." Adopting and claiming this powerful narrative of revolt enable Arabs and Arab-Americans to reconceive and renarrate their own identities, thus "rewriting the[ir] story" to incorporate the personal as well as the intersecting spheres of the national and the international.

During the revolts in Libya, Khaled Mattawa, poet, translator, and winner of an Academy of American Poets Fellowship, was prominent in his comments on the implications and effects of ousting Libya's longtime dictator, Muammar Qaddafi. Born in Benghazi and forced in 1979 at the age of fourteen to immigrate to the US with his brother, leaving his parents and sisters behind, Mattawa finds in the rebellion against and the toppling of Qaddafi's forty-two-year despotic rule a populist radicalism that holds at its center a precious expression of hope. Linking that collective demand for change to his personal experiences of exile, Mattawa states in an interview, "To witness this change, your sense of despair, which you've tried to push in a corner and ... sort of live your life around, or to walk around it, . . . that roadblock to how you perceive life and perceived it for a long time, is not there anymore" (Mattawa, "Conversation"). Such a perspective exemplifies how the hope compelling people in various Arab countries to take to the streets and to demand change extends to the Arab diaspora, infusing its members with a fresh impetus that pushes them toward new and radical futures within their countries of exile and displacement.

What is made evident by the ecstasy of hope described in Mattawa's poem "Now That We Have Tasted Hope" from this section's epigraph is that that there is no turning back to an oppressive past made bearable by willed forgetfulness and simple survival. With the promising possibilities brought about by a glimmering change, these strategies no longer work as palliatives, for they become part of a "darkness," a "thousand hopeless vistas" that have no place in the speaker's rejuvenated mental and physical terrains. The "I" of the poem, linked to the "we" of a Libyan collective and placed alongside the Libyan-American identity of the poet himself, asserts that the territoriality of hope is not restricted by geographical boundaries.[9] Such Libyan hope draws on and at the same time informs the sister revolutions in Tunisia and Egypt and extends in significant ways into the bounds of exile and loss, rejuvenating them in the process.[10]

As mentioned earlier, these significant popular movements as carried out in various Arab homelands, by enacting landmark shifts in rigid understandings of ancestral home countries and diasporas, render these spaces even more fluid and interconnected. However, these homes and homelands are still informed by a transcontinental geopolitical landscape that is rampant with militarism, oppression, violence, imperialist interventions, and governmental crackdowns. For this reason, rather than fixing the transnational paths between Arab and US homes that have shaped Arab-American belonging in the US from the second half of the twentieth century onward within predictable and well-defined patterns, this book recognizes the messiness and complexity of transnational lives, which, by virtue of being in constant motion, are thus repeatedly being revised and reconfigured. For with the protracted wars in Iraq and Afghanistan, the ongoing War on Terror, the dismal effects of the Israeli occupation in the West Bank and Gaza, as well as the brutal governmental crackdowns in many places in the Arab world that are undergoing or awaiting regime change, new narratives of immigration, exile, and displacement are continuously being scripted and lived. In other words, the perpetual displacements caused by war and conflict across the Arab world repeatedly reconfigure the makeup and outlook of immigrant, exilic, and diasporic identities. These reconfigurations continuously interrogate and undercut stable and exclusive conceptualizations of national belonging, thus pointing, in crucial and transformative ways, to the omissions and gaps in dominant narratives of the nation-state, while at the same time imagining and creating more promising and inclusive landscapes for transnational belongings in the US and elsewhere.

Notes

Introduction

1. The Pen League is a group of writers of Lebanese and Syrian background that was based in New York during the first few decades of the twentieth century. Its members included Gibran Kahlil Gibran, Ameen Rihani, Mikhail Naimy, Elia Abu Madi, Nassib 'Aridah, Nudra Haddad, and Rashid Ayyub.

2. My use of the term *Arab-American* throughout the book is meant to indicate its inclusion of, rather than its equation with, Arab Muslim identities. In this way, the Arab-American label as it is used here encompasses various religious (as well as national and political) affiliations, including Muslim ones.

3. This discourse is informed by nineteenth-century Western attitudes toward Asia and the Middle East as analyzed by Edward Said in his seminal book *Orientalism*. Further critiques of Orientalism are prevalent in Anouar Majid, *Unveiling Traditions*; Ella Shohat and Robert Stam, *Unthinking Eurocentrism*; and Mahmood Mamdani, *Good Muslim, Bad Muslim*.

4. For detailed discussions of such stereotypes, see Amira Jarmakani, Jack Shaheen, and Ronald Stockton.

5. In addition to the pervasive "terrorist" term, such labels now include, for instance, the epithet "sons or daughters of Osama."

6. For a discussion of such affirmations in American TV programs, see Evelyn Alsultany, "The Prime-Time Plight" and *Arabs and Muslims in the Media*.

7. I recognize that the presence of Arabs in the US extends well beyond the citizenship rubric, with the transnational movement of laborers, professionals, students, and even visitors forming other kinds of Arab connections to the US. My focus on Arab-American citizens here is a way to engage in a discussion of how US citizenship in general can be reformulated and reimagined by virtue of the Arab-American presence within the US. Moreover, this focus recognizes but does not directly discuss Arab-American citizens who do not reside in the US.

8. I borrow the term "enemy-alien" from David Cole's book *Enemy Aliens: Double Standards and Constitutional Freedoms in the War on Terrorism*.

9. Other types of citizenship include consumer citizenship (Ann Cronin, *Advertising and Consumer Citizenship*; Inderpal Grewal, *Transnational America*), and sexual citizenship (Nancy Cott, *Public Vows*; Lauren Berlant, *The Queen of America Goes to Washington City*).

10. Even Christian Arabs are often barred from such types of inclusions, given that the terms *Arab* and *Muslim* are predominantly seen to be one and the same in the US national imaginary. The forms of inclusion bestowed by cultural citizenship are only available to those Arab-Americans (both Christians and Muslims) who are able, and willing, to perform racial, political, and religious acts of erasure and passing.

11. Arabs immigrated to the US well before the nineteenth century, but they first started arriving en masse during this period. For accounts of pre-nineteenth-century Arab immigration to the US, see Randa Kayyali, *The Arab Americans*; and Gregory Orfalea, *The Arab Americans*.

12. I discuss some of these laws in chapter 4. See Leti Volpp, "Citizenship Undone," for a discussion of the case of two Pakistani-American men, Muhammad Ismail and his son Jabir Ismail, who were barred from reentering the US despite their US citizenship. See also Moustafa Bayoumi, "Arab America's September 11."

13. One of the earliest uses of the *transnational* term dates back to Randolph Bourne's 1916 essay "Trans-national America." For a discussion of what scholars have referred to as the transnational turn in literary studies and the debates revolving around it, see Shelley Fisher Fishkin; Donald Pease; and Paul Jay.

14. For discussions of the relationship between ethnicity and diaspora in the context of black cultural studies, see Stuart Hall; and Paul Gilroy. See also R. Radhakrishnan for a discussion of the relationship between ethnicity and nationality. For further discussions of transnationalism and diasporic identities, see the work of Khachig Tölölyan; Pnina Werbner; William Safran; Aihwa Ong; James Clifford; Arjun Appadurai; Jana Evans Braziel and Anita Mannur; Avtar Brah; Nina Glick Schiller, Linda G. Basch, and Cristina Szanton Blanc; Akhil Gupta and James Ferguson; and Smadar Lavie and Ted Swedenburg.

15. In Nadine Naber's ethnographic study of Arab-American activism, *Arab America: Gender, Cultural Politics, and Activism*, she posits "the diasporic state of consciousness" that a second generation of Arab-American activists experience as one that reflects "a sense of belonging to a diaspora of empire" (27).

16. Other scholars of Arab-American studies who have discussed the role of transnationalism in the formation of Arab-American identities starting from the first wave of Arab immigration onward include Alixa Naff, Evelyn Shakir, Michael Suleiman, Akram Fouad Khater, and Nadine Naber.

17. See Ella Shohat's "Coming to America" for a discussion of the myriad connections enacted by the immigrant body and for a distinction between what Shohat calls a "single hyphen" and a "chain of hyphens" (292).

18. Many Arab-Americans as well as other Arabs living in the diaspora cannot return to their original homelands because of a variety of political and socioeconomic factors. Palestinians, for instance, are repeatedly turned away at the Tel Aviv airport even when they are citizens of the US or other Western nations.

19. For critiques of celebratory approaches to transnational studies, see Nina Glick Schiller; and Caren Kaplan, "World without Boundaries."

20. Even though there are major differences between the concepts of *home* and *homeland*, I still conceive of them as being closely connected in the way they are often imaginatively articulated in Arab-American cultural production. I do not, however, use them interchangeably, for while I use the term *original homeland* to specifically signal an Arab national affiliation or location, the concept of *home* in the Arab-American context is more fluid, signifying a type of belonging that is shaped by its subjects' associations with both the Arab world and the US.

21. Transnational feminist readings of Middle Eastern, Arab, and Arab-American cultural texts can be found in the work of Ella Shohat, Amal Amireh, Nada Elia, Lisa Majaj, Therese Saliba, Joe Kadi, Mervat Hatem, and Sarah Husain, as well as other feminists whose work is included in Rabab Abdulhadi, Evelyn Alsultany, and Nadine Naber's *Arab and Arab American Feminisms*. Other key anti-imperialist feminist projects include Robin L. Riley, Chandra Talpade Mohanty, and Minnie Bruce Pratt's *Feminism and War*; Cynthia Enloe's *Bananas, Beaches, and Bases*; Sunaina Maira's "'Good' and 'Bad' Muslim Citizens"; and Sunera Thobani's "White Wars.'"

22. I am indebted to the excellent variety of historical, literary, sociopolitical, and ethnographic materials on Arab-Americans by scholars such as Evelyn Shakir, Lisa Suhair Majaj, Michael Suleiman, Gregory Orfalea, Steven Salaita, Carol Bardenstein, Evelyn Alsultany, Waïl Hassan, Layla Al Maleh, and Nadine Naber, to name a few.

23. For a discussion of such erasures, and for suggestions of other representative terms, see Naber, *Arab America*; and Kadi, "Introduction."

24. The member states of the Arab League include Algeria, Bahrain, Comoros, Djibouti, Egypt, Iraq, Jordan, Kuwait, Lebanon, Libya, Mauritania, Morocco, Oman, Palestine, Qatar, Saudi Arabia, Somalia, Sudan, Syria, Tunisia, the United Arab Emirates, and Yemen.

25. The contested nature of the term *Arab* is also evident within the Arab world, as exemplified, for instance, in Lebanon by some Christian groups who regard themselves as being Phoenician rather than Arab in order to distinguish themselves from the Muslim connotations they deem to be embedded in the *Arab* label.

26. For more details on these backgrounds, see Suad Joseph 260.

27. The US Census Bureau classifies US citizens with ancestral links to the Middle East and North Africa as white. According to the decennial 2000 census, there are around 1.25 million Arab-Americans in the US. The Arab American Institute (AAI), however, places that number at around 3.6 million, while others believe it be as high as 4.2 million. For the AAI estimate, see "Quick Facts about Arab Americans," http://www.aaiusa.org/pages/demographics/. See also Anan Ameri; and Gregory Orfalea, *The Arab Americans*.

28. The Six-Day War, also known as the 1967 war or as Al-Naksa (The Setback) resulted in an Arab defeat and Israel's capture of the Gaza Strip and the Sinai from Egypt, the West Bank (including East Jerusalem) from Jordan, and the Golan Heights from Syria. The period after the 1960s in the Arab world is also marked "by the rise of national liberation movements, the defeat of Arab nationalism, the fragmentation of Arab identity, and the increasing militarism of the Israeli state" (Majaj, Sunderman, and Saliba, "Introduction" xix).

29. See Gregory Orfalea's *The Arab Americans* for a more detailed discussion of the various phases of Arab-American immigration. See also Alixa Naff, *Becoming American*; and Michael Suleiman, "Introduction: The Arab Immigrant Experience."

30. This area consists of present-day Lebanon, Syria, Jordan, and Palestine/Israel.

31. In the 1920s, after the fall of the Ottoman Empire, these immigrants adopted the Lebanese label since many of them had emigrated from the Mount Lebanon region (Naff, *Becoming American* 2).

32. These predominantly Lebanese Christian immigrants were mostly of the Maronite, Melkite, and Eastern Orthodox sects, while 5 to 10 percent were Muslims (Naff, *Becoming American* 2).

33. For more detailed discussions of early formations of Arab-American identities, see Shakir, *Bint Arab* (see especially part 1); Suleiman, "Early Arab-Americans"; Kayal and Kayal; Alixa Naff, *Becoming American*; and Philip K. Hitti. Also, for focused analyses of individual Arab immigrant collectives grouped according to their original nationalities, religious affiliations, or the period in which they emigrated, see the edited collections by Sameer Y. Abraham and Nabeel Abraham, and by Ernest McCarus.

34. By the end of the second wave of Arab-American immigration, in the late 1960s, Arab countries had gained independence from their colonial British and French mandates.

35. See Melani McAlister, *Epic Encounters*; and Rashid Khalidi, *Resurrecting Empire*, for detailed depictions of the genealogies and developments of such US imperial ambitions.

36. For more detailed discussions of these organizations and their individual goals, see Gregory Orfalea's chapter "The Political Awakening" in his book *The Arab Americans*; Mervat Hatem, "How the Gulf War Changed the AAUG's Discourse"; Kathleen M. Moore; and Suad Joseph, 265–68.

37. Other, more local organizations include the Arab Community Center for Economic and Social Services (ACCESS), established in Dearborn, Michigan, in 1971. It focuses for the most part on supporting the various cultural aspects of community building, such as the establishment of the Arab American National Museum in Dearborn in 2005. The Arab American Studies Association (AASA) was launched in 2012. An affiliate organization of the Middle East Studies Organization, it is dedicated to the study of Arab-Americans' history, culture, literature, art, music, politics, and religion and other aspects of Arab-American experiences. See also my discussion of the literary organization Radius of Arab American Writers Inc. (RAWI) later in the introduction.

38. For an analysis of the 1929 lynching of Nola Romey, a "Syrian" man living with his family in Lake City, Florida, at the time, see Sarah Gualtieri, "Strange Fruit?"

39. For a more detailed discussion of such naturalization laws, see Helen Hatab Samhan, "Not Quite White" 210–13. For a history of the 1882 Chinese Exclusion Act and the 1924 Asian Exclusion Act, see Ronald Takaki, *Strangers from a Different Shore*.

40. Both Najour and Dow were Christian "Syrian" immigrants. Shahid was a Christian born in Zahle (currently Lebanon). Ahmed Hassan was a Muslim Yemeni, and Mohamed Mohriez was a Muslim born in Sanhy, Badan (in present-day Saudi Arabia). For further discussions of these cases, see Salah Hassan; Suad Joseph; Moustafa Bayoumi, "Racing Religion" 267–70; and Sarah Gualtieri, "Becoming 'White,'" as

well as Gualtieri's book-length study of early Arab-American immigration to the US, *Between Arab and White*.

41. See also Ian Haney-López for a detailed discussion of prerequisite cases.

42. According to the Census Bureau, the white category encompasses people originating in Europe, the Middle East, and North Africa.

43. See Helen Hatab Samhan, "Not Quite White" 215–16, 223–24. This ancestry question is part of what is also referred to as the long form, which in 1990 was distributed to one-sixth of US households (see De la Cruz and Brittingham).

44. See also Michael W. Suleiman, "Introduction: The Arab Immigrant Experience" 15; Therese Saliba, "Resisting Invisibility" 309; and Helen Hatab Samhan, "Not Quite White" 222–23.

45. I thank Randa Kayyali for this information and for her helpful input on the subject of Arab-American racial classification.

46. Majaj borrows this concept of "honorary whiteness" from Joseph Massad, 101, 108; and Soheir Morsy. Such conceptualizations of the social construction of race draw on Franz Fanon's *Black Skin, White Masks* and Homi Bhabha's "Of Mimicry and Man."

47. Helen Hatab Samhan argues in her essay "Politics and Exclusion" that the construction of Arabs as foreign subjects in the US is based primarily on what she calls political racism. According to her, anti-Arab racism is based "not in the traditional motives of structurally excluding a group perceived as inferior, but in politics" (14). I agree with Samhan that politics is a root cause of anti-Arab racism in the US, but there are additional factors at play in the demonization of Arabs in the US, the most important of which is religion, as Islam is perceived to be antithetical to the religious tenets of US identity.

48. For a discussion of how racial and ethnic divisions were reconfigured after 9/11, see Inderpal Grewal, 206–9.

49. For a discussion of Gibran's and Rihani's work, see Waïl Hassan's first two chapters of his book *Immigrant Narratives*. Other discussions about Pen League members such as Rihani and Naimy, especially regarding their experiences in New York City, include an essay by Michael Suleiman, "Impressions of New York City by Early Arab Immigrants" 36–41.

50. Such a transnational perspective is evident, for example, in works such as Gibran Kahlil Gibran's poem "To Young Americans of Syrian Origin" as well as Ameen Rihani's novel *The Book of Khalid*, in which he described the in-betweenness defining Arab immigrant lives.

51. See Sirène Harb; and Evelyn Shakir's essays "Pretending to be Arab" and "Mother's Milk," which focus on the works of Bourjaily, Rihbany, and Rizk.

52. D. H. Melhem, for one, exemplifies such links, with her scholarly work including *Gwendolyn Brooks: Poetry and the Heroic Voice* and *Heroism in the New Black Poetry: Introductions and Interviews*. She was also the first to organize an Arab-American poetry reading at the Modern Language Association conference in 1984 (Abinader, "Children of Al-Mahjar").

53. Some of the earlier writers addressed the struggles and crises pervading their Arab homelands, as exemplified, for instance, by Gibran Kahlil Gibran's poem "Dead Are My People" about the famine in Lebanon during World War I.

54. For a discussion of the role of gender in such early migrations from the Arab world, specifically from the Levant area, see Sarah Gualtieri, "Gendering the Chain Migration Thesis."

55. Often referred to by Israelis as the War of Independence, the 1948 war marks what Palestinians refer to as the Nakba, or the catastrophe. See Lila Abu-Lughod and Ahmad H. Sa'di's introduction to *Nakba*.

56. The publication of Nye's work, however, preceded the 1990s, with *Words under the Words* published in 1980 and *Hugging the Jukebox* and *Yellow Glove* appearing in 1982 and 1986, respectively.

57. Joseph's prior published collections include *Shouting at No One* and *Curriculum Vitae*.

58. Other books published in the 1980s and 1990s include Kathryn K. Abdul-Baki's *Tower of Dreams* (1995), Etel Adnan's *From A to Z* (1982), *The Indian Never Had a Horse and Other Poems* (1985), and *Of Cities and Women: Letters to Fawwaz* (1993), and Khaled Mattawa's *Ismailia Eclipse* (1997), among others. Although Mona Simpson does not strongly identify as an Arab-American writer, she also started publishing during this period, with her critically acclaimed novels *Anywhere but Here* and *A Regular Guy* published in 1986 and 1996, respectively.

59. See Robert Fisk, *Pity the Nation*; and David Hirst, *Beware of Small States*.

60. This anthology was preceded by the booklet titled *Wrapping the Grape Leaves: A Sheaf of Contemporary Arab-American Poets*, edited by Gregory Orfalea and published by the American-Arab Anti-Discrimination Committee in 1982. It features many of the Arab-American poets whose work was later included in *Grape Leaves: A Century of Arab American Poetry*. For further discussions of Arab-American literary history, see Lisa Suhair Majaj, "Two Worlds Emerging"; Evelyn Shakir, "Arab American Literature"; and Tanyss Ludescher.

61. Other key anthologies and collected works include those edited by D. H. Melhem and Leila Diab, *A Different Path: An Anthology of the Radius of Arab American Writers*; Susan Muaddi Darraj, *Scheherazade's Legacy: Arab and Arab American Women on Writing*; and Nathalie Handal, *The Poetry of Arab Women*, which includes the work of many Arab-American poets.

62. The past decade or so has witnessed a noted increase in book publications focusing on Arab America. The participation of Arab-American literary critics in such projects of self-representation is undertaken in a handful of books and edited collections such as Lisa Suhair Majaj and Amal Amireh's *Etel Adnan: Critical Essays on the Arab-American Writer and Artist*; Amal Talaat Abdelrazek's *Contemporary Arab American Women Writers: Hyphenated Identities and Border Crossings*; Steven Salaita's *Arab American Literary Fictions, Cultures, and Politics* and *Modern Arab American Fiction: A Reader's Guide*; Layla Al Maleh's *Arab Voices in Diaspora*; Somaya Sabry's *Arab-American Women's Writing and Performance: Orientalism, Race and the Idea of the Arabian Nights*; and Waïl Hassan's *Immigrant Narratives*. Special issues on Arab-American and Arab-diasporic literatures have been put forth by journals such as *MELUS*, *American Book Review*, and *Studies in the Humanities*.

63. For a thematic engagement with this concept, see Naomi Shihab Nye's poem "Half and Half" (*19 Varieties of Gazelle* 97) and Lisa Suhair Majaj's essay "Boundaries: Arab/American." See also Alice Evans's "Half-and-Half: A Profile of Diana Abu-Jaber."

64. Many important works had to be left out of my analysis for the sake of maintaining a clear and coherent analytical framework. Poetry and fiction by Elmaz Abinader, Nathalie Handal, Fady Joudah, Dima Shehabi, Sharif Elmusa, Katherine Abdul-Baki, Sahar Mustafah, Marian Haddad, Alia Yunis, Evelyn Shakir, Hedy Sabbagh Habra, Iman

Mersal, Hayan Charara, Glenn Shaheen, and Susan Abdulhawa are important for further discussions of transnational formations of Arab-American identities, specifically in the Lebanese and Palestinian contexts. Further analyses of the effects of military conflicts in the Arab world on Arab-American identities should include discussions of the First and Second Gulf Wars, with special reference to the work of Iraqi-American writers such as Sinan Antoon, Dunya Mikhail, Weam Namou, and Deborah Al-Najjar. The effects of military conflicts are also handled in Alicia Erian's novel *Towelhead*, which takes place in the US against the backdrop of the First Gulf War, and Philip Metres's poetry collection *Abu Ghraib Arias*, which captures different voices of Iraqi prisoners and US soldiers taken from reports on the Abu Ghraib prison scandal. Moreover, careful consideration should be given to the Maghrebi perspective, as exemplified by the award-winning works of Khaled Mattawa, Hisham Matar, Laila Lalami, and Djelloul Marbrook.

65. My use of the terms *second-generation* and *third-generation* Arab-Americans specifically refers to children of Arab immigrants who were born or raised in the US from the 1950s and 1960s onward and does not refer to earlier generations of US-born-and-raised Arab-Americans.

66. Throughout the book, I use the term *first generation* in reference to Arab immigrants to the US who become naturalized citizens.

1 / Reimagining the Ancestral Arab Homeland

1. Born in the US to a Palestinian father and an American mother, Majaj grew up partly in Amman, Jordan, and was educated in Lebanon and the US. She has published numerous journal articles and book chapters and coedited several collections on Arab and Arab-American writing. Her book of poetry *Geographies of Light* was published in 2009.

2. While this chapter focuses on discursive reconceptualizations of an Arab homeland from the diasporic vantage point of second- and third-generation Arab-American writers and their characters, chapter 2 explores representations of physical returns to these homelands of origin.

3. As I point out in the introduction, my use of the terms *second-generation* and *third-generation Arab-Americans* specifically refers to children of Arab immigrants who were born or raised in the US from the 1950s and 1960s onward and does not refer to earlier generations of US-born-and-raised Arab-Americans.

4. The designation of *older immigrant generation* specifically refers to those who arrived during the first and second waves of immigration to the US between the late nineteenth century and the mid-twentieth century.

5. Nostalgic depictions of Arab homelands are not only limited to the early waves of Arab immigration to the US. They are still alive and rampant among many new immigrants. The antinostalgic ruminations of contemporary Arab immigrants to the US are discussed in chapter 3.

6. Even though most of the works discussed in this chapter were published from the 1990s onward, the historical and political references included in these texts assert the impact of the civil rights movement in the US and the changing political climate in the Arab world following the 1967 Arab-Israeli war.

7. Such a "split vision" suggests obvious connections to W. E. B. Du Bois's concept of "double-consciousness," as he describes it in *The Souls of Black Folk* (45). This sense

of doubleness is evident in articulations of Arab-American identity, pointing to a strong link between various minority positionalities within the US. A close comparative analysis of such links lies beyond the purview of this study.

8. For a detailed discussion of earlier generations' assimilative tendencies, see Evelyn Shakir, *Bint Arab* 13–76.

9. Minnie Bruce Pratt calls this type of homelessness "feeling homesick with nowhere to go" (24). For further feminist and postcolonial interrogations of the concept of home, see Rosemary Marangoly George; Caren Kaplan, "Deterritorializations"; Bernice Johnson Reagon; Carol Haddad; and Bookda Gheisar.

10. Marianne Hirsch defines this type of inherited memory as "postmemory." In her analysis of postmemory, she focuses on how children of Holocaust survivors access the past through their parents' memories. These memories in turn shape the younger generation's present in very specific and formative ways. See Hirsch's *Family Frames* and *The Generation of Postmemory*.

11. The term "presence of absence" in the title of this section is used by Roberta Rubenstein to describe an "absence that continues to occupy a palpable emotional space" (5). As I argue in this section, the presence of the absent homeland permeating the texts discussed in this chapter takes on physical as well as emotional space in the lives of Arab-Americans. I also borrow this term from *In the Presence of Absence*, the English title of Mahmoud Darwish's poetry collection *Fi Hadrat al-Ghiyab*, translated by Sinan Antoun.

12. Lawrence Joseph was born in Detroit in 1948 and attended the University of Michigan for his BA and JD degrees. A professor of law at St. John's University School of Law, Joseph is the author of several books of poetry, including *Into It*, *Shouting at No One*, *Curriculum Vitae*, and *Before Our Eyes*, as well as the collection *Codes, Precepts, Biases, and Taboos: Poems 1973–1993*. He is also the author of *Lawyerland* (1997), a book of prose. Even though the poem "Sand Nigger" appeared in *Curriculum Vitae*, which was published in 1988, I still include it here due to its central place in Arab-American literature as well as its portrayal of various versions of an Arab homeland pervading the speaker's domestic US home.

13. See Carol Bardenstein, "Threads of Memory," for an interesting discussion of the ascendency of certain memories over others in the context of Palestinian memory-sites and memory-objects.

14. I am influenced in my analysis of immigrants' nostalgia by Svetlana Boym, *The Future of Nostalgia*.

15. In thinking through Arab-Americans' everyday expressions of generational connections and disconnections to an original Arab homeland, I draw on Michel de Certeau's *The Practice of Everyday Life* (1984).

16. Saliba is a professor of Third World feminist studies at Evergreen State College, Washington, and former Fulbright scholar in Palestine (1995–96). She is coeditor of two collections, *Gender, Politics, and Islam* (2002) and *Intersections: Gender, Nation, and Community in Arab Women's Novels* (2002), and has published various essays on Arab-Americans, feminism, and gender.

17. Green-eyed and light-skinned, Saliba's grandmother is described in her US naturalization papers as being "brown, dark brown even," by which foreignness (indicated by "darkness") is inscribed and even imposed on the immigrant body by a

majority whose myopia demands and serves to develop what Saliba calls a "monochromatic vision" ("Sittee" 8).

18. Hammad is a Palestinian-American poet, author, and political activist born in Amman, Jordan, in 1973 to Palestinian refugee parents. She immigrated with her family to Brooklyn at the age of five. She is the winner of numerous awards and is an original cast member and writer for *Russell Simmons Presents Def Poetry Jam* on Broadway. Her books of poetry include *Born Palestinian, Born Black*, *Zaatar Diva*, and *breaking poems*.

19. For a detailed discussion of the significance of national symbols such as trees, the Jaffa orange, and prickly-pear cactus in Palestinian and Israeli narratives, see Bardenstein, "Threads of Memory"; and Juliane Hammer.

20. Moreover, the alliterative repetition of the letter *p* (which does not exist in the Arabic alphabet) at the beginning of every word in this line does not make easy reading, encompassing the Arab-speaking exile's cumbersome navigation of a foreign language.

21. A prominent figure in Arab-American literature, Nye was born in St. Louis, Missouri, in 1952 to a Palestinian father and an American mother. A prolific writer, her works include several books of poetry such as *Words under the Words* (1980), *Red Suitcase* (1994), *Fuel* (1998), and *You and Yours* (2005), as well as a young-adult novel, *Habibi* (1997), and a book of nonfiction, *Never in a Hurry: Essays on People and Places* (1996).

22. I read the line "a world that was always his own" as an articulation of the Palestine that he had woven in his imagination from within his exilic location.

23. These gender roles are shaped by Arab- as well as Western-based patriarchal social and cultural constructs.

24. Arab-American literary texts are replete with grandmothers characterized by a willful, playful, and commanding presence within both the familial and public US space. From "Situe-bitue" in Frances Khirallah Noble's *The Situe Stories* and *The New Belly Dancer of the Galaxy* to the domineering Nazera in Gregory Orfalea's book of essay memoirs *Angeleno Days* and the indignant Syrian grandmother in Mohja Kahf's poem "My Grandmother Washes Her Feet in the Sink at Sears," as well as the trailblazing duo grandmothers in Evelyn Shakir's *Bint Arab*, there is much evidence that the grandmother figure in contemporary Arab-American literary texts is far from being a docile one. This pervasive grandmother figure, however, is not always physically present in the US. While several of the grandmothers portrayed in the texts discussed here are immigrants, others remain in the Arab world.

25. An example of performing this type of body memory is Kadi's grandmother making *laban* (yogurt) without the need for a recipe or a measuring cup (Kadi, "Five Steps" 233). Other Arab-American texts that exemplify the centrality of the grandmother's visceral type of "body memory" include Susan Muaddi Darraj's *The Inheritance of Exile: Stories from South Philly*, in which one of the main characters, Nadia, remembers how her "Siti's hands smelled salty, like the brine of the grape leaves she was eternally stuffing and rolling at the kitchen table while listening to her tapes of Om Kulthoum in concert" (4). Other similar memories are captured in the two pieces "Tata Olga's Hands" and "The Words under the Words" by Majaj and Nye, respectively.

26. Kadi is a writer, cultural critic, poet, musician, and activist who focuses on working-class, feminist, and ethnic concerns. Of Lebanese heritage, Kadi was born and raised in Oshawa, Canada, and has worked closely with Arab communities in Canada and the US. Essays and short fiction by Kadi have appeared in collections such as *Working Class Women in the Academy: Laborers in the Knowledge Factory* (1993) and Nathalie Handal's *The Poetry of Arab Women*.

27. For a detailed analysis of Kadi's introduction, as well as the introductions of two other anthologies, *Grape Leaves: A Century of Arab-American Poetry* (Orfalea and Elmusa) and *Post-Gibran: Anthology of New Arab American Writing* (Mattawa and Akash), see Michelle Hartman.

28. A third-generation Lebanese-American, Williams is the author of two poetry collections, *Traveling Mercies* and *Far Sides of the Only World*. His work has appeared in many journals and anthologies.

29. Born in Brooklyn to Lebanese immigrants, Melhem is the author of eight books of poetry, including *Notes on 94th Street* and *Art and Politics: Politics and Art*. She is also the coeditor of the anthology *A Different Path* and the author of several novels including *Blight*

30. Even though Kadi states that her grandmother carried a *dirbakeh* with her on the long journey to the US, she does not explicitly state that her grandmother actually played it. Even if she never did play it, I read the grandmother's determination to bring the *dirbakeh* with her to the US as an indication of her subscribing to a broader conception of cultural heritage that goes beyond strictly conceived gender roles.

31. Although less central than the grandmother and father figures, the mother also has a strong presence in literary works by contemporary Arab-American writers, including Hayan Charara's two books of poetry, *The Alchemist's Diary* and *The Sadness of Others*, Susan Muaddi Darraj's *The Inheritance of Exile*, Elmaz Abinader's *Children of the Roojme*, Laila Halaby's *West of the Jordan*, and Evelyn Shakir's *Bint Arab* (1997). A detailed discussion of this parental figure lies outside the scope of my analysis here.

32. Both writers were born to Arab fathers (Palestinian in the case of Nye and Jordanian in the case of Abu-Jaber) and American mothers, which partly explains their focus on the father figure in their negotiations of an Arab homeland. However, such a focus is not merely evident in "half and half" writers (Evans 38) but is also featured in writers whose parents are both Arab, as evident in Suheir Hammad's poems "Daddy's Song" and "Argela Remembrance," the latter of which was discussed in the previous section.

33. For a focused analysis of the representation of the father figure in other exilic Anglophone narratives, see Syrine C. Hout, "Of Fathers and the Fatherland."

34. In addition to the works discussed in this section, Abu-Jaber's fiction includes the more recent novels *Origin* and *Birds of Paradise*.

35. Even though both Hanif's and Sirine's uncles are Iraqis living in the US, their status differs one from the other since the former was coerced to leave Iraq, fleeing Saddam Hussein's regime, while the latter had immigrated as a young man to the US with his brother (Sirine's father) in pursuit of adventures and new experiences.

36. The name of the university is never mentioned in the text of the novel. However, in an interview with Andrea Shalal-Esa, Abu-Jaber names the university as being UCLA, where she taught a class in Middle Eastern culture in 1995 (Abu-Jaber, "The Only Response" 5).

37. It is worth noting here that such a past is also passed on to Sirine by her uncle's memories and intricate storytelling. For a discussion of the uncle's stories, see Nouri Gana; and Waïl Hassan, "A Thousand and One Recipes."

38. For further analysis of Abu-Jaber's *Crescent* and its depiction of what I describe as "interethnic bridges" connecting the novel's Arab-American characters to other displaced ethnic minorities, see my essay "Arab-American Literature in the Ethnic Borderland." See also Brinda Mehta; Amal Talaat Abdelrazek; and Lorraine Mercer.

39. Even though Bud's preparation of Arabic dishes by way of his fragmented and selective memory of home dominates the memoir, Abu-Jaber includes a section describing the period that she spent as a young girl with her family in Jordan and the food to which she was exposed there. She also includes recipes for the "American" comfort food her mother and grandmother used to prepare for her as a kid.

40. The production and consumption of Middle Eastern food can still reify or perpetuate apolitical and exoticized formulations of the Arab world on the part of uncritical consumers. We see such attitudes in *Language*, for instance, in Sister John's exuberant reaction to what she regards as "Food from the Holy Land" (26).

41. For an interesting analysis of the exiles' transmission of culinary knowledge and the relationship between memory, gender, food, and exile in cookbook-memoirs, see Carol Bardenstein, "Transmissions Interrupted." See specifically her analysis of Aziz Shihab's memoir *A Taste of Palestine* (1993) (Shihab being the same father figure in Nye's poem "My Father and the Figtree").

42. Despite the revisionary type of memory that both Fatima and Aunt Aya exhibit, there exists a vast difference between these two characters. Fatima, unlike Aunt Aya and despite her traumatic memories of home, still subscribes to the patriarchal order by insisting that her nieces should get married (preferably to their Arab cousins) and have children. For a more in-depth discussion of Fatima's character and the concept of gendered memory in *Arabian Jazz*, see Steven Salaita, "Sand Niggers"; Salwa Essayah Chérif; and Gómez-Vega.

43. Lisa Majaj states in her essay "Arab American Literature and the Politics of Memory" that "to remember the utopian organicism of . . . [the homeland] is to remember only part of the story" (278). In this important essay, Majaj discusses several texts by second-generation Arab-American writers not included in my discussion here, such as Sam Hamod, Eugene Paul Nassar, and Vance Bourjaily.

44. Others have addressed such representations, with Ella Shohat stating that Arabs in the US are perceived as "forever foreign" ("Gendered Cartographies of Knowledge" 6). See also Steven Salaita, "Beyond Orientalism and Islamophobia."

45. Even though writers featured in this chapter, such as Joseph Geha, Mohja Kahf, and Suheir Hammad, were born in the Arab world and immigrated to the US with their parents as young children, I still define their perspective as one representing second-generation Arab-Americans, given that their coming-of-age period occurred in the US and their exposure to an Arab homeland was mainly funneled through their parents and grandparents, as well as their immigrant milieux. These writers, caught between the first and second generation of immigrants, are often referred to as the 1.5 generation (see Peggy Levitt and Mary C. Waters, *The Changing Face of Home*).

46. Autobiographical essays that exemplify such outlooks among an earlier generation include Alixa Naff's "Growing Up in Detroit," which portrays the author's account of growing up in a Lebanese household in Detroit, where she lived with her

parents and siblings between 1930 and 1950 (107). See also sociologist Nabeel Abraham's essay "To Palestine and Back."

47. Such revisionary assertions are obviously not shared by all Arab immigrants and diasporics. Some Arab-Americans retain a view that assimilation is their path to success in the US, while others maintain a more critical, antiassimilative stance.

48. Geha was born in Lebanon and immigrated with his parents to the US in 1946. His work, published widely in journals and anthologies, has been awarded a Pushcart Prize and a National Endowment for the Arts Award. His first novel, *Lebanese Blonde*, was published in 2012.

49. For further analysis of Geha's collection, see Steven Salaita's essay "Sand Niggers, Small Shops, and Uncle Sam."

50. See the introduction for a more detailed discussion of Arab-Americans' white categorization by the US Census, an anomalous categorization that has been a source of contention among various Arab-American groups.

51. I borrow the term "bleaching" from Nada Elia's essay "The 'White' Sheep of the Family: But *Bleaching* Is Like Starvation," in which she challenges the invisibility plaguing Arab-Americans, one that she views as even being imposed by other women of color.

52. The name of the city, however, is not explicitly stated in the second half of the poem.

53. In addition to Charara's two books of poetry, *The Alchemist's Diary* and *The Sadness of Others*, he (b. 1972) is the editor of *Inclined to Speak: An Anthology of Contemporary Arab American Poetry*.

54. Abinader was born in Pennsylvania in 1954 to Lebanese parents, and she has traveled widely in the Arab world as an adult. Her other works include the nonfiction book *Children of the Roojme* (1991), the poetry collection *In the Country of My Dreams* (1999), and plays such as *Country of Origin* (1997) and *Under the Ramadan Moon* (2000).

55. Abinader records these stories in *Children of the Roojme*, which is divided into separate sections relating the stories of her grandmother, mother, father, and grandfather. In doing so, she underscores the transnational and gendered aspects of immigration, travel, and displacement.

56. In chapter 4, which focuses on Arab-American identity formations post-9/11, I discuss in more detail the processes by which religion (specifically here Islam) is racialized in discussions of US national belonging, and the counternarratives that address such racializations after 9/11.

57. I realize here that the parameters of Muslim-American identities are much wider than the Arab-American context framing my discussion of Kahf's work. I primarily read Kahf's poetry as an expression of Arab Muslim-American experiences, thus focusing on Muslim Arab-Americans as a subgroup of the Arab-American community. Kahf's other works include critical texts such as *Western Representations of the Muslim Woman* and her novel *The Girl in the Tangerine Scarf*, which I discuss in chapter 2.

58. This highly misinterpreted song is often played during right-wing political rallies and demonstrations to articulate US patriotism. Such a use is highly ironic considering that aside from the celebratory refrain, the song's lyrics portray a rather dark

and far-from-ideal Vietnam-era America. I thank Mike Goode for pointing out the relevance of the song's lyrics.

59. I thank Susan Muaddi Darraj for reminding me of the significance of Springsteen's background in the poem's context.

60. Originally established in 1932 as the Muhammad University of Islam in Detroit, Michigan, by Nation of Islam leader Elijah Mohammed, it was renamed in the 1970s by his son W. D. Mohammed as the Sister Clara Muhammad School in honor of his mother, Clara Mohammed (Mohammed Schools of Atlanta).

61. The distinction between the way I use "space" versus "place" here is that "space" is used to indicate a more ideological inclusion of Otherness, whereas "place" points to physical enactments of such inclusions, such as the prevalence of mosques, prayer rooms, etc.

62. Such policies include providing strong political and material support to Israel (which receives more aid from the US than any other country in the world), establishing permanent US army bases in various Arab countries, supporting one Arab regime against another (as in the case of the Iran-Iraq war, during which the US provided Saddam Hussein with arms to fight against Iran), and invading and occupying Iraq.

63. Muaddi Darraj herself was born in the US in 1975 to immigrant Palestinian parents, both of whom arrived in the US in 1967. Her fiction and nonfiction have appeared in several journals and anthologies, and she is the editor of *Scheherazade's Legacy* (2004).

64. UNRWA stands for the United Nations Relief and Works Agency for Palestine Refugees in the Near East, which provides assistance, protection, and advocacy for around five million registered Palestinian refugees in Jordan, Lebanon, Syria, and the occupied Palestinian territories.

65. Orfalea has written widely and prolifically on Arab-American literature and culture, with his groundbreaking coedited anthology *Grape Leaves* (1988) being the first of its kind, followed by an updated edition in 2000. Orfalea, whose grandparents immigrated from Lebanon and Syria in the early 1900s, is the author of *The Arab Americans* (2006), the book of poetry *Capital of Solitude* (1988), the collection of memoir essays *Angeleno Days* (2009), and the collection of short stories *The Man Who Guarded the Bomb* (2010).

2 / To the Arab Homeland and Back

1. For an in-depth discussion of Bourjaily's book, see Evelyn Shakir, "Pretending to Be Arab."

2. Nicholas Van Hear refers to the process of permanent returns that reestablish diasporic individuals or groups back in their original countries as "de-diasporization" (48). I am not suggesting a theory of de-diasporization as much as one that encourages a constant reassessment of Arab and US national landscapes on the basis of an Arab-American mode of belonging to both terrains and cultures simultaneously.

3. I draw here on the theoretical framework presented in the introduction to the edited collection *Uprootings/Regroundings: Questions of Home and Migration* to outline "new ways of inhabiting bodies and worlds" (Ahmed et al. 12).

4. See chapter 1 for an analysis of the ways in which this female role within the domestic space is developed and challenged in a selection of Arab-American literary texts.

5. Of course, there are other instances beyond the Palestinian case in which a return to an original or ancestral homeland is unfeasible or impossible, as in the case of asylum seekers from countries such as Iraq, as well as dissident exiles from countries governed for a long time by dictatorial regimes.

6. The phrase "reimagining the umma" is taken from the title of Peter Mandaville's book *Transnational Muslim Politics: Reimagining the Umma*.

7. Even though there are clear autobiographical resonances with Kahf's own life, this book is not presented as a memoir.

8. The word *mattawa*, which means "volunteer" in Arabic, is used to refer to members of the religious police in Saudi Arabia who enforce the Sharia law as outlined by the Saudi government.

9. Even though Khadra refers to Téta as grandmother, she is actually Khadra's father's aunt rather than his mother.

10. For a description of the Arab homeland's figurative memory of its exiled and immigrant subjects, see Kahf's poem "The Cherries" (*E-mails* 11–14). See also Samaa Abdurraqib for a discussion of the poetic representations of the homeland in Kahf's work.

11. The Baathist regime came to power in Syria in 1963, with Hafez Al-Assad becoming president in 1971 until his death in 2000. His rule is well-known for its oppressive crackdowns and persecution of religious and political dissidents, particularly those opposing the Alawite's unmitigated power in government. In the novel, Khadra's parents stand in for such opposition.

12. It is important to point out that the way Khadra constitutes Jews such as the Damascene rabbi within an "us versus them" construct is not simply internal to her own configurations. Her approach is informed by a larger political framework of structural forces and historical conflicts that shape such ideas of inclusion and exclusion. Such conflicts extend, for instance, to the establishment of Israel in 1948 and the Six-Day War of 1967, instrumental moments in the casting of Jewish identity, regardless of national affiliation, outside the boundaries of Arab homelands.

13. I borrow the term "soul-sickness" from Diana Abu-Jaber, who uses it in her memoir *The Language of Baklava* to describe the disorientation and culture shock she experiences when she returns to the US after a year-long stay in Jordan, her father's homeland (317).

14. For a comparative study of Kahf's *The Girl in the Tangerine Scarf* and other narratives about Muslim women written from the diasporic perspective, such as Azar Nafisi's *Reading Lolita in Tehran* (2003), see Ruzy Suliza Hashim and Nor Faridah Abdul Manaf. For a critique of Muslim-American texts by Kahf, Daniel Abdal-Hayy Moore, and Agha Shahid Ali, see Khaled Mattawa, "Writing Islam in Contemporary American Poetry."

15. Such conceptualizations of home are similar to what André Aciman describes as a "diaspora of memory" (qtd. in Boym 258).

16. Serageldin, born and raised in Egypt, immigrated to the US in 1980. Her other books include the collection of short stories *Love Is Like Water and Other Stories* (2009) and the novel *The Naqib's Daughter* (2010).

17. As the second president of Egypt after the monarchy was overthrown in 1952, Nasser introduced socialist reform, which disengaged land ownership from the hands of a limited few and nationalized key corporations for the purpose of wealth distribution.

18. In addition to the temporal split in Cairo's representation (between the past and the present), the novel also shows the spatial and social multiplicity of Cairene life.

19. In Gigi's case, this temporal return reflects her own experience of the past. But in other narratives, such as *The Girl in the Tangerine Scarf*, the protagonist's return familiarizes her with the past experiences of close family members such as those of her mother.

20. As Svetlana Boym suggests, "locale is not merely a context but also a remembered sensation and the material debris of past life" (258).

21. Nubians are an ethnic group originating in the south of Egypt and north of Sudan.

22. To further examine the relevance of class privilege in *The Cairo House*, see Mona Mikhail's review of the novel.

23. This difference becomes obvious in the novel's first chapter, when, upon arriving at the airport in Cairo, Gigi is asked by the passport-control officer if she has a visa to enter the country. Noting his surprise when she tells him that she is Egyptian, she acknowledges, "perhaps I do not look typically Egyptian" (5).

24. Gigi's return visit that dominates the narrative of *The Cairo House*, particularly the novel's last section, is not her first return to Egypt since her departure in the early 1980s, for she had previously returned for a short time to attend her mother's funeral.

25. Kaldas's other works include a book of poetry, *Egyptian Compass* (2006), and a collection of short stories, *The Time between Places* (2010). She also coedited with Khaled Mattawa *Dinarzad's Children: An Anthology of Contemporary Arab American Fiction* (2009).

26. These mandatory roles of translator and/or negotiator are being increasingly assigned to Arab women (especially those living in the diaspora). Such a role is especially significant given the problematic and even sexist assumption that women are nonthreatening actors in the international political arena. See Nada Elia, "Islamophobia and the 'Privileging' of Arab American Women," for a more detailed analysis of the positioning of Arab and Muslim women as cultural translators.

27. The effects of the recent regime changes in some of these Arab countries are discussed in the conclusion.

28. While some Palestinians are able to return from the diaspora to live permanently in the West Bank and Gaza (see Cainkar, "Managing Identities"), those hailing originally from the towns and villages that currently fall within the 1948 borders of the Israeli state are barred from permanent returns.

29. This line is from Mahmoud Darwish's poem "The Earth Is Closing on Us," included in his book *Victims of a Map* (1984).

30. The choice of the Arabic name Aliyah (and its specific spelling in the narrative) is noteworthy given that in Hebrew, the term *aliyah* signifies the Jewish return to Israel as embodied in the country's Law of Return. This law grants any Jew outside Israel the right to settle in Israel and to become a citizen. The choice of the name Aliyah becomes particularly ironic given that most Palestinians are barred from returning to historical Palestine.

31. An example of this problematic and erroneous link is the salient assumption in the US that all Arabs are Muslim and all Muslims are Arab.

32. As Lisa Majaj notes in her essay "On Writing and Return," critical places such as East Jerusalem, for one, are undergoing what she describes as "'ethnic cleansing,' in

an attempt to decrease the number of Palestinians in East Jerusalem and increase the number of Israeli Jews" (125n. 5). For further information on the use of the term *ethnic cleansing* in a Palestinian context, see Ilan Pappé, *The Ethnic Cleansing of Palestine* (2006).

33. This right is enshrined in the UN General Assembly Resolution 194, passed on December 11, 1948.

34. This ability to cross into Israel is of course not available to the over four million Palestinians living in refugee camps in places like Lebanon, Jordan, and Syria, as well as within the West Bank and Gaza. Moreover, a US passport does not always guarantee entry into Israel or the West Bank, as more and more Arab-Americans and specifically Palestinian-Americans have been scrutinized, humiliated, and turned away at the Israeli border. See Randa Jarrar's account of her experience at the Ben Gurion Airport in her piece "Imagining Myself in Palestine," published in *Guernica* on May 14, 2012.

35. Some writers whose work delves into thematic Palestinian returns include Mahmoud Darwish, Ghada Karmi, Mourid Barghouti, Aziz Shihab, Fawwaz Turki, Edward Said, and Lila Abu-Lughod. Abu-Lughod writes about her father, Ibrahim Abu-Lughod, and his final return to and burial in Jaffa ("Return to Half-Ruins" and "My Father's Return").

36. Aside from Muaddi Darraj's *Inheritance of Exile* discussed in this section, other texts depicting a woman's return to an ancestral Palestinian homeland include nonfictional accounts such as Lisa Majaj's "Journeys to Jerusalem," Muaddi Darraj's "My West Bank Education: 1998," and Najla Said's autobiographical one-woman play *Palestine* (about her visit to Palestine in 1992 with her father, Edward Said). Fiction by other Palestinian-American female writers that incorporates the theme of return includes Susan Abdulhawa's novel *Mornings in Jenin* (2010) and Naomi Shihab Nye's young-adult novel *Habibi* (1997).

37. Films that feature a return to the Palestinian homeland from a male perspective include Elia Abu Sleiman's *Chronicle of a Disappearance* (1996), as well as Hazim Bitar's *Jerusalem's High Cost of Living* (2001) and Kassem Hawal's groundbreaking *Return to Haifa* (1981), which is based on a novel by the Palestinian writer Ghassan Kanafani.

38. Annemarie Jacir is the cofounder of Philistine Films, a production company invested in promoting films from the Arab world and Iran, as well as cofounder of the Dreams of a Nation project, which focuses on supporting Palestinian cinema and creating a database for Palestinian films and filmmakers. In 2004, Jacir was named one of the "25 New Faces of Independent Cinema" by *Filmmaker* magazine. Her other work includes the short film *Like Twenty Impossibles* (2003) and *The Satellite Shooters* (2001). Born to Palestinian parents in 1974, Jacir was raised in Saudi Arabia and moved to the US at the age of sixteen. She attended film school at Columbia University and has taught at Bethlehem University, Birzeit University, Columbia University, and in refugee camps in Palestine, Lebanon, and Jordan.

39. We learn that despite the fact that Emad has been granted a scholarship to study in Canada, he is still denied a visa four times in a row.

40. One of the very few things we glean from Soraya's discussion of her life in the US is that she worked as a waitress at a restaurant.

41. For an incisive critique of the film's characters and what the writers describe as these characters' archetypal qualities, see Naira Antoun and Mohanad Yaquibi.

42. See Lena Jayyusi's essay "Iterability, Cumulativity, and Presence," in which she describes the centrality of *"lived geographies"* in Palestinian memory.

43. Such traces include a plaque dating to 1926 and commemorating an official event in the city presided by its Palestinian mayor and other dignitaries, as well as a shot of a gated villa with stained glasswork, on which is written the name of the villa in Arabic and the year in which it was built.

44. It is these material objects of the past that render "lived geographies" different from the "imaginative geographies" critiqued by Edward Said, which I discuss in some detail in chapter 3.

45. Emily Jacir's work spans a diverse range of media and strategies including film, photography, social interventions, installation, performance, video, writing, and sound. Jacir has shown her work extensively throughout Europe, the Americas, and the Middle East since 1994. Her awards include a Golden Lion at the 52nd Venice Biennale (2007), a Prince Claus Award from the Prince Claus Fund in The Hague (2007), the Hugo Boss Prize at the Guggenheim Museum (2008), and the Alpert Award from the Herb Alpert Foundation (2011). She has been a professor at the vanguard International Academy of Art Palestine since it opened in 2006 and served on its Academic Board from 2006 to 2012. Jacir led the first year of the Home Workspace Program in Beirut and created its curriculum and programming (2011–12).

46. As T. J. Demos points out, such a project not only reveals the desire of Palestinian exiles for family, home, and land, but it also exposes the "artist's [own] desires: to somehow provide connections through an artistic mediation that would draw together a diasporic community, that would shed light on the absurdity of displacement, that would show the privations exiles suffer over things that most of us take for granted" (70).

47. In 2003, the Israeli Parliament passed a law that prohibits Palestinians who marry Israelis from acquiring Israeli citizenship or residency. This has resulted in perpetuating the boundaries between Palestinians in the West Bank and Gaza on the one hand and Palestinians within Israel on the other hand.

48. The reference to house keys is not merely included for comedic effect, for many Palestinians, especially those who experienced dispossession and exile firsthand, still carry the keys to their homes in Palestine as well as the deeds and titles that indicate their ownership of the houses and land that they were forced to leave.

3 / Translocal Connections between the US and the Arab World

1. The Lebanese civil war incorporated national, regional, and international aspects throughout its different phases. Around one hundred thousand people died during the war, and an estimated one hundred thousand were injured, in addition to around a million who were displaced. For a history of Lebanon and its fifteen-year war, see Fawwaz Traboulsi, *A History of Modern Lebanon*; Kamal Salibi, *A House of Many Mansions: The History of Lebanon Reconsidered*; and Robert Fisk, *Pity the Nation*.

2. Chapter 2, however, does include the story of Gigi (the protagonist in *The Cairo House*), who was born and raised in Egypt. The analysis of her story within the context of the second chapter is based on the fact that the narrative includes an important focus on her return to Egypt.

3. In developing this concept of translocality, I draw on Peter Mandaville, *Transnational Muslim Politics*. Whereas Mandeville discusses the translocal primarily in the

context of political studies and international relations, I use the concept to explore its role and impact in Arab-American literary production. See pages 98 and 106–7 for a discussion of translocal spaces and identities.

4. As Edward Said states in *Culture and Imperialism*, to study things contrapuntally is to "be able to think through and interpret together experiences that are discrepant, each with its particular agenda and pace of development, its own internal formations, its internal coherence and system of external relationships, all of them coexisting and interacting with others" (36).

5. This type of consciousness is similar to the altered consciousness developed through the journeys of return and rearrival discussed in chapter 2, as well as the antinostalgic perspective discussed in chapter 1.

6. It is important to note that most of the discursive viewpoints analyzed in this chapter emanate from a privileged position, whether this privilege is informed by class, education, gender, or dual citizenship.

7. See the introduction for a brief discussion of the distinction between legal citizenship and cultural citizenship.

8. In the article "Between Memory and History: Les Lieux de Mémoire," Pierre Nora emphasizes the spatial and material dimension of memory, stating that "memory takes root in the concrete, in spaces, gestures, images and objects" (7).

9. Official acknowledgment of such histories in the US is often limited to the loss of US troops, acknowledgment that itself is limited and heavily censored.

10. For a discussion of the ways in which fiction by writers of Lebanese descent has shaped Lebanese national memory and identity, see Syrine Hout, *Post-war Anglophone Lebanese Fiction*.

11. As Syrine Hout points out in her essay "Revisiting Lebanon," there are some obvious similarities between the fictional character and her creator. Ward's father was also a professor at AUB (although he taught archeology), and her mother was a Lebanese of Armenian and Danish heritage. For further autobiographical connections, see Elise Salem's and Amira Pierce's reviews of the novel. See also Wendy Wolters for further analytical discussion of the novel; and Steven Salaita, *Modern Arab American Fiction* 27–31.

12. The role of Arab-American literary and cultural production in revising narratives about trauma resulting from political events within the sphere of the US (as in the case of 9/11) is discussed in chapter 4.

13. In fact, the post-Lebanese-civil-war era has been marked by the flagrant absence of public commemorations of the war, with this period being ostensibly characterized by a collective social amnesia vis-à-vis all civil-war referents. For a discussion of the ways in which artistic and cultural production challenges such amnesia, see Sune Haugbolle, "Public and Private Memory" and *War and Memory in Lebanon*. The investigation of such Lebanese forms of cultural production used to counter collective war amnesia lies outside the purview of this study.

14. The narrative, however, is far from evoking simplistic and nostalgic evocations of home. For other than the pure air of the mountains, Marianna's sharp spatial memories of Beirut's urban life do not leave out "the air of filthy streets and clackety-clack of chestnut vendors, beeping cars, old horse clopping misery under a whip, . . . things burned up and swept into garbage bags, heaved to the side of the road," all of which she describes as "missing" from her unfamiliar US surroundings (92).

15. In fact, the sisters take on opposite roles throughout the novel. In Lebanon, Marianna watches over her sister, Alaine, who exhibits clear signs of mental trauma and tries to commit suicide. In the US, it is Marianna who sinks into depression while Alaine takes on a positive outlook on the family's new beginnings.

16. Creating this co-conspirator is extremely important given that Marianna has very little contact in the US with people outside her immediate family. At one point in the narrative, Marianna, hospitalized after her suicide attempt, tries to connect with an Israeli nurse. This connection fails, however, when he does not respond to her question about whether he had participated in the 1982 Israeli invasion of Lebanon.

17. For a full discussion of how the image of "the stranger" is constructed in Western discourse of self and nation, see Sara Ahmed et al.

18. In the Arabian epic *Kitab Qissat al-Muqaddam Ali Al-Zaibaq*, Saisaban is portrayed as a jinn princess (see M. C. Lyons 2–16). More interestingly, Saisaban is the name of a plant that "has been introduced into Iraq and planted for windbreaks. The seeds are sold in bazaars throughout India and Iran. . . . The Hindus have a superstition that sight of the seeds will remove the pain of scorpion stings. They are used medicinally on account of their astringent properties. The seeds are beaten into a paste which is applied locally to cure eruptions" (Hooper 171).

19. Haas (Haseeb) Mroue was born in Lebanon in 1965 to Lebanese parents and after high school moved permanently to the US. He passed away in Beirut on October 6, 2007, at the age of forty-one, after suffering from a heart attack. *Beirut Seizures* was written during his MFA residency at the University of Colorado–Boulder.

20. The US space might also be conceived of as one in which different factions that took part in the Lebanese civil war can connect and come together in ways that might not be easily accessible given the continued geographical segmentation of Lebanese areas according to religious backgrounds.

21. Born in Jordan to Lebanese parents, having lived in Kuwait, Lebanon, England, and the US, and currently living between Beirut and San Francisco, Alameddine himself represents this model of transnational and translocal identification that he succeeds so well in portraying in *I, the Divine*. He is also the author of the novels *Koolaids: The Art of War* and *The Hakawati*, as well as the collection of short stories *The Perv*.

22. I distinguish Arab-Americans like *I, the Divine*'s protagonist, Sarah, from others since the ease of her transnational movements might not be readily available to other Arab-Americans, whether it be for political, legal, or socioeconomic reasons or even due to personal choice. Moreover, not all the transnational and translocal perspectives portrayed in the novel are the same. For we see Sarah's husband, Omar, struggling with an overwhelming sense of alienation during his sojourn in New York, with the conviction that he only "felt human in Beirut" (Alameddine, *I, the Divine* 212).

23. The novel also often shifts to the third-person point of view, interspersing chapters written in English with the same chapters rewritten in French, thus multiplying the narrative articulation of one experience, rendering it more linguistically nuanced. This fragmentation of *I, the Divine*'s plot also characterizes Alameddine's first novel, *Koolaids*, which equally experiments with notions of genre and representation.

24. Unlike *The Bullet Collection*'s Marianna, who at one point identifies herself as a refugee, Sarah does not move to the US to escape the Lebanese war but to be with Omar while he attends Columbia University. Once in the US, however, the return to

Lebanon for her and her husband becomes complicated due to the intensity of the war at that time (especially with the Israeli invasion in 1982).

25. Unlike Sarah, *The Bullet Collection*'s Marianna is unable to return to Beirut due to the persistence of the Lebanese war in the novel's narrative and her close connection to her relocated family.

26. Sarah's personal trauma also extends to the dissolution of her parents' marriage when she was two years old, resulting mainly from the fact that her American mother, Janet, did not provide her seemingly liberal husband with the long-awaited son, producing Sarah instead, the third daughter in a row.

27. Regarding this point, see the interview with Alameddine in *I, Divine* ("A Conversation" 313). See also Alameddine's discussion of the concept of writerly detachment in "Transcontinental Detachment." I read Alameddine's concept of detachment here as a version of the translocal consciousness discussed in this chapter.

28. At one point in the narrative Sarah says, "There will always be there," an important statement that ironically comes right after her decision to "put it [Lebanon] behind her." Instead of regarding the former statement ("There will always be there") as a flippant postponement of dealing with the feeling of being torn between here and there, I see it as one of the first signs of Sarah's complex acceptance of her transnational/translocal identity and the inevitable constant presence of the Lebanese homeland in her everyday American life.

29. Born in Beirut, Lebanon, to a Syrian Muslim father and a Greek Christian mother, Etel Adnan is one of the foremost Arab-American writers and thinkers, with her work including fiction, poetry, drama, essays, and visual art. Her novella *Sitt Marie Rose* was first published in French in 1977. Her other works include a long poem, *From A to Z*, and a collection titled *The Indian Never Had a Horse and Other Poems*, which deals with the dispossession of Native Americans, as well as *Of Cities and Women: Letters to Fawwaz*, a collection of letters revolving around gender and feminism, written by Adnan to fellow Arab writer and exile Fawwaz Traboulsi.

30. See Liz Countryman's review for a discussion of memory and displacement in the book (75).

31. This narrative section and the piece on T. E. Lawrence, "At Both Ends," are the only two essays that do not adhere to the cyclical paragraph structure adopted in the rest of the book.

32. In a review of the book, Kim Jensen describes the structure of the narrative as being "something of a palimpsest."

33. Such ambivalence does not always result in disengagement, for, as evidenced by the huge rallies around the country in 2003, there was and still remains a visible and vocal strata of US society that opposes US-led wars in the Middle East.

34. In *The Colonial Present*, Derek Gregory writes, "For us to cease turning on the treadmill of the colonial present—it will be necessary to explore other spatializations and other topologies, and to turn our imaginative geographies into geographical imaginations that can enlarge and enhance our sense of the world" (262).

35. Geographical imaginations necessitate what Said calls a critical and discursive "rethinking [of] geography," which would then enable us to reconceive the power structures imbricated in "the struggle over it" (Said et al. 21).

36. This contradiction is further exemplified by the name Edward Said itself, which, with all its implied historical and linguistic incongruities, creates in Said an identity crisis he spends most of his life analyzing.

37. Said's mother, who is herself half Lebanese, did not visit the US before 1948 and never procured US citizenship for herself.

38. This taxing insistence on adhering to a US identity is enforced almost exclusively by his father, who even carries it out within the sphere of their own home.

39. Being a student at the British-run Gezira Preparatory School (GPS) puts Said in direct contact with what he describes as the "colonial encounter" (*Out of Place* 44).

40. Echoing what Said perceives as the ahistorical US landscape that he first experienced at Mount Hermon School, he describes "Princeton in the fifties [as] unpolitical, self-satisfied, and oblivious" (*Out of Place* 278).

41. Other minorities also undergo this "battle for space." See Lisa Lowe's *Immigrant Acts: On Asian American Cultural Politics* and Patricia Chu's *Assimilating Asians: Gendered Strategies of Authorship in Asian America*.

42. After being repeatedly called on to act as the Palestinian spokesperson on US news channels, Said notes in *Selves and Others* how he became exasperated by the compromising positions in which such inclusions placed him, since he "was treated as guilty until proven innocent."

43. Alternative and interrogative types of transnational belonging are inevitably faced with skepticism and criticism. Said has been severely criticized for introducing such an alternative narrative into the US discursive landscape, with the likes of Israeli-American scholar Justus Reed Weiner attacking Said's claim that he had lived and been schooled in Jerusalem prior to 1948.

44. Said himself did not carry out a return to his family's original home in West Jerusalem till 1992, at which point he found out that it was occupied by a "right-wing fundamentalist Christian and pro-Zionist group" and could not bring himself to enter it (Said, "Palestine, Then and Now").

45. The primacy of Said's intellectual dedication and his criticism of Zionism, for example, do not only frame him as an oppositional figure in the US academic and political terrain. He was deeply critical of some of the stances upheld by Arab leaders themselves, such as Yasser Arafat, whom Said condemned for his "self-aggrandizing and opportunistic policies" (Lal 39). Said's books were banned in Palestine by the Palestinian Authority in 1995 as a result of the tensions between him and Arafat.

46. Even though Laila Halaby, born in Lebanon to a Jordanian father and an American mother and raised in Arizona, is a second-generation Arab-American writer (or more accurately of the 1.5 Arab-American generation), I include her novel here because it incorporates the immigrant perspective of Hala, who moves from Jordan to the US to pursue her studies. In addition to *Once in a Promised Land* and *West of the Jordan*, Halaby's publications include the poetry collection *My Name on His Tongue*.

47. Khadija is the only one among the four featured cousins who has not been to Nawara, because the trip is too expensive for her father to afford. Nevertheless, in the absence of physical travel, televisions, video cameras, videotapes, and VCRs are depicted throughout the novel as crucial means for maintaining translocal and transnational connections.

48. According to the US Department of State's webpage, "Individuals who hold a PA [Palestinian] ID, as well as persons judged by Israeli authorities to have claim to a

PA ID by virtue of ancestry, will be considered subject to Israeli law and to regulations that Israel applies to residents of the West Bank and Gaza, regardless of whether they also hold U.S. citizenship" (United States Department of State).

49. In the essay "Imaginative Geographies," Derek Gregory describes Said's critical output by stating, "He charts a series of mappings, sometimes discordant and sometimes compounded, through which places and identities are deterritorialized and reterritorialized" (448). I see the texts discussed in this section enacting, in many ways, the counterhegemonic strategies described by Gregory.

50. This point is addressed in more detail in chapter 2.

51. Even though Hala's father is Jordanian, she still heavily identifies with her mother's Palestinian/Nawarese identity (this sentiment is shared by her brother but not by her sister).

52. This is a very popular charm among Palestinians, featuring a full map of pre-1948 Palestine. Other similar charms might feature an olive tree, a key, or Naji Al-Ali's cartoon figure Handala.

53. Hala also claims that the *roza* would be too short if she used the belt, noting that her mother was shorter than she is.

54. By pointing out such revisionary mappings of Palestinian identity, I do not mean to undercut the continued struggle over important issues such as the right of return for Palestinians and the issue of Palestinian refugees who were displaced in 1948 and 1967. In other words, the cartographies of identity discussed in this section do not constitute an alternative agenda to Palestinian rights but might be defined as a way for Palestinian-Americans to negotiate their identities in the US while still maintaining their national and territorial rights in Palestine/Israel.

55. In my use of the term "traveling identity," I draw on Said's concept of "traveling theory." Originally suggesting that an idea or a theory can lose some of its vigor when transplanted from one location to another, Said revises this approach in a subsequent essay to propose that such mobility can also strengthen "traveling theory." See Said, "Traveling Theory" and "Traveling Theory Reconsidered"; and Moustafa Bayoumi, "Our Work Is of This World."

56. I draw here on James Clifford's concept of "dwelling-in-displacement" that he develops in his essay "Diasporas."

57. In a *Ha'aretz* interview, Said explains the origin of the word *invention*, stating, "In Latin, *inventio* is to find again. . . . It's not creating from nothing, it's reordering" ("My Right of Return" 456).

58. Hammer here is referencing Marie-Louise Weighill's essay "Palestinians in Exile."

59. Like the novel's protagonist, Jarrar was also born in the US and grew up in Kuwait, Egypt, and the US. See her short essay "Loosely Based," in which she reflects on her own background and her relationship with her father. *A Map of Home* is her first novel.

60. The short scene in the novel in which Nidali describes being in Palestine mostly focuses on retelling the stories that her grandmother narrates to her.

61. For a discussion of the significance of names in the novel, see Dina Jadallah's review of the novel (110–11).

62. The blue book is a reference to Sir Geoffrey Furlonge's *Palestine Is My Country: The Story of Musa Alami*, written about the activism of Arab Palestinian writer/thinker Musa Alami after 1948. The book includes a map that features a shaded representation

of the various Palestinian and Israeli territories after the two key years of 1948 and 1967 (218). However, this map is not necessarily the exact one that Nidali is instructed to trace in *A Map of Home* (Jarrar, "Re: question").

63. Other parts of the novel depict Palestinian characters undergoing the difficulties of politically restricted travel, including her Palestinian family's complex passage from Jenin to Egypt through Jordan in order to attend Nidali's parents' wedding (*A Map of Home* 38).

64. The ironic juxtaposition of topographic versus politically driven implementations of border restrictions is highlighted in another part of the novel, where Nidali describes her family's escape across the border from Kuwait to Iraq.

4 / Representing Arabs and Muslims in the US after 9/11

1. As I point out in the introduction, while many Americans with Arab roots embrace the Arab-American or even the Middle Eastern label (at the same time raising questions as to who should be included under these umbrella terms), many others, in the name of safety and cultural assimilation, distance themselves from what they deem to be ultimately harmful and compromising Arab labels.

2. This is not to say that only Arab-American writers offer such a critical stance, for we find non-Arab and non-Muslim intellectuals also voicing their concerns about the binary rhetoric and the violence that have typified national responses to the attacks of 9/11. See Judith Butler, *Precarious Life*; Slavoj Žižek, *Welcome to the Desert of the Real*; Joan Didion, *Fixed Ideas: America since 9.11*; and Noam Chomsky, *9-11*.

3. On September 11, 2002, the Justice Department initiated the National Security Entry-Exit Registration System. This system involves fingerprinting, interviewing, and photographing foreign or nonresident men in the US from twenty-four Muslim-majority countries and North Korea. See Salah Hassan; Leti Volpp, "The Citizen and the Terrorist"; and Moustafa Bayoumi, "Racing Religion." According to Nadine Naber, "Special registration resulted in the deportation of more than thirteen thousand individuals, none of whom was found guilty of terrorism charges" ("Look, Mohammed" 288). Moreover, Louise Cainkar notes that "in the seven days following September 11, Arabs and South Asians reported 645 cases of hate crimes" ("No Longer Invisible"). Some of these murder victims include a Sikh man, Balbir Singh Sodhi (killed on September 15 in Mesa, Arizona), the Pakistani Waqar Hasan (killed on September 15, 2001, in Mesquite, Texas), Coptic Christian Adel Karas (killed in San Gabriel, California), and the Yemeni Ali Almansoop (killed in Detroit, Michigan). These murders were part of a 1,600 percent increase in crimes against Muslims, Arabs, or South Asians in the US between 2000 and 2001 (Naber, "Look, Mohammed" 289).

4. Helen Hatab Samhan refers to such discrimination as "political racism." See her essay "Politics and Exclusion."

5. As portrayed in the other chapters, literary iterations of transnational Arab-American subjectivities have been in circulation well before 9/11.

6. Such involvement includes the military presence in the Arabian Gulf, US sanctions against Iraq starting in 1990, and US support of Israel, to name a few. For a discussion of the history of US foreign policies in the Middle East, see Rashid Khalidi, *Resurrecting Empire*; and Melani McAlister, *Epic Encounters*.

7. See Mary K. Bloodsworth-Lugo and Carmen R. Lugo-Lugo for detailed discussions of some containment strategies carried out by the US government.

212 / NOTES

8. While Mamdani interrogates the polarities and exclusions embedded in George W. Bush's distinction between "good Muslims" and "bad Muslims" within the framework of the War on Terror (15), Maira broadens Mamdani's scope by focusing on Arab and South Asian "Muslim Americans and the ways their political identities are interpreted in moral and gendered terms" ("'Good' and 'Bad' Muslim Citizens" 633).

9. The girls' father had also changed his name from Rasheed Tammouz to Richard Thomas after he divorced their mother to marry his American wife, Dusty.

10. This incident is based on real-life events that took place in Chicago's Bridgeview area in the days after 9/11. See Louise Cainkar, *Homeland Insecurity* (206).

11. This statement might seem contradictory given that Arab-Americans are officially categorized by the US Census Bureau as white. I deem such a categorization to be problematic given the fact that Arab-Americans are for the most part regarded and treated as nonwhites in the US and also given that many Arab-Americans self-identify as people of color.

12. Even though my analysis in this section addresses some textual gestures that connect the struggles shared by Arab-Americans and other minorities, it does not incorporate a full study of such thematic and theoretical intersections, which lies beyond the scope of this project. For a discussion of passing in the Arab-American context, see Wardi-Zonna and Wardi.

13. Other Arab-American texts not discussed here that address the immediate aftereffects of 9/11 include poetry by Mohja Kahf, Hayan Charara, Samuel Hazo, and D. H. Melhem. Nonfictional texts focusing on the topic of 9/11 include Moustafa Bayoumi's *How Does It Feel to Be a Problem? Being Young and Arab in America* and Naomi Shihab Nye's "An Open Letter" (2001), while short stories on the topic include Evelyn Shakir's "I Got My Eye on You," Amani Elkassabani's "Hanaan's House," Gregory Orfalea's "Get Off the Bus," Samia Serageldin's short story "It's Not about That," and Randa Jarrar's "A Frame for the Sky." Other than Laila Halaby's *Once in a Promised Land*, only a couple of Arab-American novels include direct references to 9/11 in their narrative landscape, including Alia Yunis's *The Night Counter* and Frances Khirallah Noble's *The New Belly Dancer of the Galaxy*. It can nevertheless be argued that many literary texts, even if not referencing 9/11 directly, still capture the distinct and multiple political, religious, ethnic, and transnational outlooks of the Arab-American community (such as Jarrar's novel *A Map of Home*, Rabih Alameddine's *The Hakawati* and Laila Lalami's *Secret Son*).

14. I base the concept of citizenship in crisis on the title of the study of the Arab-American community in Detroit after 9/11 conducted by the Detroit Arab American Study Team, titled *Citizenship and Crisis: Arab Detroit after 9/11*.

15. See the introduction for a discussion of the distinctions among these types of citizenship.

16. For a discussion of specific enactments of cultural citizenship, see Sunaina Maira, "Flexible Citizenship / Flexible Empire"; Aihwa Ong, "Cultural Citizenship as Subject Making"; and May Joseph.

17. See Inderpal Grewal's discussion of this type of consumer citizenship, as well as the prevalence of the flag in post-9/11 consumer culture as a sign of US patriotism and belonging, in chapter 5 of her book *Transnational America* (196–220). See also Robert Stam and Ella Shohat's use of the word "flag" in *Flagging Patriotism* (xi–xxvii).

18. Marcel Khalife is a Lebanese musician (composer, singer, and oud player) whose songs, based on the poetry of Palestinian poet Mahmoud Darwish, have been internationally recognized as commemorations of Palestinians' experience of struggle and dispossession.

19. Even though a large percentage of Jordanians are of Palestinian background, Jassim is identified in the novel solely as Jordanian, one who is nevertheless committed to the Palestinian cause. Salwa, however, even though she was born in the US, identifies herself as a Palestinian who was raised in Jordan by her refugee parents.

20. See Jasbir Puar and Amit Rai for a discussion of "docile patriots."

21. In an interesting narrative move, however, the novel integrates a dehomogenized US public response to the US government's crackdown on Arabs and Muslims after 9/11. Even though still operating on a binary axis, Jassim's boss, Marcus, refers to Amy Goodman's radio show *Democracy Now!*, pinpointing a strain of political dissent in the media that counteracts what he calls the Christian "right-wing, . . . unthinkingly flag-waving" patriotism flaunted by his office staff (Halaby, *Once in a Promised Land* 225).

22. Ironically, even with Salwa's "abandonment" of Hassan as a future husband, his calls to her cell phone in the days following 9/11 as a last bid to connect with her before he gets married are still used by the FBI as evidence of the Rashids' potential implication in the 9/11 plots.

23. See Georgiana Banita for what she refers to as "racial scapegoating" in the novel (246).

24. Such intimidating tactics used to silence political critique are enacted through direct punitive state action and the curbing of civil rights as sanctioned by the PATRIOT Act.

25. Hammad's performance of "first writing since" on the show can be viewed on YouTube: http://www.youtube.com/watch?v=SNfec7Fa2Cc.

26. For a discussion of Hammad's "first writing since" in the context of contemporary trauma theory, see Michael Rothberg.

27. In an interesting moment of ethnic recognition, Abdulhadi and the Iranian businessman choose not to reveal each other's Middle Eastern identity to the other passengers in the taxi in order to preserve each other's and each's own safety.

28. The essay also incorporates Abdulhadi's memories of visiting the Sabra and Shatila Palestinian refugee camps in Beirut.

29. For an in-depth analysis of the connections among heterosexuality, hypermasculinity, and patriotism, see M. Jacqui Alexander. For a discussion of homonormative nationalism, see Jasbir Puar's chapter titled "The Sexuality of Terrorism" in *Terrorist Assemblages* (37–78).

30. See also Amira Jarmakani for a detailed analysis of the representation of Arab and Muslim women prior to 2001.

31. Thus, we find that visual representations of the terrorist figure's perverse/failed heterosexuality abound in the period right after 9/11, with cartoons depicting Osama bin Laden, for instance, being sodomized by the Empire State Building (see Puar and Rai 126).

32. For a discussion of post-9/11 representations of Arab- and Muslim-Americans in the US media, see Evelyn Alsultany, "The Prime-Time Plight" and *Arabs and Muslims in the Media*; and Jack Shaheen.

33. *Covering Islam*, written by Edward Said, was first published in 1981 and then reprinted in 1997. *Quotations from Chairman Mao Tsetung*, or the "Little Red Book," contains some of the famous writings and sayings of Chairman Mao Tsetung and was first published in 1964. *A Manual for the Oppressed* most likely draws on works such as *Pedagogy of the Oppressed* by Paulo Freire, and *Militant Islam* might be in reference to right-wing pundit Daniel Pipes's *Militant Islam Reaches America*, published in 2003.

34. In the two months following the 9/11 attacks, over eleven hundred noncitizens were detained by the Justice Department, but such figures were no longer released by the government after November 8, 2001 (Volpp, "The Citizen and the Terrorist" 148). The detainment and incarceration of Muslim-American men in the US (including citizens) continues, with the well-known cases of Dr. Sami Al-Arian of Temple Terrace, Florida, Dr. Rafil Dhafir of Syracuse, New York, Yassin Aref and Mohammed Hossain of Albany, New York, and Fahad Hashmi of Flushing, New York, to name a few (all of whom, except Aref, are US citizens).

35. In fact, the positioning of such female characters as judges or regulators of Khaled's Arab Muslim identity has resonance with the role of women in the Abu Ghraib scandal, in which US female military personnel such as reservist Lynndie England were portrayed as primary (and independent) agents involved in torturing prisoners by using what they deemed to be nonnormative, taboo, and deviant sexual methods. For an in-depth discussion of the Abu Ghraib photographs, see Mary Ann Tétreault; for an analysis of the role of female soldiers in the war on terror, see Robin Riley, "Valiant, Vicious, or Virtuous?"

36. On the project's website, Bilal describes the technological setup of the project: "Technically, the 3rdi is an automatic photographic apparatus that is comprised of three different components: a small digital camera permanently surgically mounted to the back of my head with a USB connection, a lightweight laptop which I carry on my body connected to the camera with a USB cable, and a 3G wireless connection to access the internet" ("3rdi").

37. Rep. King is a Long Island Republican and the chairman of the House Homeland Security Committee.

Conclusion

1. I thank Khaled Mattawa for allowing me to reprint his poem "Now That We Have Tasted Hope" here in its entirety.

2. See my interview with Alameddine, "Transcontinental Detachment."

3. Mattawa is a widely acclaimed Libyan-American poet and translator. Author of four volumes of poetry, he is also coeditor of two anthologies of Arab-American literature and translator of the works of various contemporary Arab poets, including the Syrian Adonis's *Selected Poems*, which was a finalist for the 2011 Griffin Poetry Prize. Mattawa has been awarded a number of major literary awards, including a fellowship from the Academy of American Poets and two Pushcart Prizes.

4. "About Meena Magazine," Meena website, n.d., http://www.meenamag.com/about/index.htm.

5. The works of some of these playwrights appear in Holly Hill and Dina A. Amin, eds., *Salaam, Peace: An Anthology of Middle Eastern-American Drama*.

6. The acronym stands for Notoriously Offensive Male Arabs Discussing Sh*t.

7. Yassin Alsalman, better known by his stage name The Narcicyst (or Narcy), is an Iraqi-Canadian journalist and hip hop emcee. Born in Dubai in 1982, Yassin moved with his family to Montreal, Canada, in 1987.

8. Jarrar's story appeared in *Guernica* on May 14, 2012: http://www.guernicamag.com/daily/randa-jarrar-imagining-myself-in-palestine/.

9. Mattawa's poem "After 42 Years" focuses on Qaddafi's death.

10. Another diasporic Libyan writer who was vocal about the uprising in Libya is American-born Hisham Matar. His father, a diplomat, was captured by Qaddafi's men in 1990 in Cairo and was taken back to Libya. No word has been heard about him since then. Matar's two novels, *In the Country of Men* (2006) and *Anatomy of a Disappearance* (2011), both draw on his family and national backgrounds. For an interview with Matar and his reflections as a writer in the time of national revolutions, see Matar, "Libya's Reluctant Spokesman."

Works Cited

Abdelrazek, Amal Talaat. *Contemporary Arab American Women Writers: Hyphenated Identities and Border Crossings.* Youngstown, NY: Cambria, 2007.
———. "'Elsewhere-within-here/-there': Exiles and Identity of Home/s in Diana Abu-Jaber's *Crescent*." Abdelrazek, *Contemporary Arab American Women Writers* 175–223.
Abdul-Baki, Kathryn K. *Tower of Dreams.* Washington, DC: Three Continents, 1995.
Abdulhadi, Rabab. "Where Is Home? Fragmented Lives, Border Crossings, and the Politics of Exile." Afzal-Khan 71–83.
Abdulhadi, Rabab, Evelyn Alsultany, and Nadine Naber, eds. *Arab and Arab American Feminisms: Gender, Violence, and Belonging.* Syracuse: Syracuse UP, 2010.
Abdurraqib, Samaa. "Making It Survive Here and 'Dreams of Return': Community and Identity in the Poetry of Mohja Kahf." Al Maleh 449–62.
Abinader, Elmaz. "Children of Al-Mahjar: Arab American Literature Spans a Century." US Department of State, International Information Programs. Feb. 2000. Web. 1 Nov. 2003.
———. *Children of the Roojme: A Family's Journey from Lebanon.* New York: Norton, 1991.
———. "Just Off Main Street." US Department of State, International Information Programs. n.d. Web. 7 Dec. 2007.
Abraham, Nabeel. "To Palestine and Back: Quest for Place." Abraham and Shryock 425–62.
Abraham, Nabeel, and Andrew Shryock, eds. *Arab Detroit: From Margins to Mainstream.* Detroit: Wayne State UP, 2000.

Abraham, Sameer Y., and Nabeel Abraham, eds. *Arabs in the New World: Studies on Arab-American Communities.* Detroit: Wayne State UP, 1983.

Abu-Jaber, Diana. *Arabian Jazz.* New York: Harcourt, 1993.

———. *Birds of Paradise.* New York: Norton, 2012.

———. *Crescent.* New York: Norton, 2003.

———. *The Language of Baklava.* New York: Pantheon, 2005.

———. "The Only Response to Silencing... Is to Keep Speaking." Interview with Andrea Shalal-Esa. *Al-Jadid* 8.39 (2002): 4–6.

———. *Origin.* New York: Norton, 2008.

Abu-Lughod, Lila. "My Father's Return to Palestine." *Jerusalem Quarterly* 3.1 (2001): 5–10.

———. "Return to Half-Ruins: Memory, Postmemory, and Living History in Palestine." Abu-Lughod and Sa'di 77–103.

Abu-Lughod, Lila, and Ahmad H. Sa'di. "Introduction: The Claims of Memory." Abu-Lughod and Sa'di, *Nakba* 1–24.

———, eds. *Nakba: Palestine, 1948, and the Claims of Memory.* New York: Columbia UP, 2007.

Adnan, Etel. *From A to Z.* Sausalito, CA: Post-Apollo, 1982.

———. *The Indian Never Had a Horse and Other Poems.* Sausalito, CA: Post-Apollo, 1985.

———. *In the Heart of the Heart of Another Country.* San Francisco: City Lights Books, 2005.

———. *Of Cities and Women: Letters to Fawwaz.* Sausalito, CA: Post-Apollo, 1993.

Afzal-Khan, Fawzia, ed. *Shattering the Stereotypes: Muslim Women Speak Out.* Northampton, MA: Olive Branch, 2005.

Ahmed, Sara, Claudia Castañeda, Ann Marie Fortier, and Mimi Sheller. "Introduction: Uprootings/Regroundings: Questions of Home and Migration." *Uprootings/Regroundings: Questions of Home and Migration.* Ed. Sara Ahmed, Claudia Castañeda, Ann Marie Fortier, and Mimi Sheller. Oxford, UK: Berg, 2003. 1–19.

Alameddine, Rabih. "A Conversation with Rabih Alameddine." *I, the Divine: A Novel in First Chapters.* New York: Norton, 2001. 313–16.

———. *The Hakawati.* New York: Knopf, 2008.

———. *I, the Divine: A Novel in First Chapters.* New York: Norton, 2001.

———. *Koolaids: The Art of War.* New York: Picador, 1998.

———. *The Perv.* New York: Picador, 1999.

———. "Transcontinental Detachment: What Shelf Are You On?" Interview with Carol Fadda-Conrey. *Al Jadid* 9.44 (2003): 24–26, 38.

Alexander, M. Jacqui. "Not Just (Any)*body* Can Be a Patriot: 'Homeland' Security as Empire Building." Riley and Inayatullah 207–40.

Al Maleh, Layla, ed. *Arab Voices in Diaspora: Critical Perspectives on Anglophone Arab Literature.* Amsterdam: Rodopi, 2009.

Alsultany, Evelyn. *Arabs and Muslims in the Media: Race and Representation after 9/11*. New York: New York UP, 2012.

———. "The Prime-Time Plight of the Arab Muslim American after 9/11." Jamal and Naber 204–28.

Ameri, Anan. "Arab American Immigration." *Daily Life of Arab Americans in the 21st Century*. Ed. Anan Ameri and Holly Arida. Santa Barbara, CA: Greenwood, 2012. 1–28.

Amireh, Amal. "Palestinian Women's Disappearing Act: The Suicide Bomber through Western Feminist Eyes." Abdulhadi, Alsultany, and Naber 29–45.

Anthias, Floya. "Evaluating 'Diaspora': Beyond Ethnicity?" *Sociology* 3.32 (1998): 557–80.

Antoun, Naira, and Mohanad Yaquibi. "Yaffa Is Not an Orange: The Limits of Archetypes." *Jadaliyya* 25 July 2011: n.p. Web. 27 Sept. 2011.

Appadurai, Arjun. *Modernity at Large: Cultural Dimensions of Globalization*. Minneapolis: U of Minnesota P, 1996.

Awad, Joseph. *The Neon Distances*. Francestown, NH: Golden Quill, 1980.

———. *Shenandoah Long Ago*. Richmond, VA: Poet's, 1990.

Banita, Georgiana. "Race, Risk, and Fiction in the War on Terror: Laila Halaby, Gayle Brandeis, and Michael Cunningham." *Lit: Literature Interpretation Theory* 21.4 (2010): 242–69.

Bardenstein, Carol. "Threads of Memory and Discourses of Rootedness: Of Trees, Oranges and the Prickly-Pear Cactus in Israel/Palestine." *Edebiyat: The Journal of Middle Eastern Literatures* 8.1 (1998): 1–36.

———. "Transmissions Interrupted: Reconfiguring Food, Memory, and Gender in the Cookbook-Memoirs of Middle Eastern Exiles." *Signs* 28.1 (2002): 353–87.

Bayoumi, Moustafa. "Arab America's September 11." *Nation* 25 Sept. 2006: 22. Web. 20 Nov. 2012.

———. *How Does It Feel to Be a Problem? Being Young and Arab in America*. New York: Penguin, 2008.

———. "Our Work Is of This World." *Amerasia Journal* 31.1 (2005): 1–4.

———. "Racing Religion." *CR: The New Centennial Review* 6.2 (2006): 267–93.

Becker, Carol. "Introduction: Drawing the Line." Bilal and Lydersen xv–xxii.

Benson, Kathleen, and Philip M. Kayal, eds. *A Community of Many Worlds: Arab Americans in New York City*. New York: Museum of the City of New York / Syracuse UP, 2002.

Berlant, Lauren. *The Queen of America Goes to Washington City: Essays on Sex and Citizenship*. Durham: Duke UP, 1997.

Bhabha, Homi. "Of Mimicry and Man: The Ambivalence of Colonial Discourse." *The Location of Culture*. New York: Routledge. 85–92.

Bilal, Wafaa. ". . . and Counting." Wafaa Bilal's website n.d. Web. 16 Mar. 2011.

———. "3rdi." Wafaa Bilal's website n.d. Web. 2 Jan. 2011.

Bilal, Wafaa, and Kari Lydersen. *Shoot an Iraqi: Art, Life and Resistance under the Gun*. San Francisco: City Lights, 2008.

Blatty, William Peter. *Which Way to Mecca, Jack?* New York: Lancer Books, 1960.
Bloodsworth-Lugo, Mary K., and Carmen R. Lugo-Lugo. *Containing (Un) American Bodies: Race, Sexuality, and Post-9/11 Constructions of Citizenship.* Amsterdam: Rodopi, 2010.
Bourjaily, Vance. *Confessions of a Spent Youth.* 1960. New York: Arbor House, 1986.
Bourne, Randolph. "Trans-national America." *Atlantic Monthly* 18 (1916): 86–97.
Boym, Svetlana. *The Future of Nostalgia.* New York: Basic Books, 2001.
Brah, Avtar. *Cartographies of Diaspora: Contesting Identities.* London: Routledge, 1996.
Braziel, Jana Evans, and Anita Mannur, eds. *Theorizing Diaspora.* Malden, MA: Blackwell, 2006.
Butler, Judith. *Precarious Life: The Powers of Mourning and Violence.* London: Verso, 2004.
Cainkar, Louise. *Homeland Insecurity: The Arab American and Muslim American Experience after 9/11.* New York: Russell Sage Foundation, 2009.
———. "Managing Identities: 2nd Generation Arab American Youth." Unpublished paper presented at the "Diaspora I: Integration" panel, Symposium on Arab World Diasporas and Migrations. Georgetown University, Washington, DC, 21–22 Mar. 2010.
———. "No Longer Invisible: Arab and Muslim Exclusion after September 11." *Middle East Report* 224 (2002): n.p. Web. 20 Nov. 2005.
Certeau, Michel de. *The Practice of Everyday Life.* 1974. Trans. Steven Rendall. Berkeley: U of California P, 1984.
Charara, Hayan. *The Alchemist's Diary.* New York: Hanging Loose, 2001.
———. "Becoming the Center of Mystery." Abraham and Shryock 401–23.
———, ed. *Inclined to Speak: An Anthology of Contemporary Arab American Poetry.* Fayetteville: U of Arkansas P, 2008.
———. "Introduction." Charara, *Inclined to Speak* xiii–xxxiii.
———. *The Sadness of Others.* Pittsburgh: Carnegie Mellon UP, 2006.
Chérif, Salwa Essayah. "Arab American Literature: Gendered Memory in Abinader and Abu-Jaber." *MELUS* 28.4 (2003): 207–28.
Chomsky, Noam. *9-11.* New York: Open Media, 2001.
Chu, Patricia P. *Assimilating Asians: Gendered Strategies of Authorship in Asian America.* Durham: Duke UP, 2000.
Civantos, Christina. "The Middle East in North America: Questions of Identity in *Food for Our Grandmothers.*" Rev. of *Food for Our Grandmothers: Writings by Arab-American and Arab-Canadian Feminists,* ed. Joe Kadi. *Stanford Humanities Review* 5.1 (1996): n.p. Web. 6 Oct. 2002.
Clifford, James. "Diasporas." *Cultural Anthropology* 9.3 (1994): 302–38.
Cole, David. *Enemy Aliens: Double Standards and Constitutional Freedoms in the War on Terrorism.* New York: New Press, 2005.

Cott, Nancy. *Public Vows: A History of Marriage and the Nation.* Cambridge: Harvard UP, 2000.
Countryman, Liz. "In the Heart of the Heart of Another Country." Rev. of *In the Heart of the Heart of Another Country*, by Etel Adnan. *Tikkun* 21.2 (2006): 75.
Cronin, Ann. *Advertising and Consumer Citizenship: Gender, Images, and Rights.* New York: Routledge, 2000.
Darwish, Mahmoud. "The Earth Is Closing on Us." *Victims of a Map.* Trans. Abdullah al-Udhari. London: Al Saqi Books, 1984. 13.
———. *In the Presence of Absence.* Trans. Sinan Antoon. Brooklyn, NY: Archipelago, 2011.
De la Cruz, Patricia, and Angela Brittingham. "Ancestry: 2000." *Census 2000 Brief.* US Census Bureau. June 2004. 1–10. Web. 4 Sept. 2011.
Demos, T. J. "Desire in Diaspora: Emily Jacir." *Art Journal* 62.4 (2003): 68–78.
Detroit Arab American Study Team. *Citizenship and Crisis: Arab Detroit after 9/11.* New York: Russell Sage Foundation, 2009.
Didion, Joan. *Fixed Ideas: America since 9.11.* New York: New York Review of Books, 2003.
Du Bois, W. E. B. *The Souls of Black Folk.* 1903. New York: New American Library, 1982.
El Guindi, Yussef. *Back of the Throat.* New York: Dramatists Play Service, 2006.
———. "Interview with Walter Bilderback." Wilma Theater. 9 Feb. 2010. Web. 13 Dec. 2010.
Elia, Nada. "Islamophobia and the 'Privileging' of Arab American Women." *NWSA Journal* 18.3 (2006): 155–61.
———. "The 'White' Sheep of the Family: But *Bleaching* Is Like Starvation." *This Bridge We Call Home: Radical Visions for Transformation.*" Ed. Gloria E. Anzaldúa and AnaLouise Keating. New York: Routledge, 2002. 223–31.
Elkassabani, Amani. "Hanaan's House." Afzal-Khan 230–43.
Enloe, Cynthia. *Bananas, Beaches, and Bases: Making Feminist Sense of International Politics.* Berkeley: U of California P, 1990.
Erian, Alicia. *Towelhead.* New York: Simon and Schuster, 2006.
Evans, Alice. "Half and Half: A Profile of Diana Abu-Jaber." *Poets & Writers* 24.4 (1996): 38–49.
Fadda-Conrey, Carol. "Arab-American Literature in the Ethnic Borderland: Cultural Intersections in Diana Abu-Jaber's *Crescent*." Arab American Literature. Spec. issue of *MELUS* 31.4 (2006): 187–205.
Fanon, Frantz. *Black Sin, White Masks.* New York: Grove, 1967.
Fishkin, Shelley Fisher. "Crossroads of Cultures: The Transnational Turn in American Studies—Presidential Address to the American Studies Association." *American Quarterly* 12 (2004): 17–57.
Fisk, Robert. *Pity the Nation: The Abduction of Lebanon.* 1990. New York: Thunder's Mouth, 2002.

Friedman, Susan Stanford. "Bodies on the Move: A Poetics of Home and Diaspora." *Tulsa Studies in Women's Literature* 23.3 (2004): 189–212.
Furlonge, Geoffrey Warren. *Palestine Is My Country: The Story of Musa Alami.* London: Murray, 1969.
Gana, Nouri. "In Search of Andalusia: Reconfiguring Arabness in Abu-Jaber's *Crescent.*" *Comparative Literature Studies* 45.2 (2008): 228–46.
Geha, Joseph. "Almost Thirty." Geha, *Through and Through* 32–47.
———. "Alone and All Together." *Big City Cool: Short Stories about Urban Youth.* Ed. M. Jerry Weiss and Helen S. Weiss. New York: Persea Books, 2002. 51–63.
———. "Everything, Everything." Geha, *Through and Through* 19–31.
———. "Holy Toledo." Geha, *Through and Through* 82–99.
———. *Lebanese Blonde: A Novel.* Ann Arbor: U of Michigan P, 2012.
———. *Through and Through: Toledo Stories.* 1990. Syracuse: Syracuse UP, 2009.
George, Rosemary Marangoly. *The Politics of Home: Postcolonial Relocations and Twentieth-Century Fiction.* Cambridge: Cambridge UP, 1996.
Gheisar, Bookda. "Going Home." Kadi, *Food for Our Grandmothers* 192–96.
Gibran, Kahlil Gibran. "Dead Are My People." Orfalea and Elmusa 31–34.
———. *The Prophet.* 1923. New York: Knopf, 1952.
———. "To Young Americans of Syrian Origin." *Syrian World* 1.1 (July 1926): 4–5.
Gilroy, Paul. *The Black Atlantic: Modernity and Double Consciousness.* Cambridge: Harvard UP, 1993.
Gómez-Vega, Ibis. "The Memory of Loss in Diana Abu-Jaber's *Arabian Jazz.*" *South Atlantic Review* 72.3 (2007): 17–37.
Gregory, Derek. *The Colonial Present: Afghanistan, Palestine, Iraq.* Malden, MA: Blackwell, 2004.
———. "Imaginative Geographies." *Progress in Human Geography* 19.4 (1995): 447–85.
Grewal, Inderpal. *Transnational America: Feminisms, Diasporas, Neoliberalisms.* Durham: Duke UP, 2005.
Gualtieri, Sarah. "Becoming 'White': Race, Religion and the Foundations of Syrian/Lebanese Ethnicity in the United States." *Journal of American Ethnic History* 20.4 (2001): 29–58.
———. *Between Arab and White: Race and Ethnicity in the Early Syrian American Diaspora.* Berkeley: U of California P, 2009.
———. "Gendering the Chain Migration Thesis: Women and Syrian Transatlantic Migration, 1878–1924." *Comparative Studies of South Asia, Africa and the Middle East* 24.1 (2004): 68–78.
———. "Strange Fruit? Syrian Immigrants, Extralegal Violence, and Racial Formation in the United States." Jamal and Naber 147–69.
Gupta, Akhil, and James Ferguson. "Beyond 'Culture': Space, Identity, and the Politics of Difference." *Cultural Anthropology* 7 (1992): 6–23.
Haddad, Carol. "In Search of Home." Kadi, *Food for Our Grandmothers* 218–23.

Haddad, Yvonne Yazbeck. *Not Quite American? The Shaping of Arab and Muslim Identity in the United States.* Waco, TX: Baylor UP, 2004.
Halaby, Laila. *My Name on His Tongue: Poems.* Syracuse: Syracuse UP, 2012.
———. *Once in a Promised Land: A Novel.* Boston: Beacon, 2007.
———. *West of the Jordan.* Boston: Beacon, 2003.
Hall, Stuart. "Cultural Identity and Diaspora." *Colonial Discourse and Post-Colonial Theory: A Reader.* Ed. Patrick Williams and Laura Chrisman. New York: Columbia UP, 1994. 392–403.
Hammad, Suheir. "Argela Remembrance." *Born Palestinian, Born Black.* 1996. New York: UpSet, 2010. 38–39.
———. *breaking poems.* New York: Cypher, 2008.
———. "Daddy's Song." *Zaatar Diva.* New York: Cypher, 2005. 28–29.
———. "first writing since." Afzal-Khan 90–94.
Hammer, Juliane. *Palestinians Born in Exile: Diaspora and the Search for a Homeland.* Austin: U of Texas P, 2005.
Hamod, Sam. *Dying with the Wrong Name: New and Selected Poems.* New York: Anthe, 1980.
Handal, Nathalie, ed. *The Poetry of Arab Women: A Contemporary Anthology.* New York: Interlink, 2001.
Haney-López, Ian F. *White by Law: The Legal Construction of Race.* New York: New York UP, 1996.
Harb, Sirène. "Orientalism and the Construction of American Identity in Abraham Mitrie Rihbany's 'A Far Journey.'" *MELUS* 33.3 (2008): 131–45.
Hartman, Michelle. "Grandmothers, Grape Leaves, and Kahlil Gibran: Writing Race in Anthologies of Arab American Literature." Jamal and Naber 170–203.
Hashim, Ruzy Suliza, and Nor Faridah Abdul Manaf. "Notions of Home for Diasporic Muslim Women Writers." *European Journal of Social Sciences* 9.4 (2009): 545–56.
Hassan, Salah. "Arabs, Race, and the Post–September 11 National Security State." *Middle East Report* 224 (2002): n.p. Web. 15 Jan. 2008.
Hassan, Waïl. *Immigrant Narratives: Orientalism and Cultural Translation in Arab-American and Arab-British Literature.* New York: Oxford UP, 2011.
———. "A Thousand and One Recipes." Rev. of *Crescent*, by Diana Abu-Jaber. *Aljadid* 9.45 (2003): 31.
Hatem, Mervat. "How the Gulf War Changed the AAUG's Discourse on Arab Nationalism and Gender Politics." *Middle East Journal* 2 (2001): 277–96.
———. "The Political and Cultural Representations of Arabs, Arab Americans, and Arab American Feminisms after September 11, 2001." Abdulhadi, Alsultany, and Naber 10–28.
Haugbolle, Sune. "Public and Private Memory of the Lebanese Civil War." *Comparative Studies of South Asia, Africa and the Middle East* 25.1 (2005): 191–203.
———. *War and Memory in Lebanon.* Cambridge: Cambridge UP, 2010.

Hazo, Samuel. *Color of Reluctance*. Story, WY: Dooryard, 1986.
———. *A Flight to Elsewhere*. Pittsburgh: Autumn House, 2005.
———. *Just Once: New and Previous Poems*. Pittsburgh: Autumn House, 1999.
———. *Silence Spoken Here*. Marlboro, VT: Marlboro, 1988.
Hilal, Dima. "america." *Scheherazade's Legacy: Arab and Arab American Women on Writing*. Ed. Susan Muaddi Darraj. Westport, CT: Praeger, 2004. 104–6.
Hill, Holly, and Dina A. Amin, eds. *Salaam, Peace: An Anthology of Middle Eastern-American Drama*. New York: Theatre Communications Group, 2009.
Hirsch, Marianne. *Family Frames: Photography, Narrative, and Postmemory*. Cambridge: Harvard UP, 1997.
———. *The Generation of Postmemory: Writing and Visual Culture after the Holocaust*. New York: Columbia UP, 2012.
Hirst, David. *Beware of Small States: Lebanon, Battleground of the Middle East*. New York: Nation Books, 2010.
Hitti, Philip K. *The Syrians in America*. 1924. Piscataway, NJ: Gorgias, 2005.
Homsi Vinson, Pauline. "New Fiction and the Post 9/11 Arab-American Experience." Rev. of *Once in a Promised Land*, by Laila Halaby. *Al Jadid: A Review & Record of Arab Culture and Arts* 12.54–55 (2006): n.p. Web. 5 Mar. 2011.
hooks, bell. *Yearning: Race, Gender, and Cultural Politics*. Boston: South End, 1991.
Hooper, Henry. *Useful Plants and Drugs of Iran and Iraq*. Chicago: Field Museum of Natural History, 1937.
Hout, Syrine C. "Of Fathers and the Fatherland in the Post-1995 Lebanese Exilic Novel." *World Literature Today* 75.2 (2001): 285–93.
———. *Post-war Anglophone Lebanese Fiction: Home Matters in the Diaspora*. Edinburgh: Edinburgh UP, 2012.
———. "Revisiting Lebanon: Testimony, Trauma, and Transition in Patricia Sarrafian Ward's *The Bullet Collection*." *Middle Eastern Literatures* 12.3 (2009): 271–88.
Husain, Sarah, ed. *Voices of Resistance: Muslim Women of War, Faith, and Sexuality*. Berkeley, CA: Seal, 2006.
Jacir, Emily. "Stella Rollig—Emily Jacir: Interview." Jacir, Rollig, and Rückert, *Emily Jacir—Belongings* 6–19.
Jacir, Emily, Stella Rollig, and Genoveva Rückert. *Emily Jacir —Belongings: Arbeiten/Works 1998–2003*. Vienna: Folio, 2004. 46–49.
Jadallah, Dina. Rev. of *A Map of Home*. *Arab Studies Quarterly* 32.2 (2010): 109–13.
Jamal, Amaney, and Nadine Naber, eds. *Race and Arab Americans Before and After 9/11: From Invisible Citizens to Visible Subjects*. Syracuse: Syracuse UP, 2008.
Jarmakani, Amira. *Imagining Arab Womanhood: The Cultural Mythology of Veils, Harems, and Belly Dancers in the U.S.* New York: Palgrave, 2008.
Jarrar, Randa. "A Frame for the Sky." Kaldas and Mattawa 31–42.

———. "Imagining Myself in Palestine." *Guernica* 14 May 2012. Web. 2 June 2012.
———. "Loosely Based." *Utne Reader* 2 Apr. 2010. Web. 1 May 2010.
———. *A Map of Home*. New York: Penguin, 2009.
———. "Re: question." Email to the author. 10 Nov. 2010.
———. "Rewriting the Story." *Utne Reader* 1 Feb. 2011. Web. 26 Oct. 2011.
Jay, Paul. *Global Matters: The Transnational Turn in Literary Studies*. Ithaca: Cornell UP, 2010.
Jayyusi, Lena. "Iterability, Cumulativity, and Presence: The Relational Figures of Palestinian Memory." Abu-Lughod and Sa'di, *Nakba* 107–33.
Jensen, Kim. Rev. of *In the Heart of the Heart of Another Country*, by Etel Adnan. *Rain Taxi* 11 (Summer 2006): n.p. Web. 20 Dec. 2010.
Joseph, Lawrence. *Before Our Eyes*. New York: Farrar, Straus and Giroux, 1993.
———. *Codes, Precepts, Biases, and Taboos: Poems 1973–1993*. New York: Farrar, Straus and Giroux, 2005.
———. *Curriculum Vitae*. Pittsburgh: U of Pittsburgh P, 1988.
———. "Inclined to Speak." Charara, *Inclined to Speak* 164.
———. *Into It*. New York: Farrar, Straus and Giroux, 2005.
———. "Sand Nigger." *Curriculum Vitae*. Pittsburgh: U of Pittsburgh P, 1988. 27–29.
———. *Shouting at No One*. Pittsburgh: U of Pittsburgh P, 1983.
Joseph, May. "Transatlantic Inscriptions: Desire, Diaspora, and Cultural Citizenship." *Talking Visions: Multicultural Feminism in a Transnational Age*. Ed. Ella Shohat. Cambridge: MIT P, 1998. 357–67.
Joseph, Suad. "Against the Grain of the Nation—the Arab-." Suleiman, *Arabs in America* 258–71.
Kadi, Joe (formerly Joanna). "Five Steps to Creating Culture." Kadi, *Food for Our Grandmothers* 231–37.
———, ed. *Food for Our Grandmothers: Writings by Arab-American and Arab-Canadian Feminists*. Boston: South End, 1994.
———. "Introduction." Kadi, *Food for Our Grandmothers* xiii–xx.
———. *Thinking Class: Sketches from a Cultural Worker*. Boston: South End, 1996.
Kahf, Mohja. "The Cherries." Kahf, *E-mails* 11–14.
———. *E-mails from Scheherazad*. U of Central Florida Contemporary Poetry Ser. Gainesville: UP of Florida, 2003.
———. *The Girl in the Tangerine Scarf*. New York: Carroll and Graf, 2006.
———. "Lateefa." Kahf, *E-mails* 21–24.
———. "Move Over." Kahf, *E-mails* 40.
———. "My Grandmother Washes Her Feet in the Sink at Sears." Kahf, *E-mails* 26–28.
———. "The Spiced Chicken Queen of Mickaweaquah, Iowa." Kaldas and Mattawa 137–54.

———. *Western Representations of the Muslim Woman: From Termagant to Odalisque*. Austin: U of Texas P, 1999.

Kaldas, Pauline. *Letters from Cairo*. Syracuse: Syracuse UP, 2007.

Kaldas, Pauline, and Khaled Mattawa, eds. *Dinarzad's Children: An Anthology of Contemporary Arab American Fiction*. 2004. Fayetteville: U of Arkansas P, 2009.

Kaplan, Caren. "Deterritorializations: The Rewriting of Home and Exile in Western Feminist Discourse." *Cultural Critique* 6 (1987): 187–98.

———. "'A World without Boundaries': The Body Shop's Trans/national Geographics." *Social Text* 43 (1995): 45–66.

Kayal, Philip M., and Joseph M. Kayal. *The Syrian-Lebanese in America: A Study in Religious Assimilation*. Boston: Twayne, 1975.

Kayyali, Randa A. *The Arab Americans*. Westport, CT: Greenwood, 2006.

Khalidi, Rashid. *Resurrecting Empire: Western Footprints and America's Perilous Path in the Middle East*. Boston: Beacon, 2004.

Khater, Akram Fouad. *Inventing Home: Emigration, Gender, and the Middle Class in Lebanon, 1870–1920*. Berkeley: U of California, P, 2001.

Khoury, Elias. "Keynote Address: The Intellectual and the Double Exile." *Waiting for the Barbarians: A Tribute to Edward Said*. Ed. Sökmen Müge Gürsoy and Başak Ertür. London: Verso, 2008. xiii–xx.

Lal, Vinay. "The Intellectual as Exemplar: Identity, Oppositional Politics, and the Ambivalent Legacy of Edward Said." *Orientalism and the Legacy of Edward Said*. Ed. Russell C. Leong. Spec. issue of *Amerasia Journal* 31.1 (2005): 39–42.

Lalami, Laila. *Secret Son*. Chapel Hill, NC: Algonquin Books, 2009.

Lavie, Smadar, and Ted Swedenburg, eds. *Displacement, Diaspora, and Geographies of Identity*. Durham: Duke UP, 1996.

Levitt, Peggy, and Mary C. Waters. *The Changing Face of Home: The Transnational Lives of the Second Generation*. New York: Russell Sage Foundation, 2002.

Lowe, Lisa. *Immigrant Acts: On Asian American Cultural Politics*. Durham: Duke UP, 1996.

Ludescher, Tanyss. "From Nostalgia to Critique: An Overview of Arab American Literature." *MELUS* 31.4 (2006): 93–114.

Lyons, M. C. *The Arabian Epic: Heroic and Oral Story-Telling*. Vol. 3. Cambridge: Cambridge UP, 1995.

Macfarquhar, Neil. "She Carries Weapons; They Are Called Words." *New York Times* 12 May 2007: n.p. Web. 10 Nov. 2008.

Maira, Sunaina. "Flexible Citizenship / Flexible Empire: South Asian Muslim Youth in Post-9/11 America. *American Quarterly* 60.3 (2008): 697–720.

———. "'Good' and 'Bad' Muslim Citizens: Feminists, Terrorists, and U.S. Orientalisms." *Feminist Studies* 35.3 (2009): 631–56.

Majaj, Lisa Suhair. "Arab-American Ethnicity: Locations, Coalitions, and Cultural Negotiations." Suleiman, *Arabs in America* 320–36.

———. "Arab American Literature and the Politics of Memory." *Memory and Cultural Politics: New Approaches to American Ethnic Literatures*. Ed. Amritjit Singh, Joseph T. Skerret, Jr., and Robert E. Hogan. Boston: Northeastern UP, 1996. 266–90.

———. "Arab-Americans and the Meanings of Race." *Postcolonial Theory and the United States: Race, Ethnicity, and Literature*. Ed. Amritjit Singh and Peter Schmidt. Jackson: UP of Mississippi, 2000. 320–37.

———. "Beyond Silence." *Homemaking: Women Writers and the Politics and Poetics of Home*. Ed. Catherine Wiley and Fiona R. Barnes. New York: Routledge, 1996. 43–52.

———. "Boundaries: Arab/American." Kadi, *Food for Our Grandmothers* 65–86.

———. "Fifty Years On / Stones in an Unfinished Wall." *Geographies of Light*. Washington, DC: Del Sol, 2009. 88–96.

———. "Journeys to Jerusalem." *Homelands: Women's Journeys across Race, Place, and Time*. Ed. Patricia Justine Tumang and Jenesha de Rivera. Emeryville, CA: Seal, 2006. 88–101.

———. "New Directions: Arab American Writing Today." *ArabAmericas: Literary Entanglements of the American Hemisphere and the Arab World*. Ed. Ottmar Ette and Friederike Pannewick. Frankfurt: Vervuert, 2006. 123–36.

———. "Of Stories and Storytellers." *Saudi Aramco World* 56.2 (2005): 24–35.

———. "On Writing and Return: Palestinian-American Reflections." *Meridians: Feminism, Race, Transnationalism* 2.1 (2001): 113–26.

———. "Tata Olga's Hands." *An Ear to the Ground: Presenting Writers from 2 Coasts*. Ed. Scott Davis. Seattle: Cune, 1997. 280–83.

———. "Two Worlds Emerging: Arab-American Writing at the Crossroads." *Forkroads: A Journal of Ethnic-American Literature* 1.3 (1996): 64–80.

Majaj, Lisa Suhair, and Amal Amireh, eds. *Etel Adnan: Critical Essays on the Arab-American Writer and Artist*. Jefferson, NC: McFarland, 2002.

Majaj, Lisa Suhair, Paula W. Sunderman, and Therese Saliba, eds. *Intersections: Gender, Nation, and Community in Arab Women's Novels*. Syracuse: Syracuse UP, 2002.

———. "Introduction." Majaj, Sunderman, and Saliba, *Intersections* xvii–xxx.

Majid, Anouar. *Unveiling Traditions: Postcolonial Islam in a Polycentric World*. Durham: Duke UP, 2000.

Mamdani, Mahmood. *Good Muslim, Bad Muslim: America, the Cold War, and the Roots of Terror*. New York: Pantheon, 2004.

Mandaville, Peter. *Transnational Muslim Politics: Reimagining the Umma*. London: Routledge, 2001.

Marshall, Jack. *From Baghdad to Brooklyn: Growing Up in a Jewish-Arabic*

Family in Midcentury America: A Memoir. Minneapolis: Coffee House, 2005.

———. *Gorgeous Chaos: New and Selected Poems, 1965–2001*. Minneapolis: Coffee House, 2002.

Massad, Joseph. "Palestinians and the Limits of Racialized Discourse." *Social Text* 11.1 (1993): 94–114.

Matar, Hisham. "Libya's Reluctant Spokesman." *Guernica / A Magazine of Art & Politics* Oct. 2011. Web. 26 Oct. 2011.

Mattawa, Khaled. "After 42 Years." *Los Angeles Times* 25 Oct. 2011. Web. 27 Oct. 2011.

———. "Conversation: Libyan Poet Khaled Mattawa." *PBS NewsHour*. 1 March 2011. Web. 15 March 2011.

———. *Ismailia Eclipse*. New York: Sheep Meadow, 1997.

———. "Now That We Have Tasted Hope." *Arabic Literature (in English)* 26 Mar. 2011. Web. 13 Oct. 2011.

———. "Writing Islam in Contemporary American Poetry: On Mohja Kahf, Daniel Moore, and Agha Shahid Ali." *PMLA* 123.5 (2008): 1590–95.

Mattawa, Khaled, and Munir Akash. "Introduction: Post-Gibran." Mattawa and Akash, *Post-Gibran* xi–xiii.

———, eds. *Post-Gibran: Anthology of New Arab American Writing*. Syracuse: Syracuse UP, 2000.

McAlister, Melani. *Epic Encounters: Culture, Media, and U.S. Interests in the Middle East, 1945–2000*. Berkeley: U of California P, 2001.

McCarus, Ernest, ed. *The Development of Arab-American Identity*. Ann Arbor: U of Michigan P, 1994.

Mehta, Brinda. "The Semiology of Food: Diana Abu-Jaber's *Crescent*." *Rituals of Memory in Contemporary Arab Women's Writing*. Syracuse: Syracuse UP, 2007. 228–62.

Melhem, D. H. *Art and Politics: Politics and Art*. Syracuse: Syracuse UP, 2010.

———. *Blight*. Syracuse: Syracuse UP, 1995.

———. *Gwendolyn Brooks: Poetry and the Heroic Voice*. Lexington: UP of Kentucky, 1987.

———. *Heroism in the New Black Poetry: Introductions and Interviews*. Lexington: UP of Kentucky, 1990.

———. *Notes on 94th Street*. 1972. New York: Dovetail, 1979.

———. *Rest in Love*. New York: Dovetail, 1975.

Melhem, D. H., and Leila Diab, eds. *A Different Path: An Anthology of the Radius of Arab American Writers*. Detroit: Ridgeway, 2000.

Mercer, Lorraine. "Counter Narratives: Cooking Up Stories of Love and Loss in Naomi Shihab Nye's Poetry and Diana Abu-Jaber's *Crescent*." *MELUS* 32.4 (2007): 33–46.

Metres, Phil. *Abu Ghraib Arias*. Denver: Flying Guillotine, 2011.

Mikhail, Mona. "A Review of *The Cairo House* by Samia Serageldin." *Middle East Journal* 55.3 (2001): 514–16.

Mohammed Schools of Atlanta. "History." Web. 23 Oct. 2011.

Moore, Anne Elizabeth. "Where We Come From: A Profile of Palestinian Artist Emily Jacir." *Progressive* 73.10 (2009): 37–39.

Moore, Kathleen M. "A Closer Look at Anti-Terrorism Law: *American-Arab Anti-Discrimination Committee v. Reno* and the Construction of Aliens' Rights." Suleiman, *Arabs in America* 84–99.

Morsy, Soheir. "Beyond the Honorary 'White' Classification of Egyptians: Societal Identity in Historical Context." *Race*. Ed. Steven Gregory and Roger Sanjek. New Brunswick: Rutgers UP, 1994. 175–98.

Mroue, Haas. *Beirut Seizures*. Berkeley, CA: New Earth, 1993.

———. "Beirut Survivors Anonymous." Mroue, *Beirut Seizures* 11–13.

———. "Beirut Survivors Anonymous II." Mroue, *Beirut Seizures* 69–71.

Muaddi Darraj, Susan. *The Inheritance of Exile: Stories from South Philly*. Notre Dame, IN: U of Notre Dame P, 2007.

———. "My West Bank Education: 1998." *Little Patuxent Review* 9 (2011): 74–80.

———. "Personal and Political: The Dynamics of Arab American Feminism." Abdulhadi, Naber, and Alsultany 248–60.

———, ed. *Scheherazade's Legacy: Arab and Arab American Women on Writing*. Westport, CT: Praeger, 2004.

Naber, Nadine. *Arab America: Gender, Cultural Politics, and Activism*. New York: New York UP, 2012.

———. "Arab-American In/visibility." *AAUG Monitor* 13.3 (1998): 1–16.

———. "Introduction: Arab Americans and U.S. Racial Formations." Jamal and Naber 1–45.

———. "'Look, Mohammed the Terrorist Is Coming!' Cultural Racism, Nation-Based Racism, and the Intersectionality of Oppressions after 9/11." Jamal and Naber 276–304.

Naff, Alixa. *Becoming American: The Early Arab Immigrant Experience*. Carbondale: Southern Illinois UP, 1985.

———. "Growing Up in Detroit: An Immigrant Grocer's Daughter." Abraham and Shryock 107–48.

Nassar, Eugene Paul. *Wind of the Land: Two Prose Poems*. 1979. Syracuse: Syracuse UP, 2002.

Noble, Frances Khirallah. *The New Belly Dancer of the Galaxy*. Syracuse: Syracuse UP, 2007.

———. *The Situe Stories*. Syracuse: Syracuse UP, 2000.

Nora, Pierre. "Between Memory and History: Les Lieux de Mémoire." *Representations* 26 (1989): 7–24.

Nye, Naomi Shihab. "Blood." Nye, *19 Varieties of Gazelle* 136–37.

———. "Half and Half." Nye, *19 Varieties of Gazelle* 97.

———. *Hugging the Jukebox*. New York: Dutton, 1982.

———. "My Father and the Figtree." Nye, *19 Varieties of Gazelle* 6–7.

———. *19 Varieties of Gazelle: Poems of the Middle East*. New York: Greenwillow Books, 1994.
———. "An Open Letter from Naomi Shihab Nye to Any Would-Be Terrorists." *About.com* 9 Oct. 2001. Web. 15 Sept. 2005.
———. *Red Suitcase: Poems*. Rochester, NY: BOA, 1994.
———. "The Words under the Words." Nye, *19 Varieties of Gazelle* 14–15.
———. *Words under the Words*. Portland, OR: Eighth Mountain, 1995.
———. *Yellow Glove*. Portland, OR: Far Corner Books, 1986.
Ong, Aihwa. "Cultural Citizenship as Subject Making: Immigrants Negotiate Racial and Cultural Boundaries in the United States." *Current Anthropology* 37.5 (1996): 737–62.
———. *Flexible Citizenship: The Cultural Logics of Transnationality*. Durham: Duke UP, 1999.
Orfalea, Gregory. *Angeleno Days: An Arab American Writer on Family, Place, and Politics*. Tucson: U of Arizona P, 2009.
———. *The Arab Americans: A History*. Northampton, MA: Olive Branch, 2006.
———. *Before the Flames: A Quest for the History of Arab Americans*. Austin: U of Texas P, 1988.
———. "The Bomb That Fell on Abdu's Farm." Charara, *Inclined to Speak* 266.
———. "Get Off the Bus." *The Man Who Guarded the Bomb*. Syracuse: Syracuse UP, 2010. 35–42.
———, ed. *Wrapping* the *Grape Leaves: A Sheaf of Contemporary Arab-American Poets*. Washington, DC: American-Arab Anti-Discrimination Committee, 1982.
Orfalea, Gregory, and Sharif Elmusa, eds. *Grape Leaves: A Century of Arab American Poetry*. 1988. New York: Interlink, 2000.
Pappé, Ilan. *Ethnic Cleansing of Palestine*. Oxford, UK: Oneworld, 2006.
Patton, Cindy, and Benigno Sánchez-Eppler, eds. *Queer Diasporas*. Durham: Duke UP, 2000.
Pease, Donald. "Introduction." *Re-framing the Transnational Turn in American Studies*. Hanover, NH: Dartmouth College P, 2011. 1–46.
Pierce, Amira. Rev. of *The Bullet Collection*, by Patricia Sarrafian Ward. *Arab Studies Journal* 12–13 (2004–5): 223–25.
Pratt, Minnie Bruce. "Identity: Skin, Blood, Heart." *Yours in Struggle: Three Feminist Perspectives on Anti-Semitism and Racism*. Ed. Elly Bulkin, Minnie Bruce Pratt, and Barbara Smith. New York: Long Haul, 1984. 11–63.
Puar, Jasbir. *Terrorist Assemblages: Homonationalism in Queer Times*. Durham: Duke UP, 2007.
Puar, Jasbir, and Amit S. Rai. "Monster, Terrorist, Fag: The War on Terrorism and the Production of Docile Patriots." *Social Text* 20.3 (2002): 117–48.
Radhakrishnan, R. "Ethnicity in an Age of Diaspora." *Theorizing Diaspora*. Ed. Jana Evans Braziel and Anita Mannur. Malden, MA: Blackwell, 2006. 119–31.

Reagon, Bernice Johnson. "Coalition Politics: Turning the Century." Smith, *Home Girls* 343–56.
Rihani, Ameen. *The Book of Khalid*. New York: Dodd, Mead, 1911.
Rihbany, Abraham Mitrie. *A Far Journey*. Boston: Houghton Mifflin, 1914.
Riley, Robin L. "Valiant, Vicious, or Virtuous? Representation, and the Problem of Women Warriors." Riley and Inayatullah 183–205.
Riley, Robin L., and Naeem Inayatullah, eds. *Interrogating Imperialism: Conversations on Gender, Race, and War*. New York: Palgrave Macmillan, 2006.
Riley, Robin L., Chandra Talpade Mohanty, and Minnie Bruce Pratt, eds. *Feminism and War: Confronting U.S. Imperialism*. New York: Zed Books, 2008.
Rizk, Salom. *Syrian Yankee*. New York: Doubleday, 1943.
Rosaldo, Renato. "Cultural Citizenship, Inequality, and Multiculturalism." *Latino Cultural Citizenship: Claiming Identity, Space, and Rights*. Ed. William Vincent Flores and Rina Benmayor. Boston: Beacon, 1997. 27–38.
Rothberg, Michael. "'There Is No Poetry in This': Writing, Trauma, and Home." *Trauma at Home after 9/11*. Ed. Judith Greenberg. Lincoln: U of Nebraska P, 2003. 147–57.
Rubenstein, Roberta. *Home Matters: Longing and Belonging, Nostalgia and Mourning in Women's Fiction*. New York: Palgrave, 2001.
Sabry, Somaya Sami. *Arab-American Women's Writing and Performance: Orientalism, Race and the Idea of the Arabian Nights*. London: I. B. Tauris, 2011.
Safran, William. "Diasporas in Modern Societies: Myths of Homeland and Return." *Diaspora* 1.1 (1991): 83–99.
Said, Edward W. *Culture and Imperialism*. New York: Vintage, 1993.
———. "Emily Jacir—Where We Come From." Jacir, Rollig, and Rückert, *Emily Jacir—Belongings* 46–49.
———. "My Right of Return." Interview with Ari Shvit. *Ha'aretz* 18 Aug. 2000. Rpt. in *Power, Politics, and Culture: Interviews with Edward W. Said*. Ed. Gauri Viswanathan. New York: Vintage, 2001. 443–58.
———. *Orientalism*. New York: Vintage, 1978.
———. *Out of Place*. New York: Vintage, 1999.
———. "Palestine, Then and Now: An Exile's Journey through Israel and the Occupied Territories." *Harper's* Dec. 1992: 47–51.
———. "Traveling Theory." *The World, the Text, and the Critic*. Cambridge: Harvard UP, 1983. 226–47.
———. "Traveling Theory Reconsidered." *Reflections on Exile and Other Essays*. Cambridge: Harvard UP, 2000. 436–52.
Said, Edward W., Bruce Robbins, Mary Louise Pratt, Jonathan Arac, and R. Radhakrishnan. "Edward Said's *Culture and Imperialism*: A Symposium." *Social Text* 40 (1994): 1–24.
Salaita, Steven. *Arab American Literary Fictions, Cultures, and Politics*. New York: Palgrave Macmillan, 2007.

———. "Beyond Orientalism and Islamophobia." *CR: The New Centennial Review* 6.2 (2006) 245–66.

———. "Ethnic Identity and Imperative Patriotism: Arab Americans before and after 9/11." *College Literature* 32.2 (2005): 146–68.

———. *Modern Arab American Fiction: A Reader's Guide*. Syracuse: Syracuse UP, 2011.

———. "Sand Niggers, Small Shops, and Uncle Sam: Cultural Negotiation in the Fiction of Joseph Geha and Diana Abu-Jaber." *Criticism* 43.4 (2001): 423–44.

———. "Split Vision: Arab American Literary Criticism." *Al-Jadid* 6.32 (2000): n.p. Web. 20 Nov. 2009.

Salem, Elise. Rev. of *The Bullet Collection*, by Patricia Sarrafian Ward. *Literary Review* 46.4 (2003): 769–70.

Saliba, Therese. "Resisting Invisibility: Arab Americans in Academia and Activism." Suleiman, *Arabs in America* 304–19.

———. "Sittee (or Phantom Appearances of a Lebanese Grandmother)." Kadi, *Food for Our Grandmothers* 7–17.

Saliba, Therese, Carolyn Allen, and Judith A. Howard, eds. *Gender, Politics and Islam*. Chicago: U of Chicago P, 2002.

Salibi, Kamal S. *A House of Many Mansions: The History of Lebanon Reconsidered*. 1988. London: I. B. Tauris, 2009.

Salt of this Sea. Dir. Annemarie Jacir. Perf. Suheir Hammad, Saleh Bakri, and Riyad Ideis. Augustus Film, 2008. Film.

Samhan, Helen Hatab. "Not Quite White: Race Classification and the Arab-American Experience." Suleiman, *Arabs in America* 209–26.

———. "Politics and Exclusion: The Arab American Experience." *Journal of Palestine Studies* 16.2 (1987): 11–28.

Saunders, Rebecca, and Kamran Aghaie. "Introduction: Mourning and Memory." *Comparative Studies of South Asia, Africa and the Middle East* 25.1 (2005): 16–29.

Schiller, Nina Glick. "The Situation of Transnational Studies." *Identities* 4 (1997): 155–66.

Schiller, Nina Glick, Linda G. Basch, and Cristina Szanton Blanc, eds. *Nations Unbound: Transnational Projects, Postcolonial Predicaments and De-territorialized Nation-States*. Amsterdam: Gordon and Breach, 1994.

———, eds. *Towards a Transnational Perspective on Migration: Race, Class, Ethnicity, and Nationalism Reconsidered*. New York: New York Academy of Sciences, 1992.

Selves and Others: A Portrait of Edward Said. Dir. Emmanuel Hamon. Wamip Films, 2003. DVD.

Serageldin, Samia. *The Cairo House*. Syracuse: Syracuse UP, 2000.

———. "It's Not about That." Kaldas and Mattawa 161–69.

Shaheen, Jack G. *Reel Bad Arabs: How Hollywood Vilifies a People*. New York: Olive Branch, 2001.

Shakir, Evelyn. "Arab-American Literature." *New Immigrant Literatures in the United States*. Ed. Alpana Sharma Knippling. Westport, CT: Greenwood, 1996. 3–18.

———. "Arab Mothers, American Sons: Women in Arab-American Autobiographies." *MELUS* 17.3 (1991–92): 5–15.

———. *Bint Arab: Arab and Arab American Women in the United States*. Westport, CT: Praeger, 1997.

———. "I Got My Eye on You." *Remember Me to Lebanon: Stories of Lebanese Women in America*. Syracuse: Syracuse UP, 2007. 128–44.

———. "'Imaginary Homelands'—Lebanese-American Prose." *Al Jadid* 9.42–43 (2003): 21–23.

———. "Mother's Milk: Women in Arab-American Autobiography." *MELUS* 15.4 (1988): 39–50.

———. "Pretending to Be Arab: Role-Playing in Vance Bourjaily's 'The Fractional Man.'" *MELUS* 9.1 (1982): 7–21.

Shohat, Ella. "Coming to America: Reflections on Hair and Memory Loss." *Going Global: The Transnational Reception of Third World Women Writers*. Ed. Amal Amireh and Lisa Suhair Majaj. New York: Garland, 2000. 284–300.

———. "Gendered Cartographies of Knowledge: Area Studies, Ethnic Studies, and Postcolonial Studies." Shohat, *Taboo Memories* 1–16.

———. *Taboo Memories: Diasporic Voices*. Durham: Duke UP, 2006.

Shohat, Ella, and Robert Stam. *Unthinking Eurocentrism: Multiculturalism and the Media*. New York: Routledge, 1994.

Shryock, Andrew. "Family Resemblances: Kinship and Community in Arab Detroit." Abraham and Shryock 573–610.

Simpson, Mona. *Anywhere but Here*. New York: Knopf, 1986.

———. *A Regular Guy*. New York: Vintage, 1996.

Smith, Barbara, ed. *Home Girls: A Black Feminist Anthology*. 1983. New Brunswick: Rutgers UP, 2000.

Sobelle, Stefanie. "The Paris-of-the-Middle-East-Effect: Beirut's Culture of Forgetting." *Daily Star* 3 Apr. 2004: n.p.

Spivak, Gayatri. "Can the Subaltern Speak?" *Marxism and the Interpretation of Culture*. Ed. Cary Nelson and Lawrence Grossberg. Urbana: U of Illinois P, 1988. 271–313.

Stam, Robert, and Ella Shohat. *Flagging Patriotism: Crises of Narcissism and Anti-Americanism*. New York: Routledge, 2007.

Stockton, Ronald. "Ethnic Archetypes and the Arab Image." *The Development of Arab-American Identity*. Ed. Ernest McCarus. Ann Arbor: U of Michigan P, 1996. 119–53.

Suleiman, Michael W., ed. *Arabs in America: Building a New Future.* Philadelphia: Temple UP, 1999.

——. "Early Arab-Americans: The Search for Identity." *Crossing the Waters: Arabic-Speaking Immigrants in the United States.* Ed. Eric J. Hooglund. Washington, DC: Smithsonian Institution, 1987. 37–54.

——. "Impressions of New York City by Early Arab Immigrants." *A Community of Many Worlds: Arab Americans in New York City.* Ed. Kathleen Benson and Philip M. Kayal. New York: Museum of the City of New York, 2002. 28–45.

——. "Introduction: The Arab Immigrant Experience." Suleiman, *Arabs in America* 1–21.

Takaki, Ronald. *Strangers from a Different Shore: A History of Asian Americans.* New York: Penguin, 1989.

Tétreault, Mary Ann. "The Sexual Politics of Abu Ghraib: Hegemony, Spectacle, and the Global War on Terror." *NWSA Journal* 18.3 (2006): 33–50.

Thobani, Sunera. "White Wars: Western Feminism and the 'War on Terror.'" *Feminist Theory* 8.2 (2007): 169–85.

Tölölyan, Khachig. "The Contemporary Discourse of Diaspora Studies." *Comparative Studies of South Asia, Africa and the Middle East* 27.3 (2007): 647–55.

——. "Rethinking *Diaspora*(s): Stateless Power in the Transnational Moment." *Diaspora* 5.1 (1996): 1–36.

Traboulsi, Fawwaz. *A History of Modern Lebanon.* 2007. London: Pluto, 2012.

United States Department of State. *Israel, the West Bank and Gaza: Country Specific Information.* n.d. Web. 24 Nov. 2010.

Van Hear, Nicholas. *New Diasporas: The Mass Exodus, Dispersal and Regrouping of Migrant Communities.* London: U College London P, 1998.

Volpp, Leti. "The Citizen and the Terrorist." *September 11 in History: A Watershed Moment?* Ed. Mary L. Dudziak. Durham: Duke UP, 2003. 147–62.

——. "Citizenship Undone." *Fordham Law Review* 75 (2007): 2579–86.

Ward, Patricia Sarrafian. *The Bullet Collection.* St. Paul, MN: Graywolf, 2003.

Wardi-Zonna, Katherine, and Anissa Janine Wardi. "In Passing: Arab America and the Politics of Race." *Ethnic Studies Review* 28.2 (2005): 17–36.

Wehr, Hans. *Arabic-English Dictionary.* Ithaca, NY: Spoken Language Services, 1994.

Weighill, Marie-Louise. "Palestinians in Exile: Legal, Geographical and Statistical Aspects." *The Palestinian Exodus 1948–1998.* Ed. Ghada Karmi and Eugene Cotran. Reading, UK: Ithaca, 1999. 7–36.

Werbner, Pnina. "Introduction: The Materiality of Diaspora—Between Aesthetic and 'Real' Politics." *The Materiality of Diaspora.* Ed. Karen Leonard and Pnina Werbner. Spec. issue of *Diaspora* 9.1 (2000): 5–20.

Williams, David. *Far Sides of the Only World.* Durham, NC: Carolina Wren, 2004.

———. "My Grandmother and the Dirbakeh." *Traveling Mercies*. Cambridge, MA: Alice James Books, 1993. 6–7.
Wolters, Wendy E. "A 'Bridge between My Memories and Yours.'" *Transformations: The Journal of Inclusive Scholarship and Pedagogy* 16.2 (2005): 118–26.
Yunis, Alia. *The Night Counter*. New York: Shaye Areheart, 2009.
Žižek, Slavoj. *Welcome to the Desert of the Real: Five Essays on 11 September and Related Dates*. London: Verso, 2002.
Zogby, John. "Arab Americans and Law Enforcement." *Huffington Post* 12 Nov. 2012. Web. 13 Nov. 2012.

Index

Page numbers in italics refer to images.

. . . *and Counting* (Bilal), 172–73, *175*
"#Jan25," 183

Abdulhadi, Rabab, 27, 141, 157; "Where is Home?," 162–64
Abinader, Elmaz, 19, 22, 26, 31, 50, 200n54; *Children of the Roojme*, 21; gender, 200n55; "Just off Main Street," 54–55
Abraham, Nabeel: *Arabs in the New World*, 21
Abraham, Sameer Y.: *Arabs in the New World*, 21
Abu Ghraib, 165; gender, 215n35
Abu-Jaber, Diana, 21, 26, 31, 38, 198n32; *Arabian Jazz*, 46–47; *Birds of Paradise*, 180; *Crescent*, 42–43; father figures, 41–47; *The Language of Baklava*, 43–46; *Origin*, 180
Adnan, Etel, 22, 26, 108, 137, 180, 208n29; *In the Heart of the Heart of Another Country*, 121–23
Afghanistan, 2, 10; US invasion of (2001), 1, 2, 24, 140, 152, 164, 187
Aghaie, Kamran, 108–9
Ahmed, Ahmed: *Axis of Evil*, 182
Akash, Munir: *Post Gibran*, 22
Alameddine, Rabih, 26, 108, 137, 178, 180; *I, the Divine*, 117–20; *Koolaids*, 21

Alexander, M. Jacqui, 142
"Alone and All Together" (Geha), 139, 141, 143–47, 148
Alsultany, Evelyn, 189n6, 191nn21–22, 213n32
"america" (Hilal), 141, 160–62
American-Arab Anti-Discrimination Committee (ADC), 13, 14
Anthias, Floya, 6
Antoon, Sinan, 181, 195n64, 196n11
Appadurai, Arjun, 107
Ashcroft, John, 14
Arab: pan-Arab identification, 122–24, 144; as term, 10–12; trans-Arab solidarities, 11, 13, 17; uprisings, 177–87 (*see* Arab Spring). *See also* representations of Arabs and Muslims
Arab-American: domestic spaces, 30–49; as "forever foreign," 5, 66–67, 150, 165, 199n44; homogenization of, 91, 142–56; hyphenated identities, 43, 53, 90, 118–19, 185, 190n17; public articulations of identity, 48–64; racialization of, 12–16, 23, 25, 51–54, 139–76; as term, 10–11, 14, 24; translocality, 105–38; as transnational, 1–27; vulnerability, 1–2, 11, 21, 61, 128, 144. *See also* Arab-American literature; belonging;

Arab-American (*continued*)
  citizenship: antihegemonic; translocal; transnational
Arab American Institute (AAI), 13
Arab-American literature: anti-Orientalist, 3, 5; as discursive site, 24; common themes, 19–20, 24–25; generic diversity of, 2, 23, 26; historical development of, 17–24; political dimensions of, 48–64. *See also* Arab-American writers
Arab American National Museum, 181. *See* "DIWAN"
Arab-American writers: contemporary generation of, 18–20; early immigrant (*mahjar*), 12, 17–18. *See also* RAWI
Arab homelands: as absent presence, 31–38, 73; embodied, 26; fragments of, 31–38, 97–98; gendered immigrant memories of, 39–47; inaccessibility, 33, 88; multinational displacement, 124–37; narratives of physical return, 65–104; nostalgic memories of, 20, 28, 31–47; transgenerational links to, 28–64; translocal connections, 105–38; transnational reimagining, 28–64; traumatic histories of, 89, 105–38. *See also* Arab League; Arab world; rearrivals
Arab-Israeli wars: 1973 War, 2; Six-Day War (1967), 2, 12, 105, 127–28, 140, 191n28
Arab League, 12, 191n24
Arab Oil Embargo (1973), 2, 140
Arab world: Arab League states, 2, 191n24; US involvement in, 2–3, 7–8, 68, 139–42, 211n6; wars and conflicts, 1–2, 51–53, 63, 108–24. *See also* Arab homelands; Arab-Israeli wars; Egypt; Lebanon; Palestine; Syria
Arabian Jazz (Abu-Jaber), 21; gendered memories, 46–47
Arabs in America (Suleiman), 21
Arabs in the New World (Abraham/Abraham), 21
Arab Spring, 184
Arab Summit, 183; *Fear of an Arab Planet*, 183
"Argela Remembrance" (Hammad), 35–36, 37
Association of Arab American University Graduates (AAUG), 13
Awad, Joseph, 19

Axis of Evil, 182
Ayah, 183; "#Jan25," 183
Aziz, Barbara Nimri, 22. *See* RAWI

Back of the Throat (El Guindi), 142; citizenship, 167; sexuality, 166, 168–71
Bakri, Saleh, 97
Bardenstein, Carol, 196n13, 197n19, 199n41
Becoming American (Naff), 21
"Becoming the Center of Mystery" (Charara), 53
Before Our Eyes (Joseph), 21
Before the Flames (Orfalea), 21
Beirut Seizures (Mroue), 108; "Beirut Survivors Anonymous," 114–16, 118; "Beirut Survivors Anonymous II," 114, 116–17. *See also* Lebanese civil war
belonging: as term, 26, 67; translocal, 105–38; transnational articulations of, 1–27; binary constructs of, 3–4, 29–30, 86–88. *See also* citizenship; translocal; transnational
Ben Ali, Zine El Abidine, 184
Bilal, Wafaa, 27, 142, 165; *. . . and Counting*, 172–73, 175; *Domestic Tension*, 172, 174; *Shoot an Iraqi*, 172; *3rdi*, 173–74
bint/ibn Arab (daughter/son of Arabs), 19, 48; nostalgia, 19; shame, 19, 48–49
Birds of Paradise (Abu-Jaber), 180
Blatty, William, 18; *Which Way to Mecca, Jack?*, 65–66
"Blood" (Nye), 60–61
bodies: "body memory," 39, 197n25; gendered, 39, 88–89, 164–75; racialized, 143–47. *See also* translocal mobility
"Bomb That Fell on Abdu's Farm, The" (Orfalea), 63
Book of Khalid, The (Rihani), 17
Born Palestinian, Born Black (Hammad), 21
Bourjaily, Vance, 18, 19; *Confessions of a Spent Youth*, 65–66
Boym, Svetlana: nostalgia, 196n14
Bullet Collection, The (Ward), 108; traumatic memories of Lebanon, 109–14; translocal consciousness, 110, 113; transforming exilic space, 110–11. *See also* Lebanese civil war
Bush, George W., 142, 150, 170, 212n8
Butterfly's Burden, The (Darwish), 181

Cairo House, The (Serageldin), 68, 90; Egypt, 79–85; gender, 83–85; politics, 79–80; race, 82–83
Charara, Hayan, 23, 31, 58; "Becoming the Center of Mystery," 53; *Inclined to Speak*, 23, 60
Chelala, Elie, 181
Children of the Roojme (Abinader), 21
Chung, Won Ho: *Axis of Evil*, 182
citizenship: antihegemonic, 3–5, 18–25, 100, 140–42; consumer, 190n9; cultural, 4, 49; gendered, 164–70; legal, 4, 49; political, 157–64; post 9/11, 139–64; as term, 4, 49; transnational enactments of, 47, 51–52, 106, 114, 157–64; US citizenship, 3–11, 108–9, 140–56. *See also* belonging; race; religion; transnational
Civantos, Christina, 39
class, 147–50; and race, 79–89; and religion, 90–91
Clifford, James, 107
Confessions of a Spent Youth (Bourjaily), 18, 65–66
Cordoba House crisis (2010), 175
Crescent (Abu-Jaber), 44, 179; father figures, 42–43; food, 43

Darwish, Mahmoud, 181, 204n35; "absence of presence," 196n11; *The Butterfly's Burden*, 181; *In the Presence of Absence*, 181; Palestinian return, 204n35
Def Poetry Jam (Simmons), 157
diasporic: as label, 6–10; narratives of return, 64–104; studies, 6. *See also* Arab homelands; ethnic
Dinarzad's Children (Kaldas/Mattawa), 23
"DIWAN." *See* Arab American National Museum
Domestic Tension (Bilal), 172, *174*
Dow, George (trial of, 1914), 14

Egypt, 20, 25, 57, 68; literary depictions of, 79–90. *See also* Arab world
El Guindi, Yussef, 27, 142, 165–71, 182; *Back of the Throat*, 165–71
Elmusa, Sharif: *Grape Leaves*, 22, 23
E-mails from Scheherazad (Kahf): "Lateefa," 56–58; "Move Over," 58
ethnic: and cross-racial alliances, 8, 23, 49, 51, 55, 183; enclaves, 49–50, 54; as label, 5–8, 10; studies, 6. *See also* diasporic

Facebook. *See* social networks
Far Journey, A (Rihbany), 19
FBI, 14, 152
Fear of a Black Planet (Public Enemy), 183
Fear of an Arab Planet (Arab Summit), 183
"Fifty Years On / Stones in an Unfinished Wall" (Majaj), 64
First Gulf War, 2, 21, 105, 136, 140, 172, 195n64
"first writing since" (Hammad), 141, 149, 163; 9/11, 157–60; transnational rubric, 157–58; US citizenship, 158–60
Food for Our Grandmothers (Kadi), 11, 22, 23, 24, 39
Free the P (Offendum/Ragtop), 183
Freeway, 183; "#Jan25," 183
Friedman, Susan Stanford, 118

Gana, Nouri, 199n37
Gass, William, 121
Geha, Joseph, 21, 26–27, 56, 139, 141; "Alone and All Together," 143–47; *Through and Through*, 49–50
gender: anticolonialist feminism, 93–104; father figures, 42–47, 198n32; grandmothers, 34–35, 39–42, 74, 197nn24–25; in national security state, 164–75; and religion, 69–79; and sexuality, 164–70
George, Rosemary Marangoly, 82, 85
Gibran, Gibran Kahlil: *The Prophet*, 17. *See* The Pen League
Girl in the Tangerine Scarf, The (Kahf), 68, 83, 85, 90; *al-ghurba*, 73; Baathist Party, 75; hijab, 76–78; nationality and religion, 69–79; spiritual homecomings, 70–71; Syria, 69–79
Golden Thread Productions, 182
Grape Leaves (Orfalea, Elmusa), 22, 23
Gregory, Derek, 125, 130, 208n34, 210n49
Grewal, Inderpal, 150, 156, 193n48, 212n17
Ground Zero crisis (2010), 175
Gualtieri, Sarah, 9, 12, 16, 192n38, 193n54
Guantanamo Bay, 165

Ha'aretz, 128
Haddad, Yvonne, 14
Halaby, Laila, 27, 108, 125, 137, 141; *Once in a Promised Land*, 150–55; *The West of Jordan*, 129–33

Hammad, Suheir, 26, 27, 30, 141, 162, 163, 178, 179; "Argela Remembrance," 35–36; *Born Palestinian, Born Black*, 21; *Def Poetry Jam*, 157; "first writing since," 157–60; in *Salt of this Sea*, 93, 97
Hammer, Juliane, 73; *Palestinians Born in Exile*, 133
Hamod, Sam, 22
Handal, Nathalie, 182
Harb, Sirène, 193n51
Hartman, Michelle, 23
Hassan, Ahmed (trial of, 1942), 15
Hassan, Waïl, 12, 17, 18, 193n49, 199n37
Haugbolle, Sune, 110, 206n13
Hazo, Samuel, 19
Hilal, Dima, 27, 141, 157; "america," 160–62
home and homeland, 191n20; "imaginative geographies" of, 123–37. *See also* Arab-American: domestic spaces; Arab homelands
Hout, Syrine, 198n33, 206nn10–11
Huntington, Samuel, 158
Hussein, Saddam, 172

I, The Divine (Alameddine), 108; traumatic memories of Lebanon, 118–20; translocality, 117–20. *See also* Lebanese civil war
immigration: assimilative tendencies, 12–13, 51–52, 66–67; causes of, 12–14; first wave, 4, 9, 12–13; second wave, 13; third wave, 13–14.
Inclined to Speak (Charara), 23, 60
"Inclined to Speak" (Joseph), 64
Inheritance of Exile, The (Muaddi Darraj), 62, 69; Palestinian space, 89–92; religion and class, 90–91
In the Presence of Absence (Darwish), 181
Iraq, 20, 172; US invasion of, 2, 140, 187. *See also* Operation Iraqi Freedom
Islam. *See* Muslims
Islamophobia. *See* representations of Arabs and Muslims
Israel, 183; establishment of (1948), 2, 47, 105. *See also* Arab-Israeli wars; Palestinian-Israeli conflict
Israeli-Palestinian conflict, 68; Israeli Occupation, 88–89, 104, 157, 187; "Resolution 184," 68. *See also* Oslo Accords

Jacir, Annemarie, 26, 69, 103–4; *Salt of this Sea*, 92–100
Jacir, Emily, 26, 29; Palestinian right of return, 92–3; *Sexy Semite*, 102–3; *Where We Come From*, 100–102
Jarrar, Randa, 27, 108, 125, 183; *A Map of Home*, 133–37; "Rewriting the Story," 185
Jayyusi, Lena, 96, 98
Jayyusi, Salma Khadra, 18
Jobrani, Maz: *Axis of Evil*, 182
Joseph, Lawrence, 21, 24, 28, 39, 50, 178, 196n12; *Before Our Eyes*, 21; "Inclined to Speak," 64; "Sand Nigger," 31–33, 51–53
Joudah, Fady, 181; translating Darwish, 181
"Journeys to Jerusalem" (Majaj), 28
"Just Off Main Street" (Abinader), 54–55

Kadi, Joe (Joanna), 26, 31, 33, 38; *Food for Our Grandmothers*, 11, 22, 23, 24, 39; *Thinking Class*, 41–42
Kahf, Mohja, 22, 26, 27, 31, 50, 62, 85, 87, 91, 104, 141, 150, 178, 200n57; *E-Mails from Scheherazad*, 55–59; *The Girl in the Tangerine Scarf*, 69–79; "Lateefa," 56–58; "Move Over," 58; "The Spiced Chicken Queen of Mickaweaquah, Iowa," 147–49
Kaldas, Pauline, 26, 68, 90, 91, 104; *Dinarzad's Children*, 23; *Letters from Cairo*, 86–88
Koolaids (Alameddine), 21
Kuwait, 20, 133–34, 137, 172; US Invasion of (1991), 21

LA 8 (trial of, 1987), 14
Language of Baklava, The (Abu-Jaber), 42; father figures, 43–46; food, 44–45
"Lateefa" (Kahf), 59, 62; inclusive belongings, 57–58; nationality and religion, 56–57
Lebanese civil war, 2, 20–21, 25, 105, 107–24, 205n1, 207n20; traumatic memories of, 109–23
Lebanon: Israeli invasion of, 2, 35, 111, 207n16, 208n24; literary versions of, 31–35, 109–24. *See also* Arab world; Lebanese civil war
Letters from Cairo (Kaldas), 68, 79, 86–88; cultural perspectives, 87–88; immigrant bodies, 86–7; Egypt, 86–88
Leys, Ruth, 109

INDEX / 241

Madi, Elia Abu, 17. *See also* The Pen League
Maira, Sunaina, 143, 212n16
Majaj, Lisa Suhair, 12, 14, 15, 16, 18, 19, 24, 29, 63, 199n43, 203n32; "Fifty Years On / Stones in an Unfinished Wall," 64; "Journeys to Jerusalem," 28
Mamdani, Mahmoud, 143
Map of Home, A, 108, 125; centrality of Palestine, 134–35; remapping home, 135–36
Mathaf, The, 173; "Told/Untold/Retold," 23. *See* Qatar's Arab Museum of Modern Art
Mattawa, Khaled: *Dinarzad's Children*, 23; "Now That We Have Tasted Hope," 176, 186; *Post-Gibran*, 22
Melhem, D.H., 19, 26, 31, 38, 193n52, 198n29; *Rest in Love*, 41
memory: gendered, 34–35, 39–47; nostalgic fragments of, 31–47; postmemory, 196n10; US amnesiac landscapes, 113, 125. *See also* Arab homelands: traumatic memories of
Middle East: complex histories of, 116; conflicts, 2, 63, 110; as racial designation, 16; as region, 10, 12, 189; studies, 6; US involvement in, 4, 59–60, 68. *See also* Arab world
Mohriez, Mohamed (trial of, 1944), 15
"Move Over" (Kahf), 58
Mroue, Haas, 26, 109, 118, 137; *Beirut Seizures*, 108, 114–17; "Beirut Survivors Anonymous," 114–16, 118; "Beirut Survivors Anonymous II," 114, 116–17
Muaddi Darraj, Susan, 26, 31, 62, 68, 104, 165; *The Inheritance of Exile*, 89–92
Muslims: bias against, 1, 75–76; as term, 11–12. *See also* representations of Arabs and Muslims
"My Father and the Fig Tree" (Nye), 45, 60; father figures, 37–38
"My Grandmother and the Dirbakeh" (Williams), 40–41

Naber, Nadine, 12, 13, 14, 140, 190n15, 211n3
Naff, Alixa: *Becoming American*, 21
Naimy, Mikhael, 17. *See also* The Pen League
Najour, George (trial of, 1909), 14
Nakba, 20, 25, 105, 128
Narcyicst, the: "#Jan25," 183. *See also* Arab Summit

Nassar, Eugene Paul, 19
Nasser, Gamal Abdel, 127
National Association for Arab Americans (NAAA), 13
National Security Entry-Exit Registration System, 140, 143, 211n3
Nibras, 182
9/11: 2, 5, 14, 16, 23, 27, 63, 138, 182; patriotism, 140, 143, 147–48, 155–56, 166; security state, 164–75
19 Varieties of Gazelle (Nye): "Blood," 60–61
N.O.M.A.D.S., 182. *See also* Offendum, Omar
Noor Theater, The, 182
nostalgia: antinostalgia, 28–64; fragmented memories, 31–37; gendered, 39–47. *See also* Arab homelands
"Now That We Have Tasted Hope" (Mattawa), 176, 186
Nye, Naomi Shihab, 22, 26, 30, 50, 178, 197n21; father figures, 37–38, 42, 45; "Blood," 60–61; "My Father and the Fig Tree," 37–38; *19 Varieties of Gazelle*, 60; *Red Suitcase*, 21; *Words under the Words*, 20

Obeidallah, Dean: *Axis of Evil*, 182
Occupy Movements, 184
Odeh, Alex (murder of, 1986), 14
Offendum, Omar: "#Jan25," 183; *Free the P*, 183. *See also*, Arab Summit; N.O.M.A.D.S.
Once in a Promised Land (Halaby), 141; class, 150–52; "good Arab/bad Arab" label, 152–56
Ong, Aihwa, 4, 212n16
Operation Enduring Freedom, 164. *See also* Afghanistan
Orfalea, Gregory: *Before the Flames*, 21; "The Bomb That Fell on Abdu's Farm," 63; *Grape Leaves*, 22, 23
Orientalism, neo-Orientalism, 2, 3, 5, 11, 31, 106, 115, 125, 132, 143, 164
Orientalism (Said), 124, 189n3
Origin (Abu-Jaber), 180
Oslo Accords (1993), 21, 92. *See also* Palestinian-Israeli conflict
Otherness: national, 2, 15, 48, 142, 164–65; racial, 1, 52, 145; religious, 1–2, 16, 142, 145, 164–65
Out of Place (Said), 108, 125–29, 134

Palestine: Gaza, 92–93, 101, 130, 157, 183, 187; historical, 92–93; West Bank, 89, 157, 183, 187. *See also* Nakba; Palestinian-Israeli conflict
Palestinian right of return, 68–69, 89–103
Palestinians Born in Exile (Hammer), 133
Patton, Cindy, 6
Pen League, The, 1, 17–18, 189n1, 193n49
Philistines, 182, 183. *See also* Arab Summit
Post-Gibran (Akash/Mattawa), 22
Prophet, The (Gibran), 17
Puar, Jasbir, 165, 213n20, 213n29
Public Enemy: Fear of a Black Planet, 183

Qaddafi, Muammar, 184, 186
Qatar's Museum of Modern Art. *See* The Mathaf

Rabita al-Qalamiyya, Al-. *See* The Pen League
race: 49–55, 143–47; and class, 79–89. *See also* Arab-American; Muslims; representations of Arabs and Muslims
Radius of Arab American Writers Inc (RAWI), 22
Raffo, Heather, 182
Ragtop: Free the P, 183. *See also* Arab Summit; Philistines
Rai, Amit S., 165, 213n20
rearrivals: 67–104; as term, 26, 67; remapping US spaces, 65–69, 77–79, 89,104. *See also* Arab homelands
Red Suitcase (Nye), 21
religion: and citizenship, 139–75; gender, 55–56, 76–78; hijab, 76–78
representations of Arabs and Muslims: counterhegemonic, 63–79, 142–56; demonization of, 16, 21, 23, 59, 154, 193n47; gendered, 55–56, 96, 142, 165–70; homogenization of, 142–56; Islamophobia, 139–76; as Other, 66; post-9/11, 139–76, 182; racist, 5, 182; stereotypes, 2, 5, 115, 185
Rest in Love (Melhem), 41
"Rewriting the Story" (Jarrar), 185
Rihani, Ameen, 22; *The Book of Khalid*, 17. *See also* The Pen League
Rihbany, Abraham Mitrie, 18–19; *A Far Journey*, 19
Rizk, Salom, 19; *Syrian Yankee*, 18

Rosaldo, Renato, 4
Rubenstein, Roberta, 36, 196n11

Sabra and Shatila massacres (1982), 61
Said, Edward, 27, 101, 108, 133, 134, 137; *Culture and Imperialism*, 134, 206n4; "Emily Jacir," 101; *Orientalism*, 124; *Out of Place*, 124–29
Salaita, Steven, 24, 29, 165, 191n22; "imperative patriotism," 155
Saliba, Therese, 13, 16, 26, 30, 39; "Sittee," 33–35
Salloum, Jackie, 183; *Slingshot Hip Hop*, 183
Salt of this Sea (Jacir, A.), 26, 69; Palestinian right of return, 92–100
Samhan, Helen Hatab, 15, 192n39, 193n43, 193n47
Sánchez-Eppler, Benigno, 6
"Sand Nigger" (Joseph), 26, 34, 35; Lebanon, 31–33; race, 33, 51–53
Saunders, Rebecca, 108–9
Serageldin, Samia, 26, 68, 87, 91, 104, 178, 202n16; *The Cairo House*, 79–85
sexuality: and post-9/11 security state, 164–70
Sexy Semite (Jacir, E.), 102–3
Shahid, Faras (trial of, 1913), 14
Shakir, Evelyn, 17, 29, 39, 66, 201n1
Shamieh, Betty, 182
Shohat, Ella, 5, 124
Shoot an Iraqi (Bilal), 172
Shyrock, Andrew, 48
Silk Road Rising, 169, 171, 182
Simmons, Russell, 157; *Def Poetry Jam*, 157
"Sittee (or Phantom Appearances of a Lebanese Grandmother)" (Saliba), 33–35
Six-Day War (1967). *See* Arab-Israeli wars
Slingshot Hip Hop (Salloum), 183
Sobelle, Stefanie, 110
social networks, 184. *See* Facebook; Twitter
"Spiced Chicken Queen of Mickaweaquah, Iowa, The" (Kahf), 141, 147–49, 150
Spivak, Gayatri, 165
Sulaiman, Amir: "#Jan25," 183
Suleiman, Michael: *Arabs in America*, 21
Syria, 9, 25; literary depictions of, 69–79. *See also* Arab world
Syrian Yankee (Rizk), 18

Tahrir Square, 183
Thinking Class (Kadi), 41–42

Through and Through (Gcha), 21, 49–50
"Told/Untold/Retold." *See* The Mathaf
Tölölyan, Khachig, 6, 107
translocal: as term, 106–7, 205n3; belonging, 106–8, 112, 123; consciousness, 106–8, 113, 117; mobility, 107–8, 130, 136–37; reconfigurations of US citizenship, 105–38
transnational: belonging, 1–27, 39–48, 114; citizenship, 22–23, 26–27, 67–69; frameworks of knowledge, 29–31; movement, 67–69; political framework, 157–64. *See also* Arab-American; Arab homelands; belonging; citizenship
trauma, 108–9. *See* Arab homelands; Lebanese civil war
Twin Cities Arab Film Festival, 181
Twitter. *See* social networks

United States: foreign policies, 7–8, 16, 140; as home, 18, 74; Immigration and Nationality Act (1965), 4, 12; Immigration Quota Act (1925), 12; memory-scapes, 108, 114; Operation Abscam, 14; Operation Boulder, 14; presidential elections (2008), 175; racial and ethnic minorities, 48, 55, 59; USA PATRIOT Act, 14, 140, 143; US Census Bureau, 15, 51, 191n27, 193n42, 200n50, 212n11; US Department of Homeland Security, 140, 143; War on Terror, 1, 187. *See also* Arab world: US involvement in; citizenship; 9/11

Ward, Patricia Sarrafian, 26, 108, 117, 118, 137; *The Bullet Collection*, 109–14
West of the Jordan (Halaby), 108, 125; centrality of Palestine, 129–33
"Where is Home?" (Abdulhadi), 141, 162–64
Where We Come From (Jacir, E.), 100–101, 102
Which Way to Mecca, Jack? (Blatty), 18, 65
Williams, David, 26, 31, 38; "My Grandmother and the Dirbakeh," 40–41
Words under the Words (Nye), 20
World Trade Center bombing (1993), 21, 140

Zayid, Maysoon, 182
Zogby, John, 14

About the Author

Carol Fadda-Conrey is Assistant Professor of English at Syracuse University, where she teaches a variety of graduate and undergraduate courses on race and ethnic studies and Arab and Arab-American literatures and cultures. A recipient of an NEH summer grant and a Future of Minority Studies Fellowship, her essays on gender, race, ethnicity, war trauma, and transnational citizenship have appeared in *Modern Fiction Studies, College Literature, MELUS, Studies in the Humanities,* and *Al-Raida,* as well as in a variety of edited collections on Arab and Arab-American literature.